THE
WORLD
ATLAS

The RANDOM HOUSE
LIBRARY OF KNOWLEDGE™

THE WORLD ATLAS

MAPS BY

Hammond Incorporated

 RANDOM HOUSE

NEW YORK

Globe on cover and title pages reproduced with permission
of Scan-Globe A/S Denmark. Photos by Edward P. Diehl

Copyright © 1982 by Hammond Incorporated. All rights reserved under
International and Pan-American Copyright Conventions. Published in the
United States by Random House, Inc., New York, and simultaneously in
Canada by Random House of Canada Limited, Toronto. No part of this book
may be reproduced or utilized in any form or by any means, electronic or
mechanical, including photocopying, recording, or by any information stor-
age and retrieval system, without permission in writing from the Publisher.

Library of Congress Cataloging in Publication Data:

Hammond Incorporated.
  The World atlas.

  1. Atlases.   I. Random House (Firm)   II. Title.
G1021.R52   1982   912   AACR2   82–675036
ISBN: 0–394–84663–X (pbk.); 0–394–94663–4 (lib. bdg.)

Manufactured in the United States of America   6 7 8 9 0

CONTENTS

PAGE
Introduction and How to Use This Atlas . .6 – 7
The Water Planet — Seven Global Views 8 – 9
The World . . . . .10 – 11

NORTH AMERICA

North America . . . . .12 – 13
United States . . . . .14 – 15
U.S. — Western Part . . . . .16 – 17
U.S. — Central Part . . . . .18 – 19
U.S. — Eastern Part . . . . .20 – 21
Alaska 22
Hawaii 23
Canada . . . . .24 – 25
Mexico 26
Central America 27
The West Indies . . . . .28 – 29

SOUTH AMERICA

South America . . . . .30 – 31
South America — Northern Part . . . . . .32 – 33
South America — Southern Part 34

EUROPE AND THE SOVIET UNION

Europe . . . . .36 – 37
Scandinavia .38 – 39
United Kingdom and Ireland . . . . .40 – 41
Netherlands, Belgium,
and Luxembourg . . . . .42 – 43
France . . . . .44 – 45
Germany . . . . .46 – 47
Austria, Czechoslovakia,
and Hungary . . . . .48 – 49
Switzerland and Liechtenstein 50
Poland 51
Spain and Portugal . . . . .52 – 53
Italy . . . . .54 – 55
The Balkan States . . . . .56 – 57
Union of Soviet Socialist Republics . . . .58 – 59
U.S.S.R. — European Part . . . . .60 – 61

AFRICA

Africa . . . . .78 – 79
Northeastern Africa . . . . .80 – 81
Western Africa . . . . .82 – 83
Central Africa . . . . .84 – 85
Southern Africa . . . . .86 – 87

PACIFIC OCEAN AND AUSTRALIA

Pacific Ocean . . . . .88 – 89
Australia . . . . .90 – 91
Southeastern Australia . . . . .92 – 93
New Zealand and Tasmania . . . . .94 – 95

ASIA

Asia . . . . .62 – 63
China and Mongolia . . . . .64 – 65
Japan and Korea . . . . .66 – 67
Mainland Southeast Asia . . . . .68 – 69
Southeast Asia . . . . .70 – 71
Southern Asia . . . . .72 – 73
Near and Middle East . . . . .74 – 75
Israel and Jordan . . . . .76 – 77

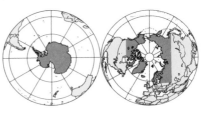

POLAR REGIONS

Antarctica 35
Arctic Regions 96

TABLES AND INDEX

Geographical Statistics 97
Gazetteer of the World . . . . .98 – 99
Introduction to Index and List of
Abbreviations 100
Index . . . . .101 – 112

A collection of maps and related charts and tables is called an atlas. The term comes from a figure in Greek mythology. Atlas was one of the Titans, or elder gods, who with the other Titans made war on the young but powerful god Zeus. Zeus won the war, and Atlas was condemned to hold the world on his shoulders forever—or so the story goes.

During the sixteenth century (some 2,000 years after the story of Atlas was first told), an Italian publisher named Lafreri put an engraving of Atlas holding up Earth on the title page of a book of maps. Other publishers liked the idea and copied it. Before long, any collection of maps became known as an atlas.

Early mapmakers drew the maps by hand in every one of their atlases. These mapmakers had a vague idea of what the world looked like—an incorrect idea. They believed that the world was flat and that the ocean circled it like the outer rim of a wheel. They did not suspect that either North or South America existed. Today cartographers have exact pictures of Earth—taken from satellites flying high above us.

The hard part of modern mapmaking is keeping up with the changes in political boundaries and with the names of countries that become independent or are taken over by other governments. With the world changing more and more rapidly these days, it is important to keep up-to-date maps. The maps in this book have been revised right up to the moment of printing, so each one is as comprehensive and timely as any map can possibly be.

HOW TO USE THIS ATLAS

Maps are like photographs of the world taken from a point in space. They show us where places are located in terms of distances and direction and tell us something about their surroundings. From high above Earth, physical and cultural features take on a special appearance. Broad rivers become narrow, winding ribbons; cities and towns become clusters of dots; mountains and valleys flatten out until only shadows remain to indicate unevenness of terrain. Differences in vegetation become vague, and one type merges with another. In a way, a map improves upon a photograph of a part of Earth by clarifying the image and showing only the most important aspects.

CONTINENT MAPS

To show the three-dimensional quality of the real world, each of the major divisions of this atlas opens with a relief/vegetation map of a continent as viewed from space. These maps are based on raised-relief models painted to show predominant vegetation types for each area. The color key provided below indicates the color tones used on the maps to represent vegetation classifications such as grassland, forest, desert and tundra, and so on. Opposite each relief/vegetation map is a political map of that continent drawn to the same scale.

POLITICAL MAPS

The core of this atlas is contained in the collection of detailed political maps for countries of the world. These are the maps that the reader is most likely to refer to when faced with such questions as Where? How big? What is it near? Each political map stresses *political* facts—international boundaries, internal political divisions, administrative centers, cities and towns. Countries of political, economic, or tourist importance are shown at a larger scale than less important nations. Areas of dense settlement or special significance are sometimes enlarged and portrayed in detailed inset maps. When there are rival claims to territory, the boundaries that actually exist are shown. This does not mean that every country in the world recognizes these boundaries, but simply shows the nations that are administering the areas at the time of printing of the atlas. As a special feature of this atlas each political map is accompanied by a global view that pinpoints the subject area. In addition, a diagram shows the size of the subject area relative to all or part of the United States.

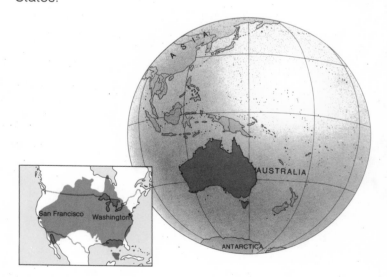

MAP SCALES

Each map has been drawn to a scale that goes hand-in-hand with the amount of detail that is presented. No attempt to standardize scales has been made. In certain cases a whole map unit may be devoted to a single nation if that nation is considered to be of prime interest to most atlas users. In other cases several nations will be shown on a single map. As mentioned before, highly populated

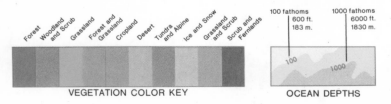

VEGETATION COLOR KEY   OCEAN DEPTHS

or otherwise important areas are often enlarged and presented as detailed maps along with the general map. The reader is advised to refer to the linear or "bar" scales in miles and kilometers, which accompany each general map or inset map. In the title box a representative fraction or natural scale ratio gives the relationship of a unit distance on the main map to the corresponding distance on Earth measured in those same units. For example, the title box for the map of Canada shows a ratio of 1:15,200,000. This means that one inch on the map of Canada equals approximately 15,200,000 inches on Earth.

MAP PROJECTIONS

To present all or part of Earth's curved surface on a flat plane, cartographers have developed *projections*. There are well over 200 types of projections, but each must sacrifice some accuracy for convenience. Only a globe can show Earth accurately. A map projection may show true shape, true direction, or equal area; however, not all can be shown at the same time. The projection selected depends on the scale and purpose for which the map is intended.

Most map projections are related to projecting a sphere onto a cylinder, a cone, or a flat plane (see illustrations below). The actual projections are usually slightly different from the original geometrical conceptions. Often, only a small portion of the projection, that which is most accurate, will be used in the final map. Different projections will be used for areas of different size or areas at different latitudes. The projection system used for each map appears below the title of the map.

MAP SYMBOLS

Since a map cannot show things as they are on Earth in their true form, cartographers have created symbols to represent cities, political capitals, canals, mountain peaks, boundaries, and so on. Some of the more widely used symbols found in the atlas appear below. Special symbols for a particular map are explained in the legend that appears under the title for that map

A SELECTION OF MAP SYMBOLS USED IN THIS ATLAS

Symbol	Meaning	Symbol	Meaning
— ·· —	International Boundaries		River
— · —	Provincial or State Boundaries		Seasonal River
— — —	Other Boundaries		Lake
☆ ✵	Capitals of Countries		Seasonal Lake
◉ ⌀	Other Capitals		Dry Lake Bed
○ ●	City or Town		Swamp
∴	Ruins		Desert
ᴗ	Oasis		Lava Field
□	Point of Interest	▲	Mountain Peak
— — —	Canal	Ⅺ	Mountain Pass

A comprehensive map index with an explanation of its use begins on page 100. Also at the back of the atlas are two reference aids: A table of Comparative Geographical Statistics (page 97) gives precise data on the world's physical features—the largest seas and islands, longest rivers, highest mountains, and so on. For quick reference, the concise Gazetteer of the World (pages 98–99) provides page numbers, capital cities, and population and area figures for all countries, major political entities and continents.

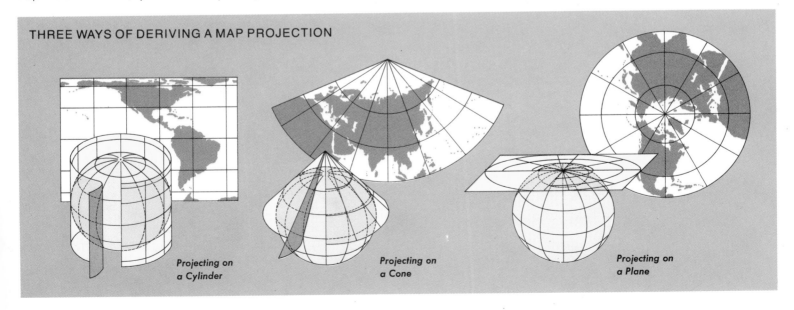

THREE WAYS OF DERIVING A MAP PROJECTION

Projecting on a Cylinder

Projecting on a Cone

Projecting on a Plane

THE WATER PLANET

Earth is unique among the planets of our solar system because of its abundance of water—nearly seventy percent of the surface is covered by it. The continents take up only thirty percent of the globe. The oceans are continuous; that is, they are really sections of one great sea that surrounds all the landmasses.

Geographers recognize four great divisions: the Pacific, Atlantic, Indian, and Arctic oceans. Of these, the Pacific Ocean is by far the largest and deepest, followed by the Atlantic and Indian oceans. Where the three larger oceans all come together around Antarctica, they form what is sometimes called the Antarctic Ocean. The Arctic Ocean is the smallest and shallowest of the four.

Our early ancestors often viewed the ocean as a hostile environment. But today the sea is a prime source of food and may become even more vital as a source of energy. The seas, once the means of exploration and conquest, today play a major role in the transportation of people and goods. The global views on these two pages present different aspects of Earth's water-land relationship.

Most of Earth's landmass is concentrated in a one-island world made up of Europe, Asia, and Africa.

The Atlantic and Pacific oceans isolate the American continents on two sides.

The Atlantic Ocean remains a barrier between the Old and the New World.

The great expanses of the Pacific Ocean make a half-world that is almost all water.

The Arctic Ocean is ringed by land areas, making it more like a shallow sea.

The waters of the Indian Ocean wash four continents: Asia, Africa, Australia, and Antarctica.

In the Antarctic the view in every direction is of the sea, with only tips of other continents on the horizon.

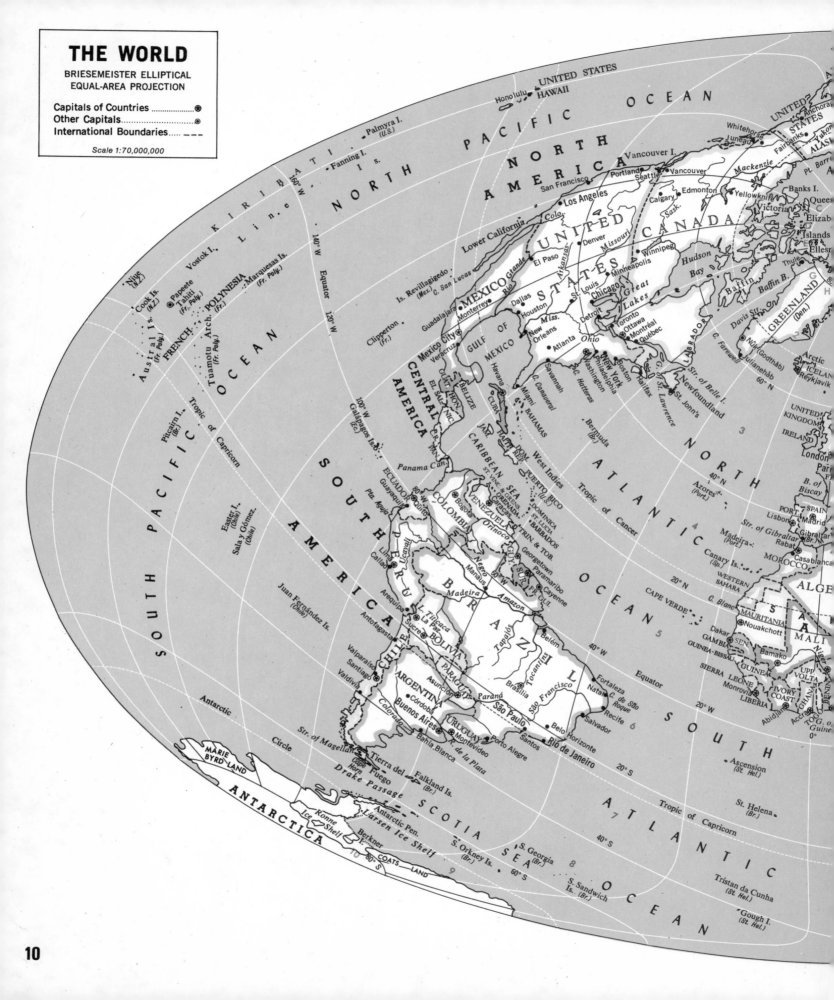

WORLD

POPULATION	4,415,000,000
LAND AREA	57,609,000 sq. mi.
	(149,208,000 sq. km.)
WATER AREA	139,341,000 sq. mi.
	(360,892,500 sq. km.)
TOTAL AREA	196,950,000 sq. mi.
	(510,100,500 sq. km.)

11

NORTH AMERICA

LAMBERT AZIMUTHAL EQUAL-AREA PROJECTION

SCALE OF MILES

0 100 200 400 600 800

SCALE OF KILOMETERS

0 200 400 600 800

Capitals of Countries..............★

International Boundaries..........

Other Boundaries.....................

Canals..

Scale 1:34,000,000

© Copyright HAMMOND INCORPORATED, Maplewood, N.J.

UNITED STATES
Western Part

POLYCONIC PROJECTION

SCALE OF MILES

| 0 | 50 | 100 | 200 |

SCALE OF KILOMETERS

| 0 | 50 | 100 | 200 |

Scale 1:6,700,000

Capitals of Countries ⊛
State and Provincial Capitals △
International Boundaries
State and Provincial Boundaries

COLORADO

Aspen ▲Leadville 14,264 ft.
(4348 m.)
Pueblo
Colorado Springs
Salida
Pikes Peak 14,110 ft.
4301 m.
Canon City
Saguache
Center
Aguilar
Gunnison
Blanca Pk. ▲14,317 ft.
(4364 m.)
Montrose
Ouray
Saguache
Paonia
Delta
Grand Junction
Silverton
Telluride
Ouray
Montrose
Durango
Aztec
Farmington

NEW MEXICO

Park View Wheeler Pk.
N. Truchas Pk. 13,161 ft.
(4011 m.) 13,110 ft.
(3996 m.)
Questa ▲Taos
Santa Rosa
Las Vegas
Santa Fe
Espanola
Los Alamos
Albuquerque
Bernalillo
Pecos
Vaughn
Fort Sumner
Roswell
Hagerman
Artesia
Carlsbad
CARLSBAD CAVERNS NAT'L PK.
Carrizozo
Estancia
Mountainair
Belen
Grants
Magdalena
Socorro
San Marcial
Truth or Consequences
Hatch
Deming
Las Cruces
Anthony
El Paso
Silver City
Bayard
Lordsburg
Columbus
GUADALUPE MTS. NAT'L PK.
Guadalupe Mts.
Dell City
Van Horn
McNary

TEXAS (TEX.)

Presidio
BIG BEND NAT'L PK.
Marfa

ARIZONA

MESA VERDE NAT'L PARK
Cortez
Carrizo Mts.
Kayenta
Chaco R.
CONTINENTAL DIVIDE
PETRIFIED FOREST NAT'L PARK
Gallup
Zuni
Saint Johns
Holbrook
Snowflake
Springerville
Clifton
Morenci
Safford
Willcox
Douglas
Bisbee
Nogales
Heroica Nogales

CALIFORNIA

Los Angeles
Long Beach
San Diego

17

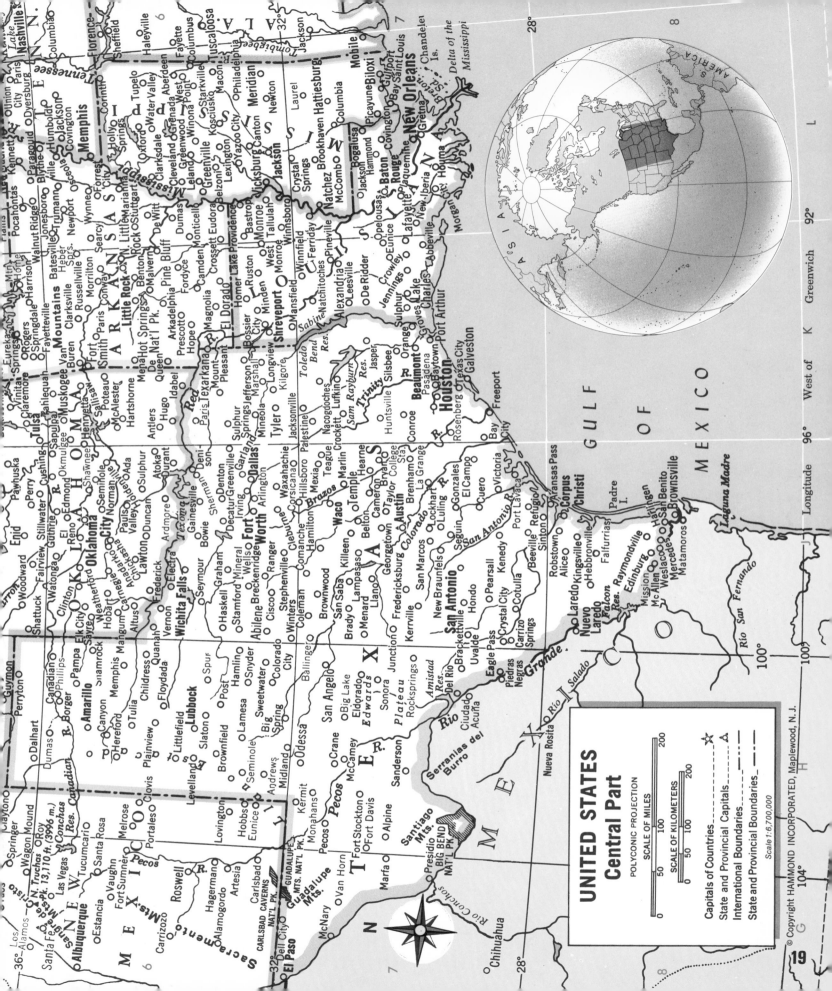

UNITED STATES
Central Part

POLYCONIC PROJECTION

SCALE OF MILES
0   50   100   200

SCALE OF KILOMETERS
0   50   100   200

Capitals of Countries _____ ⊛
State and Provincial Capitals _____ ⚐
International Boundaries _____ —··—··—
State and Provincial Boundaries _____ —·—·—

Scale 1:6,700,000

© Copyright HAMMOND INCORPORATED, Maplewood, N.J.

19

UNITED STATES
Eastern Part

POLYCONIC PROJECTION

SCALE OF MILES

0   50   100   200

SCALE OF KILOMETERS

0 50 100   200

Capitals of Countries _____ ☆
State and Provincial Capitals _____ ⊙
International Boundaries _____
State and Provincial Boundaries _____

Scale 1:6,700,000

21

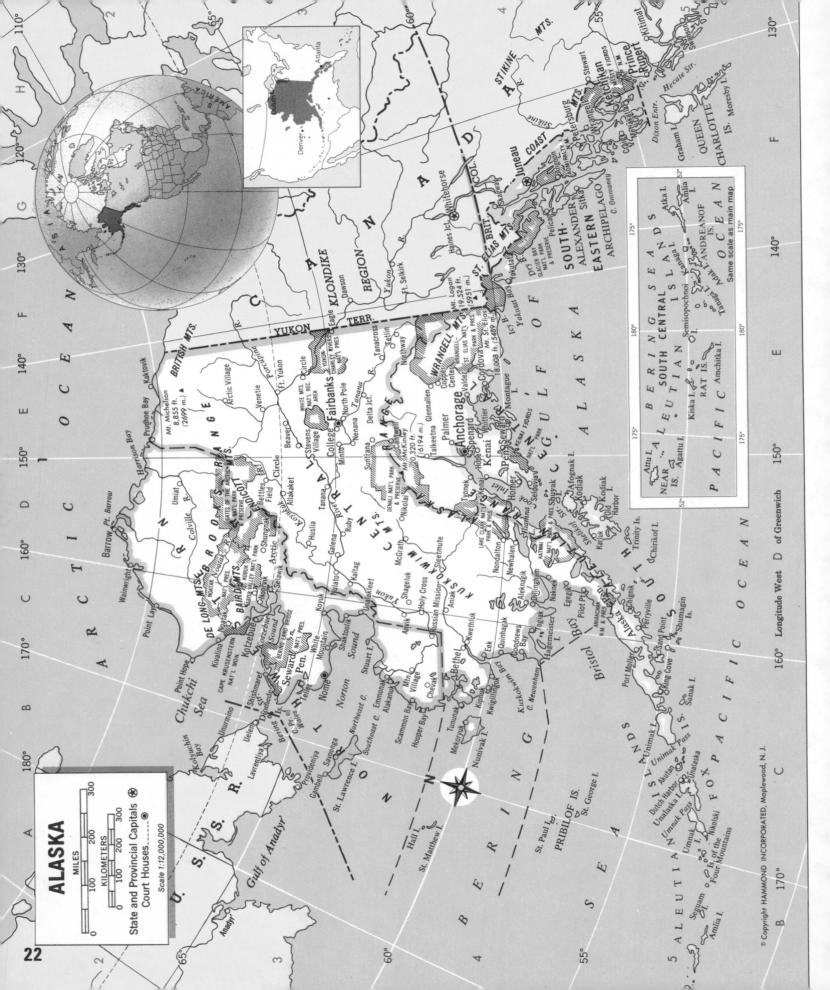

ALASKA

MILES
300 / 200 / 100 / 0

KILOMETERS
300 / 200 / 100 / 0

Scale 1:12,000,000

State and Provincial Capitals ⊛
Court Houses ⊙

22

® Copyright HAMMOND INCORPORATED, Maplewood, N.J.

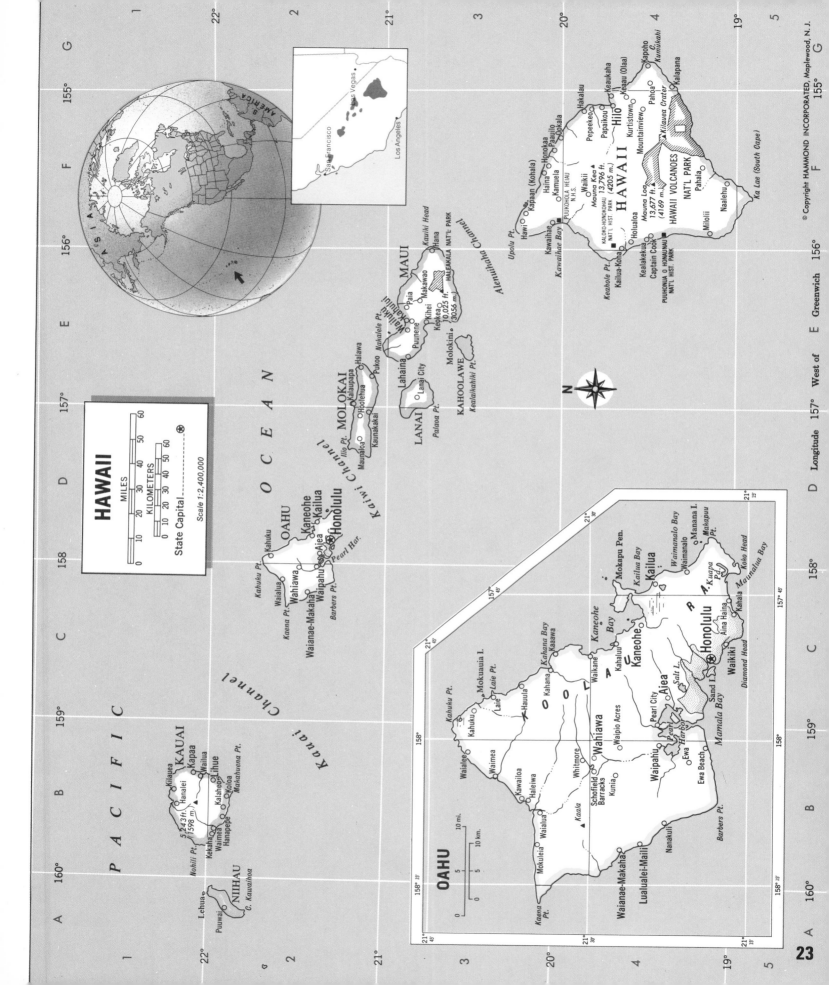

HAWAII

MILES
KILOMETERS

State Capital........... ⊛

Scale 1:2,400,000

© Copyright HAMMOND INCORPORATED, Maplewood, N.J.

OAHU

Kaena Pt.
Mokuleia
Waialua
Kahuku Pt.
Kahuku
Mokuauia I.
Laie Pt.
Laie
Hauula
Kahana
Kahana Bay
Kaaawa
Kaena
Kaneohe Bay
Waikane
Kahaluu
Waialee
Waimea
Haleiwa
Kawailoa
Whitmore
Wahiawa
Schofield Barracks
Kaala
Kunia
Waipio Acres
K O O L A U
Mokapu Pen.
Kailua Bay
Kailua
Waimanalo
Waimanalo Bay
Manana I.
Makapuu Pt.
Kuapa Pd.
Koko Head
Kahala
Maunalua Bay
Diamond Head
Waikiki
HONOLULU ⊛
Aina Haina
Sand I.
Salt L.
Aiea
Pearl City
Pearl Harbor
Ewa
Ewa Beach
Barbers Pt.
Mamala Bay
Waipahu
Nanakuli
Lualualei-Maili
Waianae-Makaha

OCEAN
PACIFIC

Kaena Pt.
Kahuku Pt.
Kahuku
Waialua
Wahiawa
Waipahu
Aiea
Honolulu ⊛
Pearl Har.
Barbers Pt.
Kaena Pt.
Waianae-Makaha
Kailua
Kaneohe
OAHU

MOLOKAI
Halawa
Kalaupapa
Hoolehua
Kaunakakai
Pukoo
Kalae Pt.
Ilio Pt.
Kamalo Channel
Maunaloa
Kahalui Channel
Mahalele Pt.

LANAI
Lanai City
Palaoa Pt.

KAHOOLAWE
Kealaikahiki Pt.

MAUI
Wailuku
Kahului
Paia
Makawao
Kihei
Keokea
Puunene
Lahaina
Molokini
Kauiki Head
Hana
HALEAKALA NAT'L PARK
10,025 ft.
(3056 m.)
Alenuihaha Channel

Kaiwi Channel

Kauai Channel

PACIFIC

NIIHAU
Lehua
Puuwai
C. Kawaihoa

KAUAI
Kilauea
Hanalei
Kapaa
Wailua
Lihue
Kalaheo
Koloa
Kekaha
Waimea
Hanapepe
Makahuena Pt.
Nohili Pt.
5,243 ft.
(1598 m.)

HAWAII
Upolu Pt.
Hawi
Kapaau (Kohala)
Kawaihae
Kawaihae Bay
Haina
Honokaa
Paauilo
Ookala
Papaikou
Kurtistown
Mountainview
Kukuihaele
Waimea
Kamuela
PUUKOHOLA HEIAU N.H.S.
Mauna Kea
13,796 ft. (4205 m.)
KALOKO-HONOKOHAU NAT'L HIST. PARK
Keahole Pt.
Kailua-Kona
Kealakekua
Captain Cook
PUUHONUA O HONAUNAU NAT'L HIST. PARK
Holualoa
Kainaliu
Milolii
Ka Lae (South Cape)
Naalehu
Pahala
Mauna Loa
13,677 ft. (4169 m.)
HAWAII VOLCANOES NAT'L PARK
Kilauea Crater
Kalapana
Kumukahi
Kapoho
Pahoa
Keaau (Olaa)
Keaukaha
Hakalau
Pepeekeo
Hilo

Hilo Pt.

D Longitude 157° West of E Greenwich 156° G

23

CANADA

CONIC PROJECTION

SCALE OF MILES

0   50   100   200   300

SCALE OF KILOMETERS

0   50 100   200   300   400   500

Capitals of Countries .... ☆

Provincial & Territorial Capitals ..... △

International Boundaries ._._._.

Provincial Boundaries _._._.

Scale 1:15,200,000

24

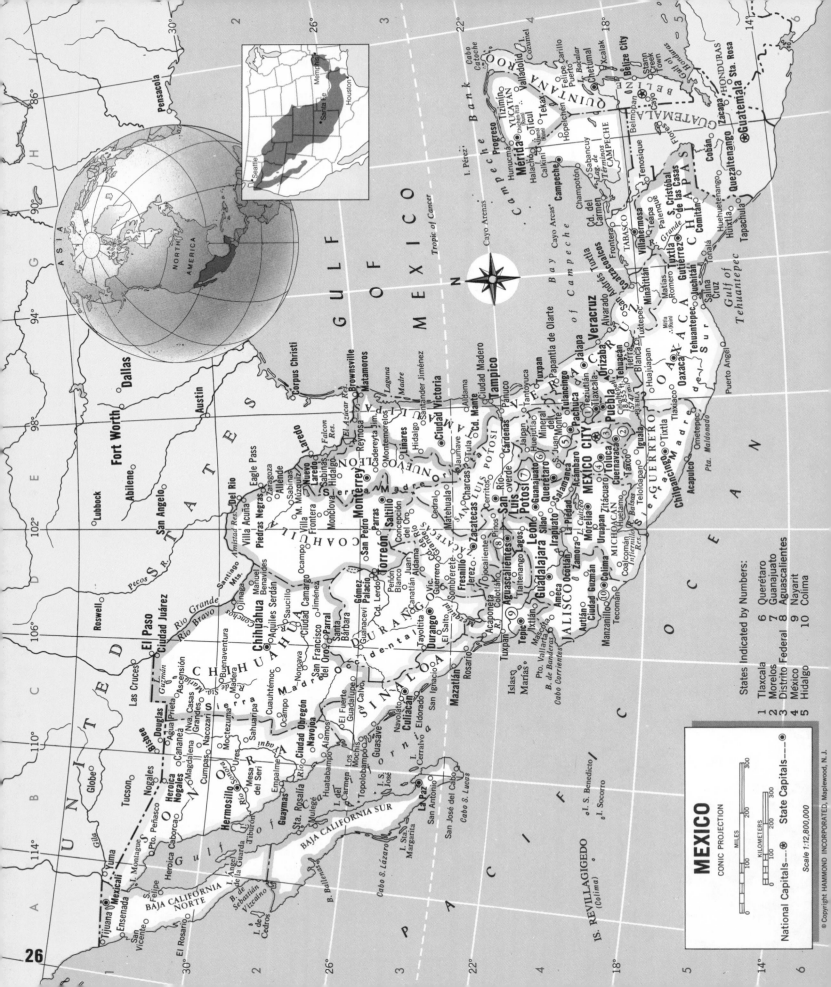

MEXICO

CONIC PROJECTION

States Indicated by Numbers:

1 Tlaxcala   6 Querétaro
2 Morelos   7 Guanajuato
3 Distrito Federal   8 Aguascalientes
4 México   9 Nayarit
5 Hidalgo   10 Colima

National Capitals ---- ⊛
State Capitals ---- ◉

Scale 1:12,800,000

MILES
0   100   200   300

KILOMETERS
0   100   200   300

© Copyright HAMMOND INCORPORATED, Maplewood, N.J.

26

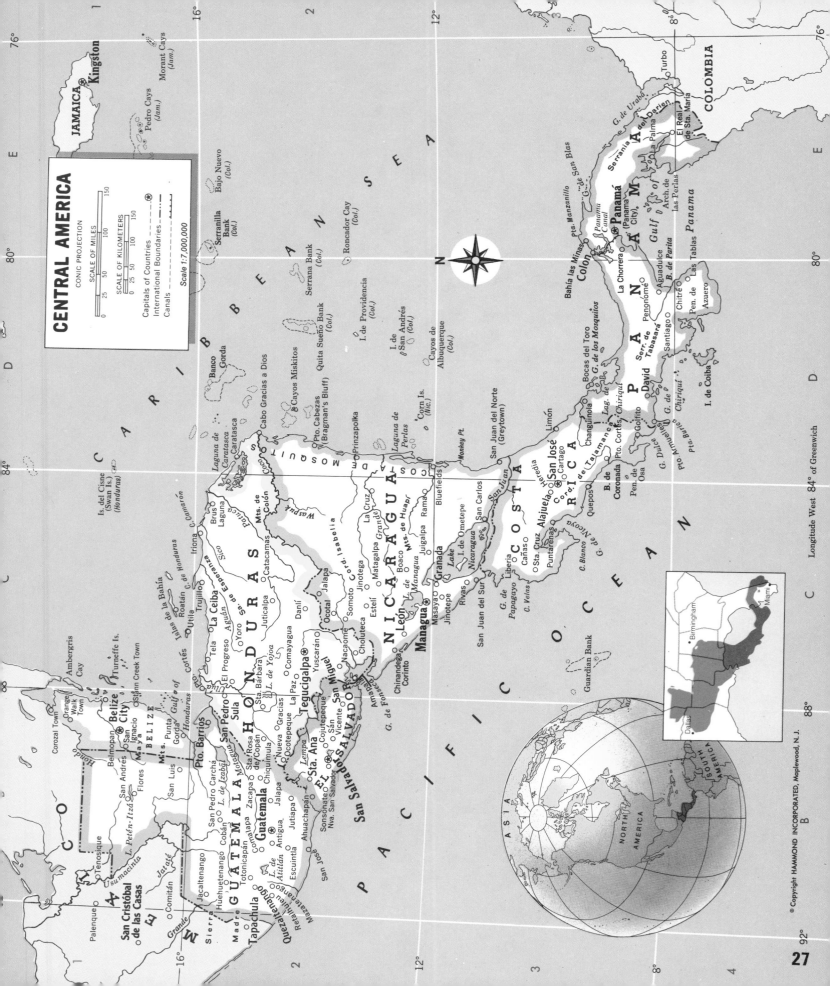

CENTRAL AMERICA

CONIC PROJECTION

SCALE OF MILES
0   25   50   100   150

SCALE OF KILOMETERS
0   25   50   100   150

Capitals of Countries ⊕
International Boundaries -----
Canals .....

Scale 1:7,000,000

JAMAICA
⊕ Kingston

Morant Cays
(Jam.)

Pedro Cays
(Jam.)

Bajo Nuevo
(Col.)

Serranilla
Bank
(Col.)

Banco
Gorda

Serrana Bank
(Col.)

Quita Sueño Bank
(Col.)

Roncador Cay
(Col.)

I. de Providencia
(Col.)

I. de
San Andrés
(Col.)

Cayos de
Albuquerque
(Col.)

C A R I B B E A N   S E A

Is. del Cisne
(Swan Is.)
(Honduras)

Laguna de
Caratasca
C. Caratasca

Cabo Gracias a Dios

Cayos Miskitos

Pto. Cabezas
(Bragman's Bluff)

Pto. Prinzapolka

Laguna de
Perlas

Corn Is.
(Nic.)

Monkey Pt.

San Juan del Norte
(Greytown)

Bluefields

Rama

Turbo

COLOMBIA

G. de Urabá

El Real
de Sta. María

La Palma

Serranía   del   Darién

Bahía las Minas Pta. Manzanillo G. de San Blas

Colón   Panamá Canal ⊕ Panamá
(Panama City)

La Chorrera

P A N A M A

Gulf of
Panama

Arch. de
las Perlas

Penonomé Aguadulce B. de Parita
Santiago   Chitré   Pen. de
Serr. de   Las Tablas   Azuero
Tabasará   Panama
Bocas del Toro G. de los Mosquitos
David
Chiriquí   G. de º I. de Coiba
Pto. Armuelles Pto. Cortés Chiriquí
Golfito
G. Dulce
B. de
Coronada Pto. Cortés
Pen. de
Osa

Changuinola Laguna de Chiriquí

Limón

Quepos

San José ⊕
Heredia
Alajuela Cartago
COSTA RICA
Coronada
San Carlos
I. de Ometepe
Liberia

N   O   R   T   H

N

COSTA DE MOSQUITOS

H O N D U R A S

Mts. de
Colón

Catacamas

Juticalpa

Jalapa

Mts. de Huapí
Cord. Isabelia
Matagalpa
Grande

Juigalpa
Boaco
L. de
Managua
Masaya
Jinotepe
Rivas

N I C A R A G U A

León
Managua ⊗
Granada
Lake
Nicaragua
San Juan del Sur
G. de
Papagayo
C. Velas
Guardian Bank
Sta. Cruz
Cañas
Puntarenas
Nicoya
G. de Nicoya
C. Blanco

Ocotal
Somoto
Estelí
Jinotega
La Cruz
Chinandega Corinto

Danlí
Choluteca
Nacaome
San
Amapala
G. de Fonseca

Brus
Laguna

Iriona C. Camarón
Trujillo
Tela La Ceiba
Utila Islas de la Bahía
Roatán
Cortés
Yoro Aguán
El Progreso
San Pedro
Sula
Sta. Bárbara
L. de Yojoa
Comayagua
La Paz
Tegucigalpa ⊗
Yuscarán

Waspuk
Coco
Patuca
Sico
Mts. de
Esperanza

Belize
⊕ City
B E L I Z E
Belmopan
San Ignacio
San
San Andrés Creek Town
Orange
Walk Town
Corozal Town
Ambergris
Cay
Turneffe Is.

Hondo

Tenosique

Palenque

San Cristóbal
de las Casas

Comitán

Jataté

Usumacinta

M a d r e

G U A T E M A L A

Flores
L. Petén-Itzá
San Luis
San Pedro Carchá
Cobán
Totonicapán
Huehuetenango
Jacaltenango
Quezaltenango
Guatemala ⊗
Antigua
Escuintla
San José
Mazatenango
Jutiapa

Sierra

Tapachula

Quezaltenango

Pto. Barrios
Punta
Gorda
Gulf of
Honduras
L. de Izabal
Motagua
Zacapa
Chiquimula
Sta. Rosa
de Copán
Nueva
Ocotepeque
Jalapa

Lempa

Nueva
San Salvador
San Salvador ⊗
E L   S A L V A D O R
Ahuachapán
Sta. Ana
Cojutepeque
Sonsonate
Usulután
San Vicente
San Miguel

Comalapa

Grande

L. de
Atitlán

P A C I F I C   O C E A N

Longitude West 84° of Greenwich

⊗ Copyright HAMMOND INCORPORATED, Maplewood, N.J.

ASIA
NORTH
AMERICA
SOUTH
AMERICA

Birmingham
Dallas
Miami

27

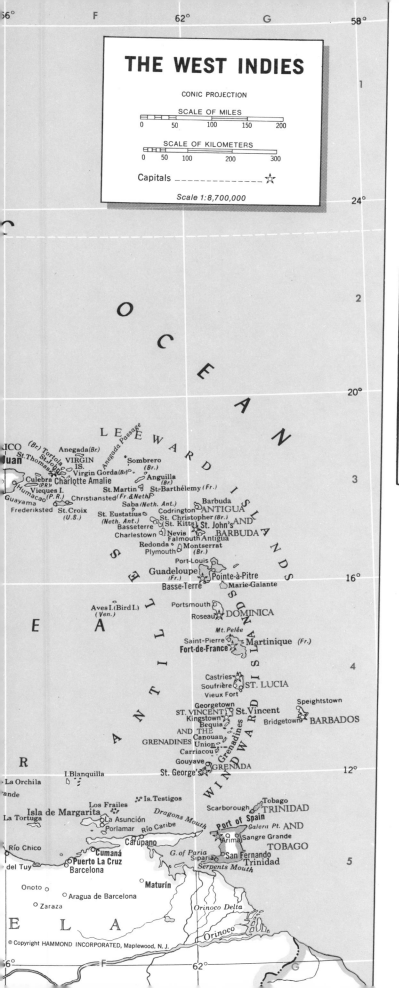

THE WEST INDIES

CONIC PROJECTION

SCALE OF MILES

0   50   100   150   200

SCALE OF KILOMETERS

0   50   100   200   300

Capitals — — — — — — ☆

Scale 1:8,700,000

O C E A N

L E E W A R D   I S L A N D S

RICO (Br.) Tortola (Br.)

St.Thomas Anegada (Br.)

Juan VIRGIN

St.Thomas IS. Sombrero (Br.)

Culebra Charlotte Amalie Virgin Gorda (Br.)

(P.R.) Anguilla (Br.)

Vieques I. (P.R.) St. Martin St-Barthélemy (Fr.)

Humacao Christiansted (Fr.&Neth.)

Guayama (U.S.) Saba (Neth. Ant.) Barbuda

Frederiksted St.Croix Codrington ANTIGUA

St. Eustatius St. Christopher (Br.)

(Neth. Ant.) (St. Kitts) St. John's

Basseterre BARBUDA

Charlestown Nevis Falmouth Antigua

Redonda Montserrat

Plymouth (Br.)

Port-Louis

Guadeloupe Pointe-à-Pitre

(Fr.)

Basse-Terre Marie-Galante

Aves I.(Bird I.) Portsmouth

(Ven.) Roseau DOMINICA

Mt. Pelée

Saint-Pierre

Fort-de-France Martinique (Fr.)

E

A

N

T

I

L

L

E

S

Castries

Soufrière ST. LUCIA

Vieux Fort

Georgetown

ST. VINCENT St. Vincent Speightstown

Kingstown

Bequia Bridgetown BARBADOS

AND THE

GRENADINES Canouan

Union

Carriacou

Gouyave

I.Blanquilla GRENADA

St. George's

La Orchila

rande Is. Testigos

Los Frailes Tobago

Isla de Margarita Scarborough TRINIDAD

La Tortuga La Asunción Dragons Mouth AND

Porlamar Galera Pt.

Río Caribe TOBAGO

Río Chico Carúpano Arima Sangre Grande

Cumaná G. of Paria

del Tuy Puerto La Cruz Siparia San Fernando

Barcelona Trinidad

Serpents Mouth

Onoto Maturín

Aragua de Barcelona

Zaraza

E L A Orinoco Delta

Orinoco

© Copyright HAMMOND INCORPORATED, Maplewood, N.J.

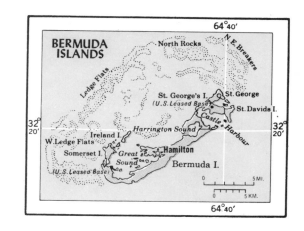

BERMUDA ISLANDS

North Rocks N.E. Breakers

Ledge Flats

St. George's I. St. George

(U.S. Leased Base) St. Davids I.

Castle Harbour

Ireland I. Harrington Sound

W. Ledge Flats

Somerset I. Hamilton

Great Bermuda I.

Sound

(U.S. Leased Base)

64°40'

0   5 MI.

0   5 KM.

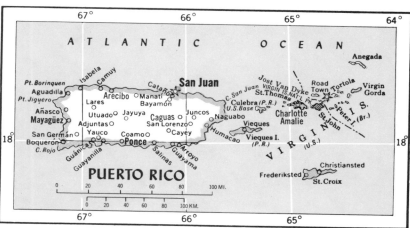

A T L A N T I C   O C E A N

Anegada

Pt. Borinquen Isabela Camuy

Aguadilla Cataño San Juan

Pt. Jiguero Arecibo Manati Jost Van Dyke Road

Bayamón C. San Juan VIRGIN IS. Town Tortola Virgin

Añasco Lares St.Thomas Gorda

Mayagüez Utuado Jayuya Caguas Juncos Culebra (P. R.) Charlotte

Adjuntas San Lorenzo U.S. Base St. John Amalie

Boquerón Yauco Coamo Cayey Naguabo Peter I. (Br.)

San Germán Guánica Ponce Vieques

C. Rojo Guayanilla Salinas Arroyo Humacao Vieques I. V I R G I N (P. R.)

Guayama Guayama (U.S.)

PUERTO RICO Frederiksted Christiansted

St. Croix

0   20   40   60   80   100 MI.

0   20   40   60   80   100 KM.

ASIA

Butte

Sacramento Denver

Houston

NORTH AMERICA

SOUTH AMERICA

© Copyright HAMMOND INCORPORATED, Maplewood, N.J.

SOUTH AMERICA

LAMBERT AZIMUTHAL EQUAL AREA PROJECTION

SCALE OF MILES
0   100   200   400   600

SCALE OF KILOMETERS
0 100 200   400   600

Capitals of Countries.................☆
International Boundaries............ — · —
Canals.............................

Scale 1:30,000,000

31

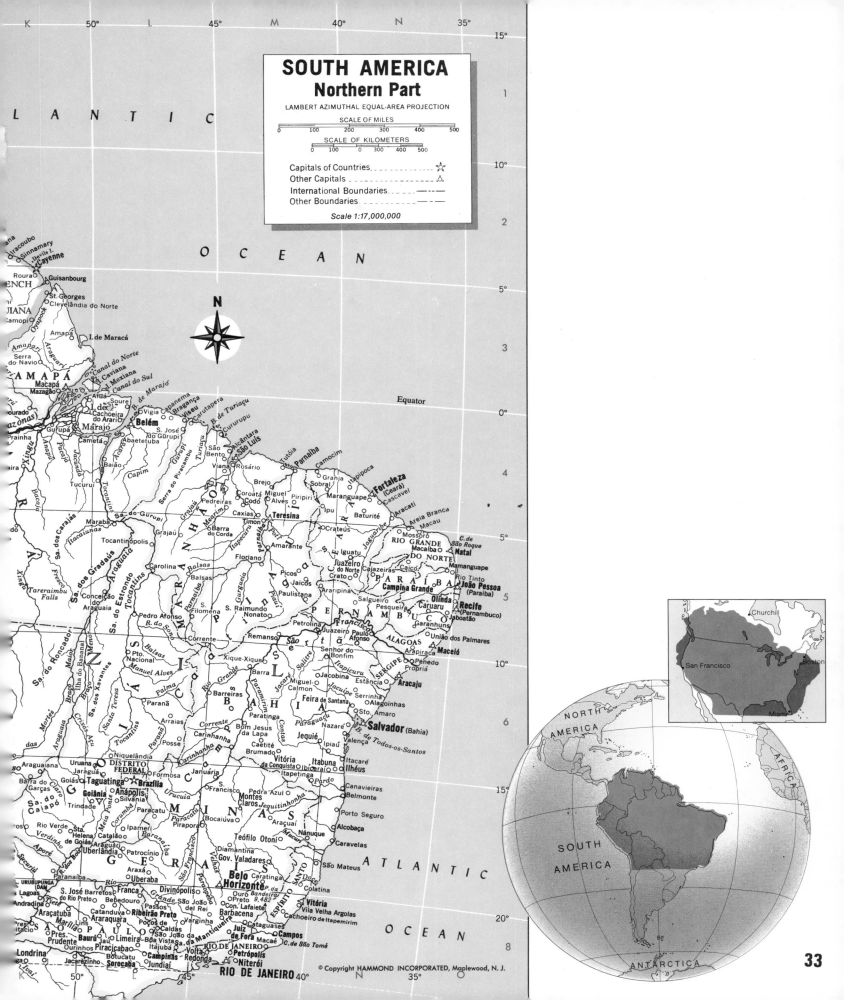

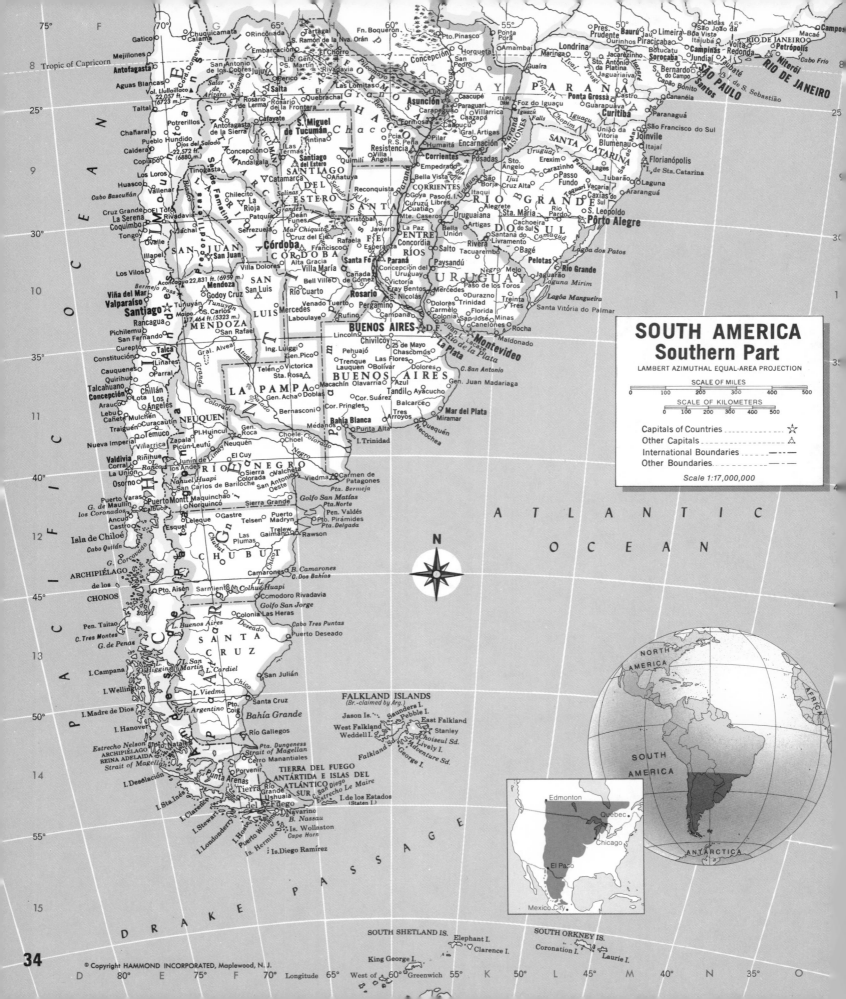

SOUTH AMERICA
Southern Part

LAMBERT AZIMUTHAL EQUAL-AREA PROJECTION

SCALE OF MILES
0   100   200   300   400   500

SCALE OF KILOMETERS
0   100 200 300 400 500

Capitals of Countries .... ☆
Other Capitals .... △
International Boundaries _____
Other Boundaries _ _ _ _ _ _ _ _ _

Scale 1:17,000,000

34

ATLANTIC OCEAN

PACIFIC OCEAN

DRAKE PASSAGE

FALKLAND ISLANDS
(Br.-claimed by Arg.)

Tropic of Capricorn

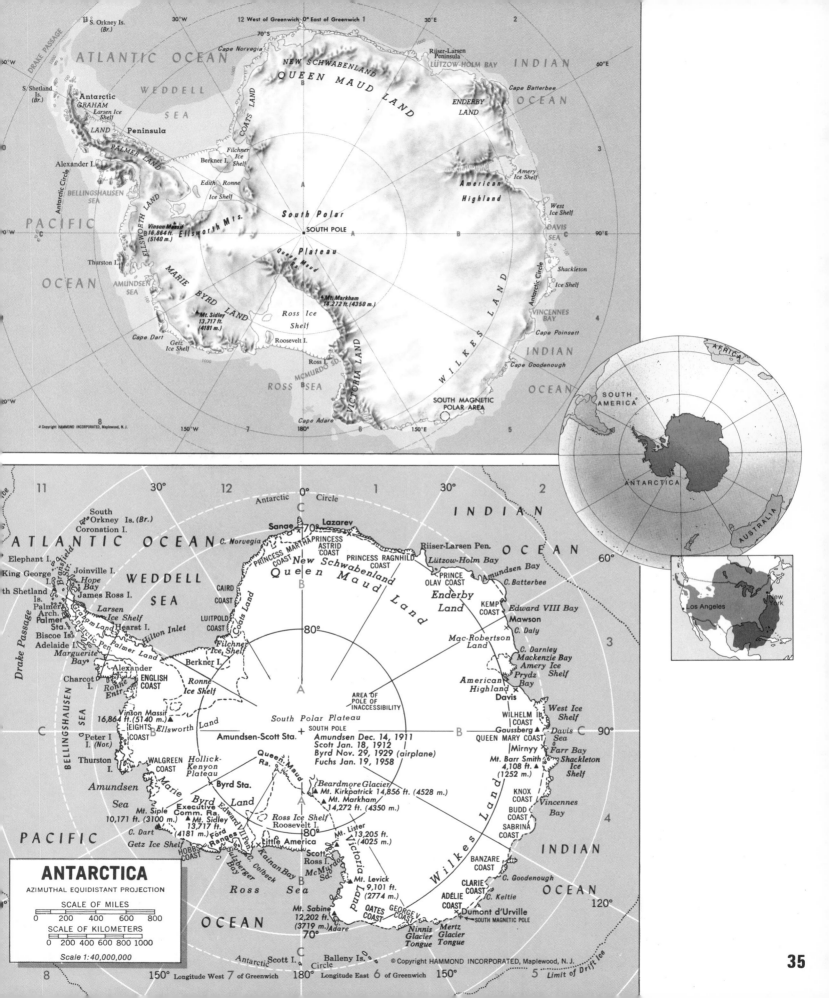

ANTARCTICA

AZIMUTHAL EQUIDISTANT PROJECTION

SCALE OF MILES

0   200   400   600   800

SCALE OF KILOMETERS

0   200 400 600 800 1000

Scale 1:40,000,000

© Copyright HAMMOND INCORPORATED, Maplewood, N.J.

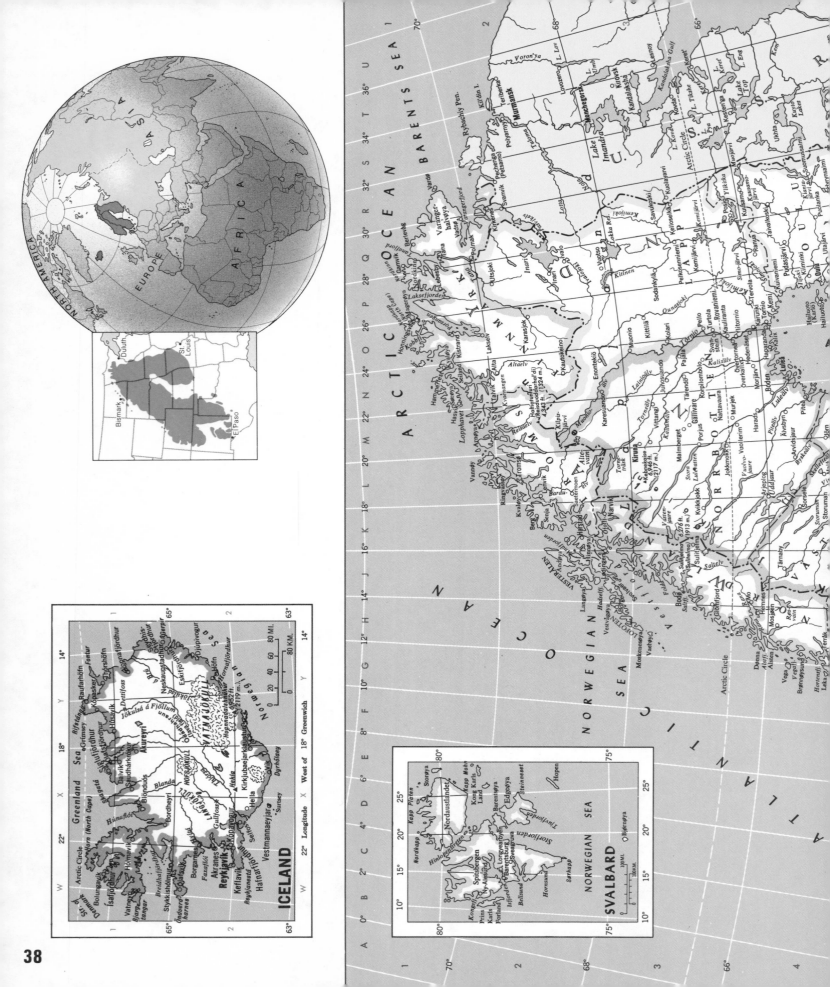

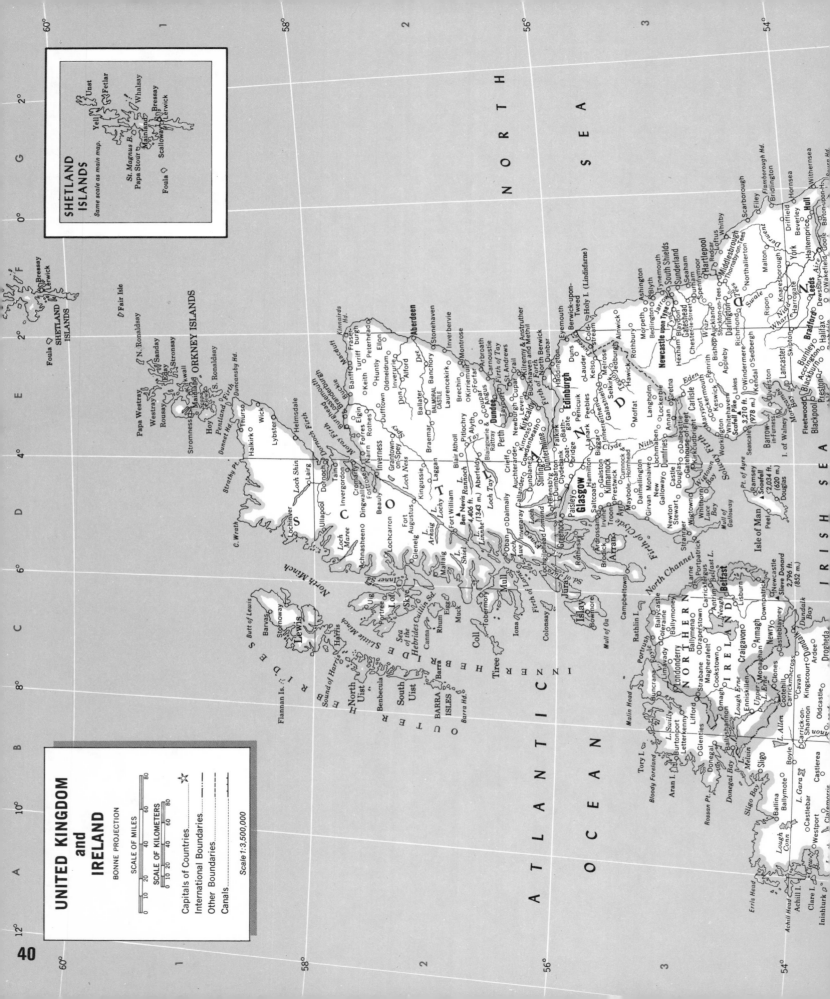

UNITED KINGDOM and IRELAND

BONNE PROJECTION

SCALE OF MILES
0 10 20   40   60   80

SCALE OF KILOMETERS
0 10 20   40   60   80

Capitals of Countries................☆
International Boundaries..............
Other Boundaries.....................
Canals...............................

Scale 1:3,500,000

SHETLAND ISLANDS

Same scale as main map.

Unst
Yell
Fetlar
Whalsay
Mainland
Bressay
St. Magnus B.
Papa Stour
Scalloway
Lerwick
Foula

60° 58° 56° 54°

NORTH SEA

ATLANTIC OCEAN

IRISH SEA

SCOTLAND

Aberdeen
Edinburgh
Glasgow
Dundee

OUTER HEBRIDES
INNER HEBRIDES

ORKNEY ISLANDS
SHETLAND ISLANDS

NORTHERN IRELAND
Belfast
Londonderry

IRELAND

Isle of Man
Douglas

North Channel

North Minch

Ben Nevis 4,406 ft. (1343 m.)
Scafell Pike 3,210 ft. (978 m.)
Snaefell 2,034 ft. (620 m.)
Slieve Donard 2,796 ft. (852 m.)

Newcastle upon Tyne
Middlesbrough
Hartlepool
Leeds
Bradford
Hull
York

40

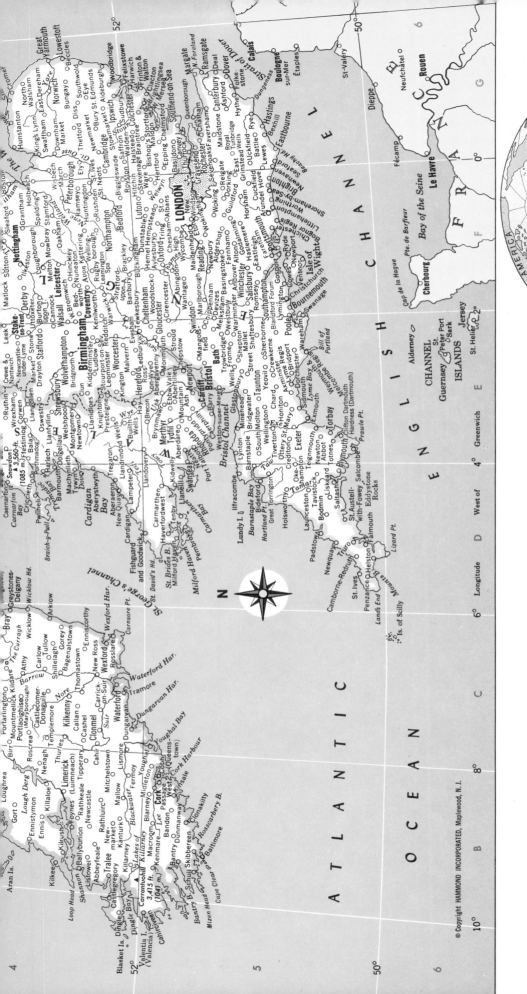

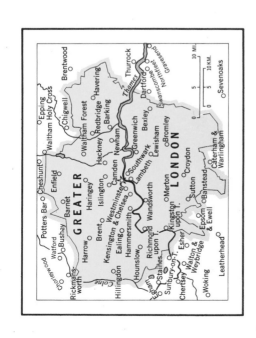

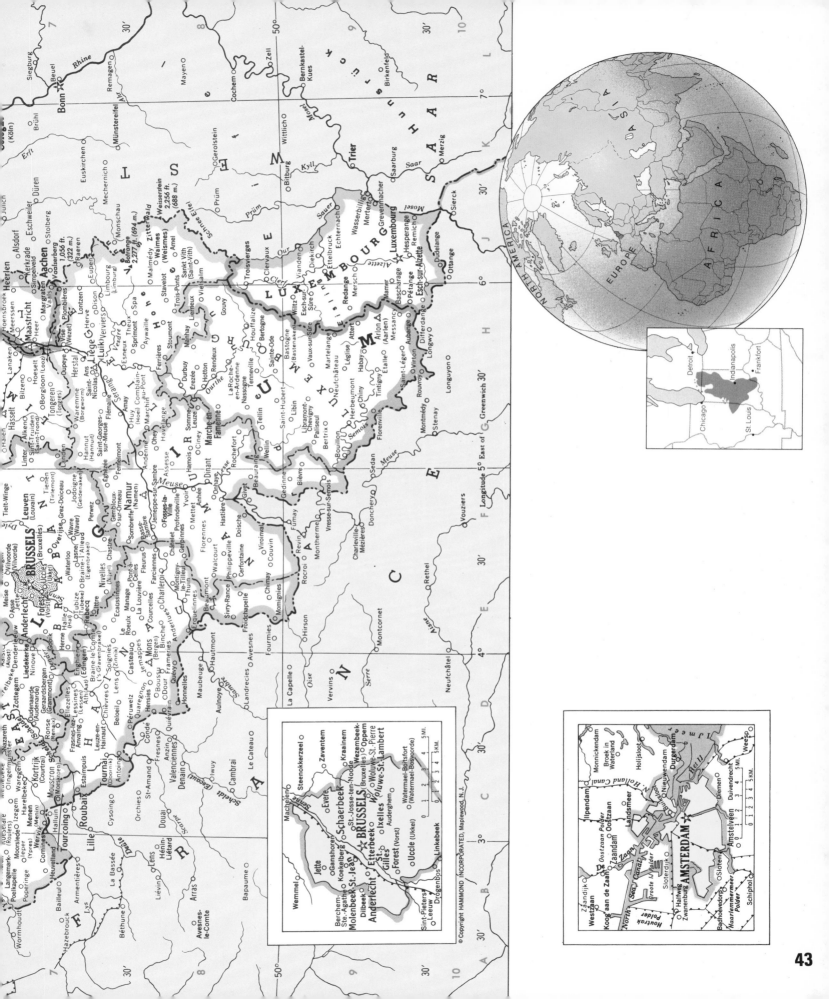

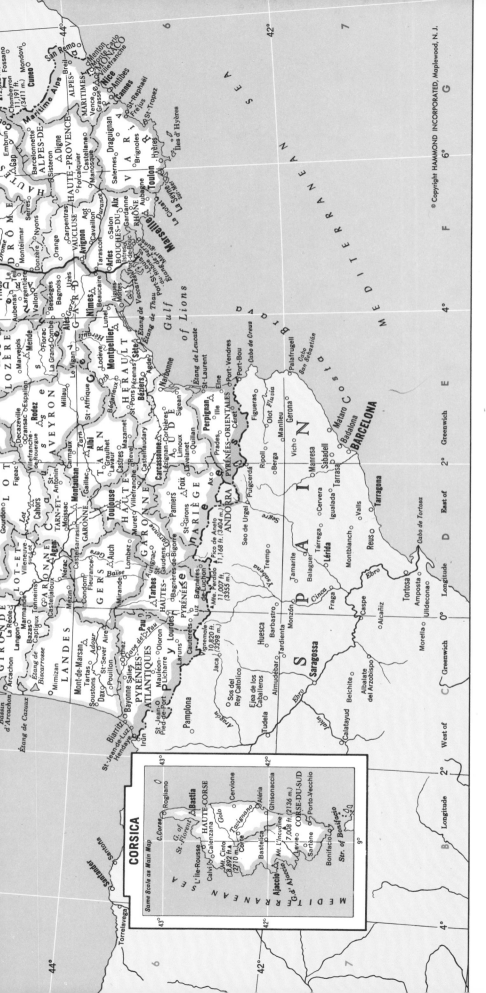

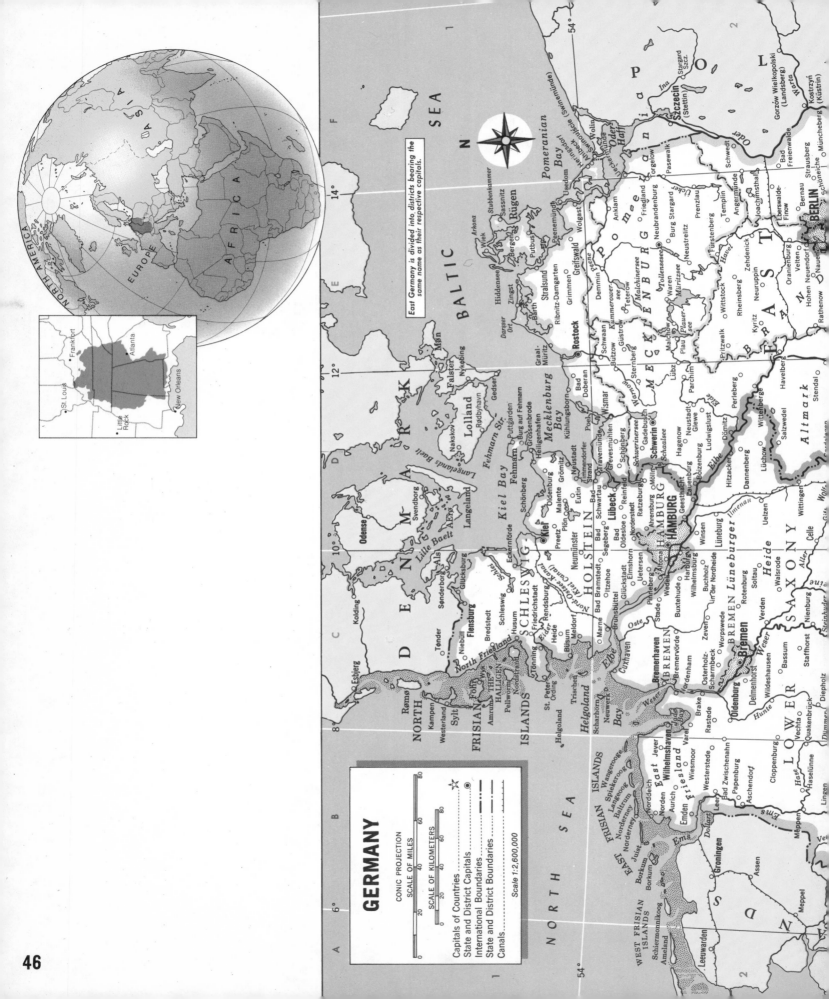

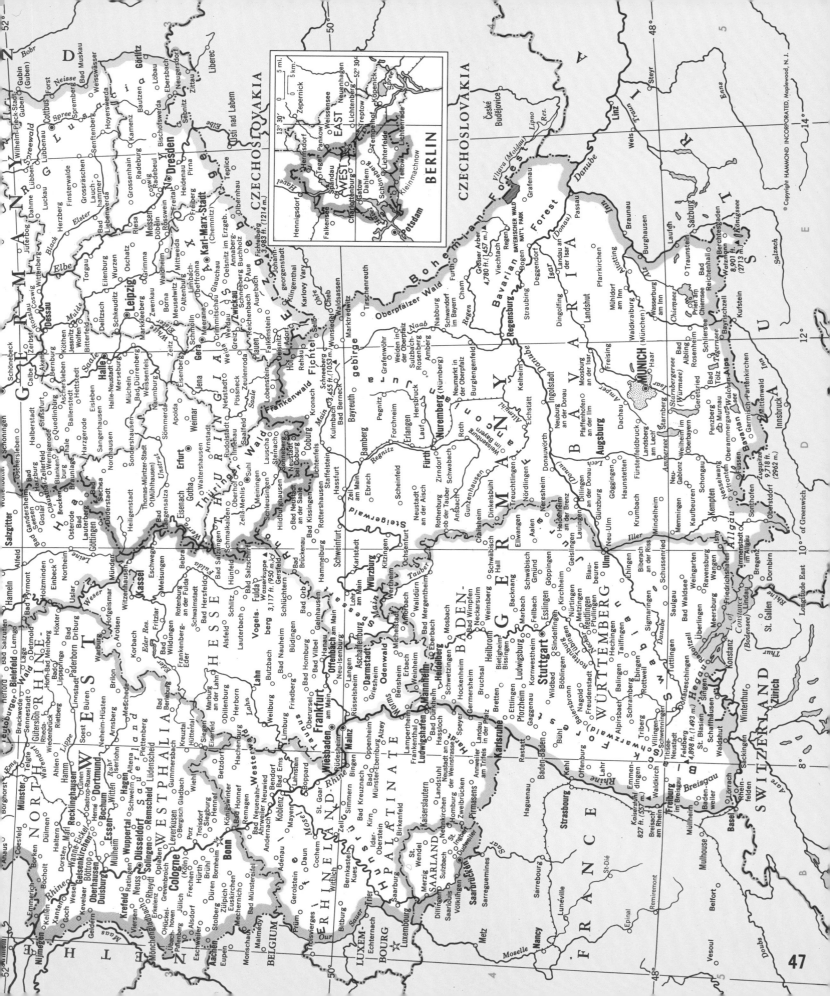

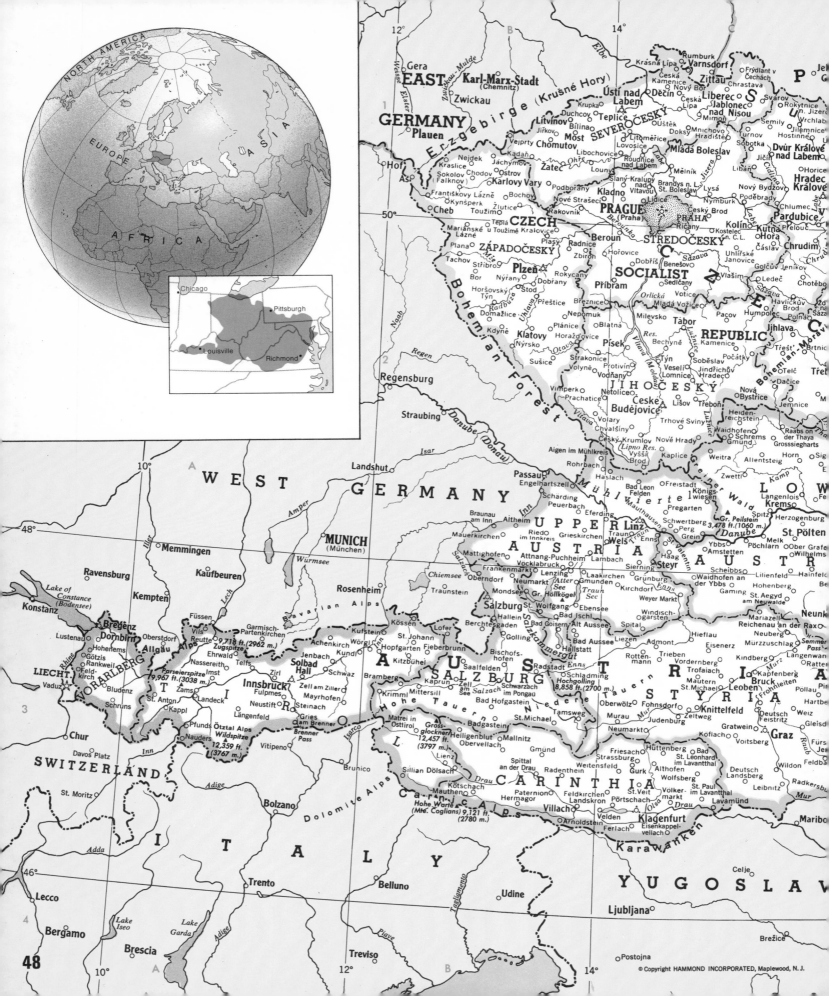

NORTH AMERICA
EUROPE
ASIA
AFRICA

Chicago
Pittsburgh
Louisville
Richmond

EAST
GERMANY
Gera
Weisse — Mulde
Zwickau-Mulde
Plauen
Karl-Marx-Stadt (Chemnitz)
Zwickau
Erzgebirge (Krušné Hory)
Elster
Elbe

Hof
As
Kraslice
Jáchymov
Nejdek
Kadaň
Chodov
Žatec
Sokolov
Falknov
Karlovy Vary
Ostrov
Bochov
Žlutice
Kynšperk
Františkovy Lázně
Toužim
Cheb
Teplá
Mariánské Lázně
Mariánské u Toužimě
Plana
Mže
Bor
Stříbro
Tachov
Radbuza
ZÁPADOČESKÝ
Plzeň
Nýřany
Dobřany
Horšovský Týn
Stod
Domažlice
Kdyně
Klatovy
Nýrsko
Sušice
Otava

Rumburk
Varnsdorf
Zittau
Krásná Lípa
Frýdlant v Čechách
Kamenice
Nový Bor
Chrastava
Liberec
Ústí nad Labem
Děčin
Jablonec nad Nisou
Krupka
Bílina
Česká Lípa
Mimoň
Semily
Jilemnice
Vrchlab
Teplice
Duchcov
Doksy
Mnichovo Hradiště
Turnov
Hostinné
Litvínov
Most
Chomutov
SEVEROČESKÝ
Libochovice
Lovosice
Litoměřice
Jičín
Libán
Dvůr Králové nad Labem
Veprty
Jirkov
Roudnice nad Labem
Mělník
Jizera
Cídlina
Horice
Hradec Králové
Slaný
Kralupy nad Vltavou
Brandys n. L.
Lysá
Nový Bydžov
Poděbrady
Kladno
Podbořany
Nové Strašecí
St. Boleslav
Nymburk
Chlumec
Pardubice
Lidice
Český Brod
Kolín
PRAGUE (Praha)
PRAHA
Kostelec n. C. L.
Kutná Hora
Přelouč
Rakovník
Beroun
Říčany
STŘEDOČESKÝ
Sázava
Čáslav
Chrudim
Hořovice
Benešov
Uhlířské Janovice
Golčův Jeníkov
CZECH
Radnice
Plasy
Dobříš
Sedlčany
Vlašim
Ledeč
Chotěbor
Zbiroh
Březnice
Mladá Vožice
Orlická
Příbram
Milevsko
Havlíčkův Brod
Humpolec
Polná
Sázava
SOCIALIST
Nepomuk
Blatná
Tábor
Pacov
Jihlava
Plánice
Res.
Bechyně
Kamenice
Třešť
Brtnic
Horažďovice
Počátky
Písek
Protivín
Týn
Soběslav
Jindřichův Hradec
Lomnice
REPUBLIC
Strakonice
Veselí
Dačice
Telč
Volyně
Vodňany
Bohemian Morava
Vimperk
Netolice
České
Lišov
Třeboň
Nová Bystřice
Jemnice
Prachatice
JIHOČESKÝ
Budějovice
Heidenreichstein
Volary
Chvalšiny
Trhové Sviny
Waidhofen
Český Krumlov
Lipno Res.
Nové Hrady
Schrems
Raabs on der Thaya
Grosssiegharts
Vyšší Brod
Kaplice
Weitra
Gmünd
Horn

WEST GERMANY
Regensburg
Naab
Regen
Straubing
Danube (Donau)
Isar
Landshut
Amper
MUNICH (München)
Würmsee
Memmingen
Iller
Kaufbeuren
Kempten
Lech
Ravensburg
Lake of Constance (Bodensee)
Konstanz
Bregenz
Dornbirn
Lustenau
Hohenems
Oberstdorf
VORARLBERG
Allgäu
Bavarian Alps
Füssen
Vils
Reutte
Ehrwald
9,718 ft. (2962 m.) Zugspitze
Garmisch-Partenkirchen
Rosenheim
Traunstein
Chiemsee
Braunau am Inn
Inn
Altheim
Ried im Innkreis
Grieskirchen
Mauerkirchen
Mattighofen
Frankenmarkt
Vöcklabruck
Attnang-Puchheim
Lambach
UPPER AUSTRIA
Schärding
Peuerbach
Eferding
Pregarten
Mauthausen
Schwertberg
Perg
Gr. Peilstein 3,478 ft. (1060 m.)
LOWER
Freistadt
Königswiesen
Mühlviertel
Greiner Wald
Kamp
Langenlois
Krems
Herzogenburg
St. Pölten
Passau
Engelhartszell
Aschach
Haslach
Rohrbach
Aigen im Mühlkreis
Linz
Wels
Enns
St. Valentin
Steyr
Grein
Ybbs
Pöchlarn
Melk
Amstetten
Ober Grafendorf
Wilhelmsburg
Scheibbs
Lilienfeld
Hainfeld
Waidhofen an der Ybbs
Hohenberg
Gaming
St. Aegyd am Neuwalde
Mariazell
Neunkirchen
Windischgarsten
Reichenau an der Rax
Neuberg
Mürzzuschlag
Semmering Pass
AUSTRIA

Ravensburg
Kempten
Rosenheim
Lenzing
Attersee
Mondsee
Gr. Höllkögel
Traun See
Kirchdorf
Grünburg
Salzburg
St. Wolfgang
Bad Ischl
Alt Aussee
Spital
Hieflau
Eisenerz
Admont
Liezen
Rottenmann
Trieben
Vordernberg
Leoben
Kindberg
Langenwang
Kapfenberg
Mürz
Bruck
Frohnleiten
Pollau
Hartberg
Weiz
Gleisdorf
Graz
Fürstenfeld
Feldbach
Wildon
Deutsch Landsberg
Leibnitz
Radkersburg
Mur

SALZBURG
Hallein
Berchtesgaden
Golling
Bischofshofen
Saalfelden
Radstadt
Hochgolling 8,858 ft. (2700 m.)
Schladming
Niedere Tauern
Hohe Tauern
STYRIA
Tamsweg
Oberwölz
Fohnsdorf
Knittelfeld
Judenburg
Neumarkt
Murau
Zeltweg
Köflach
Voitsberg
Gratwein
Deutsch Feistritz
Kötschach

Kössen
Lofer
St. Johann
Hopfgarten
Fieberbrunn
Zell am See
Schwarzach im Pongau
Bad Hofgastein
Gastein
Badgastein
Mallnitz
Obervellach
Spittal an der Drau
Gmünd
Radenthein
Friesach
Strassburg
Weitensfeld
Gurk
Althofen
Feldkirchen
St. Veit
Wolfsberg
Bad St. Leonhard im Lavantthal
St. Paul im Lavantthal
Lavamünd

Wörgl
Kufstein
Achenkirch
Jenbach
Schwaz
Kundl
Brixlegg
Brandberg
Mayrhofen
Zell am Ziller
Steinach
Kitzbühel
Mittersill
Krimml
Kaprun
Grossglockner 12,457 ft. (3797 m.)
Heiligenblut
Matrei in Osttirol
Lienz
Sillian
Dölsach
Mauthen
Hermagor
Hohe Warte (Mte. Coglians) 9,121 ft. (2780 m.)
Carnic Alps
Paternion
Villach
Velden
Klagenfurt
Pörtschach
Völkermarkt
Ferlach
Eisenkappel
Vellach
Arnoldstein
Karawanken

INNSBRUCK
Fulpmes
Neustift
Hall
Solbad Hall
Zirl
Telfs
TIROL
Steinach
Gries am Brenner
Brenner Pass
Vitipeno
Isarco
CARINTHIA

Chur
Davos Platz
St. Moritz
SWITZERLAND
LIECHT.
Vaduz
Feldkirch
Rankweil
Götzis
Bludenz
Schruns
Bregenz
Rhine
Inn
Landeck
St. Anton
Kappl
Pfunds
Nauders
Ötztal Alps
Wildspitze 12,359 ft. (3767 m.)
Parseierspitze 9,967 ft. (3038 m.)
Nassereith
Imst
Zams
Längenfeld
Brunico
Bruneck

ITALY
Bolzano
Dolomite Alps
Adige
Trento
Belluno
Udine
Tagliamento
Piave
Treviso
Brescia
Bergamo
Lecco
Lake Iseo
Lake Garda
Adda

YUGOSLAVIA
Maribor
Celje
Ljubljana
Brežice
Postojna

48

© Copyright HAMMOND INCORPORATED, Maplewood, N.J.

AUSTRIA, CZECHOSLOVAKIA and HUNGARY

CONIC PROJECTION

SCALE OF MILES

0 10 20   40   60   80

SCALE OF KILOMETERS

0 10 20   40   60   80

Capitals of Countries..........☆   International Boundaries.......—··—··—
Republic Capital..................◉   Internal Boundaries............—·—·—
Administrative Centers........⌂   Canals................................

Czechoslovakia is divided into two socialist republics, Czech (capital-Prague) and Slovak
(capital-Bratislava), ten regions (Kraj) and the independent cities of Prague and Bratislava.

Scale 1:2,360,000

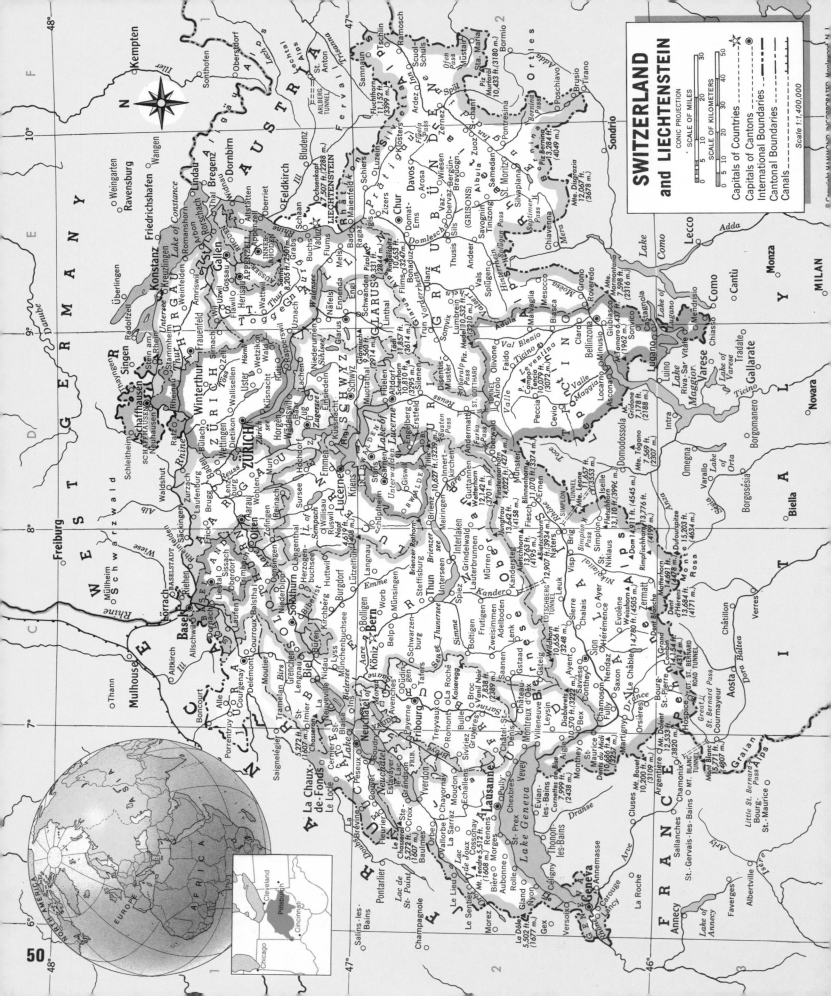

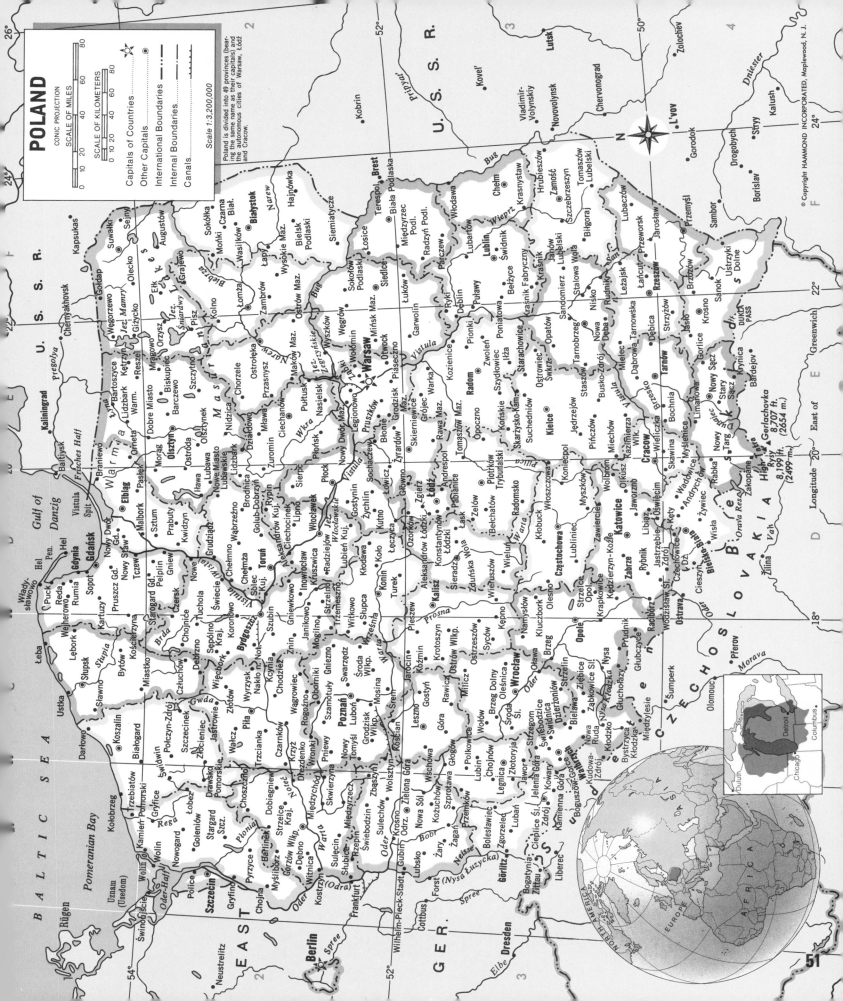

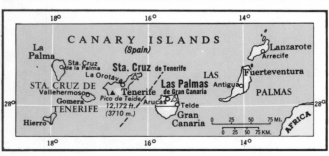

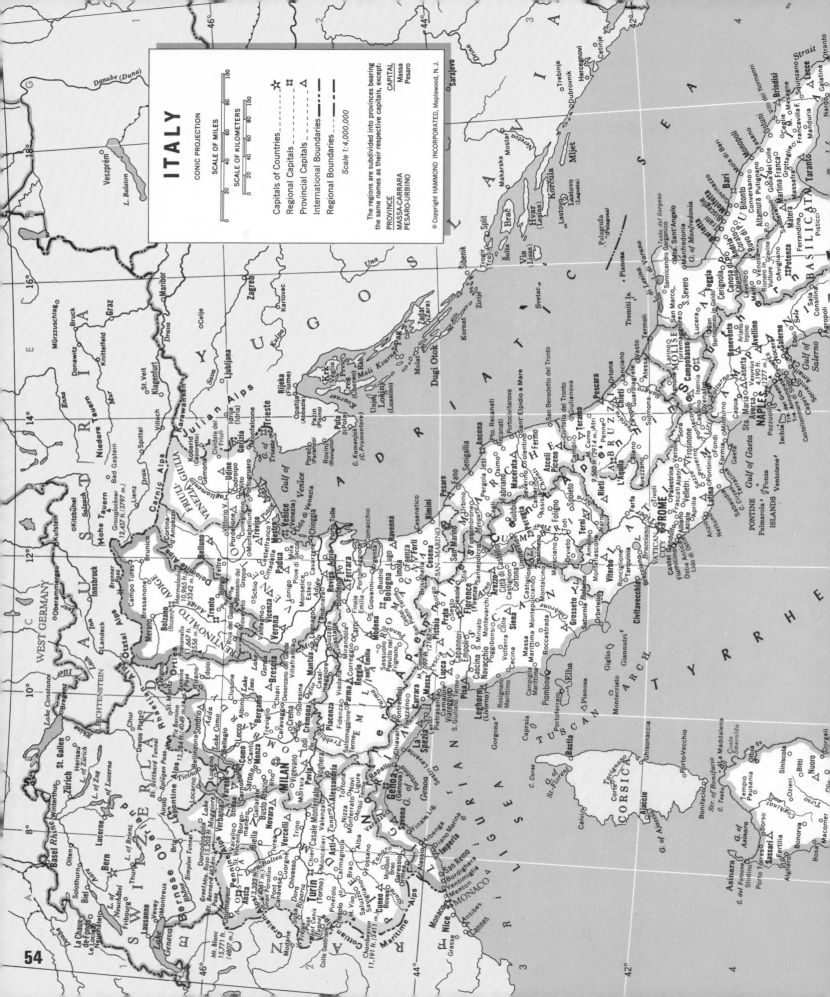

ITALY

CONIC PROJECTION

SCALE OF MILES

SCALE OF KILOMETERS

Capitals of Countries .... ⚝
Regional Capitals .... ⌘
Provincial Capitals .... △
International Boundaries .... —·—·—
Regional Boundaries .... —··—··—

Scale 1:4,000,000

The regions are subdivided into provinces bearing
the same names as their respective capitals, except:

PROVINCE	CAPITAL
MASSA-CARRARA	Massa
PESARO-URBINO	Pesaro

54

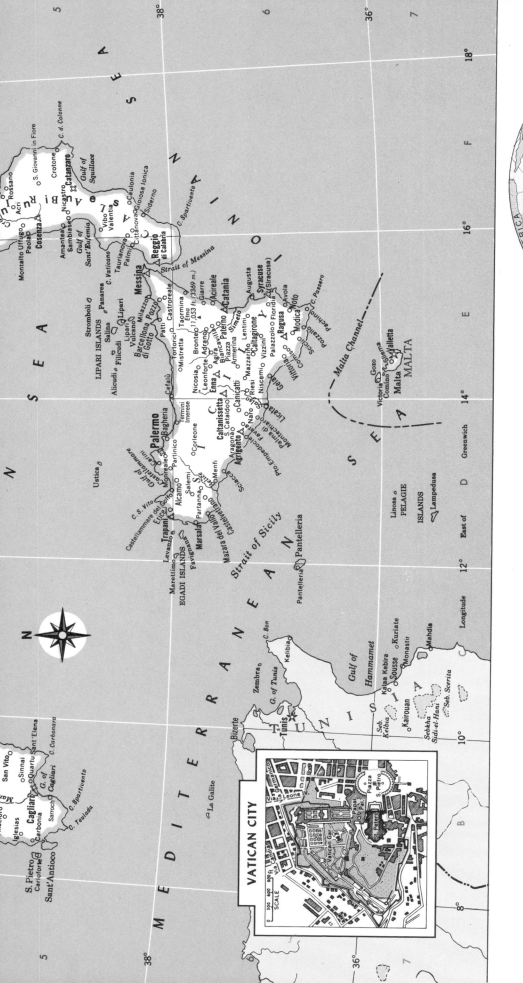

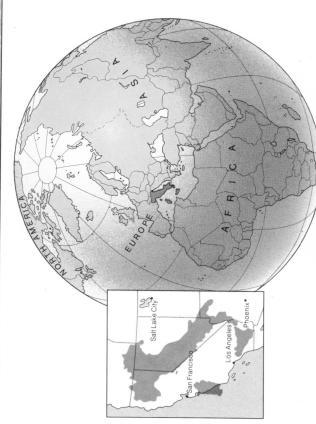

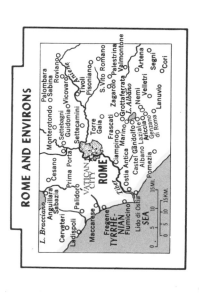

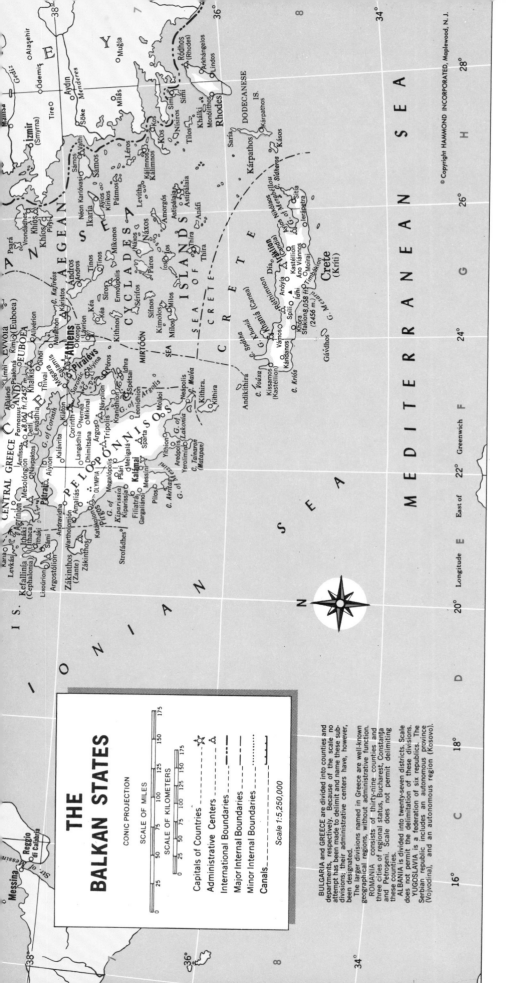

THE BALKAN STATES

CONIC PROJECTION

SCALE OF MILES

0   25   50   75   100   125   150   175

SCALE OF KILOMETERS

0   25   50   75   100   125   150   175

Capitals of Countries ---------- ☆
Administrative Centers ---------- ⌂
International Boundaries ————
Major Internal Boundaries — — —
Minor Internal Boundaries ·········
Canals ————

Scale 1:5,250,000

BULGARIA and GREECE are divided into counties and departments, respectively. Because of the scale no attempt has been made to delimit and name these sub-divisions; their administrative centers have, however, been designated.
The larger divisions named in Greece are well-known geographical regions, without administrative function.
ROMANIA consists of thirty-nine counties and three cities of regional status, Bucharest, Constanța and Petroșeni. Scale does not permit delimiting these counties.
ALBANIA is divided into twenty-seven districts. Scale does not permit the delimitation of these divisions.
YUGOSLAVIA is a federation of six republics. The Serbian republic includes an autonomous province (Vojvodina), and an autonomous region (Kosovo).

© Copyright HAMMOND INCORPORATED, Maplewood, N.J.

57

ADMINISTRATIVE DIVISIONS NOT NAMED ON MAP

Division	Ref.	Division	Ref.
1. Abkhaz A.S.S.R.	E5	13. Khakass Aut. Oblast	J4
2. Adygey Aut. Oblast	D5	14. Komi-Permyak Aut. Okrug	F4
3. Adzhar A.S.S.R.	E5	15. Mari A.S.S.R.	E4
4. Aginsk Buryat		16. Mordivian A.S.S.R.	E4
Autonomous Okrug	M4	17. Nagorno-Karabakh Aut. Oblast	E5
5. Chechen-Ingush A.S.S.R.	E5	18. Nakhichevan' A.S.S.R.	E6
6. Chuvash A.S.S.R.	E4	19. North Ossetian A.S.S.R.	E5
7. Gorno-Altay Aut. Oblast	J4	20. South Ossetian Aut. Oblast	E5
8. Gorno-Badakhshan Aut. Oblast	H6	21. Tatar A.S.S.R.	F4
9. Jewish Aut. Oblast	O5	22. Tuvinian A.S.S.R.	K4
10. Kabardin-Balkar A.S.S.R.	E5	23. Udmurt A.S.S.R.	F4
11. Karachay-Cherkess Aut. Oblast	E5	24. Ust'-Ordynsk Buryat	
12. Karakalpak A.S.S.R.	G5	Autonomous Okrug	L4

® Copyright HAMMOND INCORPORATED, Maplewood, N.J.

UNION OF SOVIET SOCIALIST REPUBLICS
European Part

CONIC PROJECTION

SCALE OF MILES
0   50   100   200   300

SCALE OF KILOMETERS
0   50 100   200   300

National Capitals
Capitals of Union Republics
Administrative Centers
International boundaries
Union Republic boundaries
A.S.S.R., Oblast, Kray boundaries
Autonomous Oblast boundaries
Autonomous Okrug boundaries
Canals

Scale 1:11,000,000

The government of the United States has not recognized the incorporation of Estonia, Latvia and Lithuania into the Soviet Union.

60

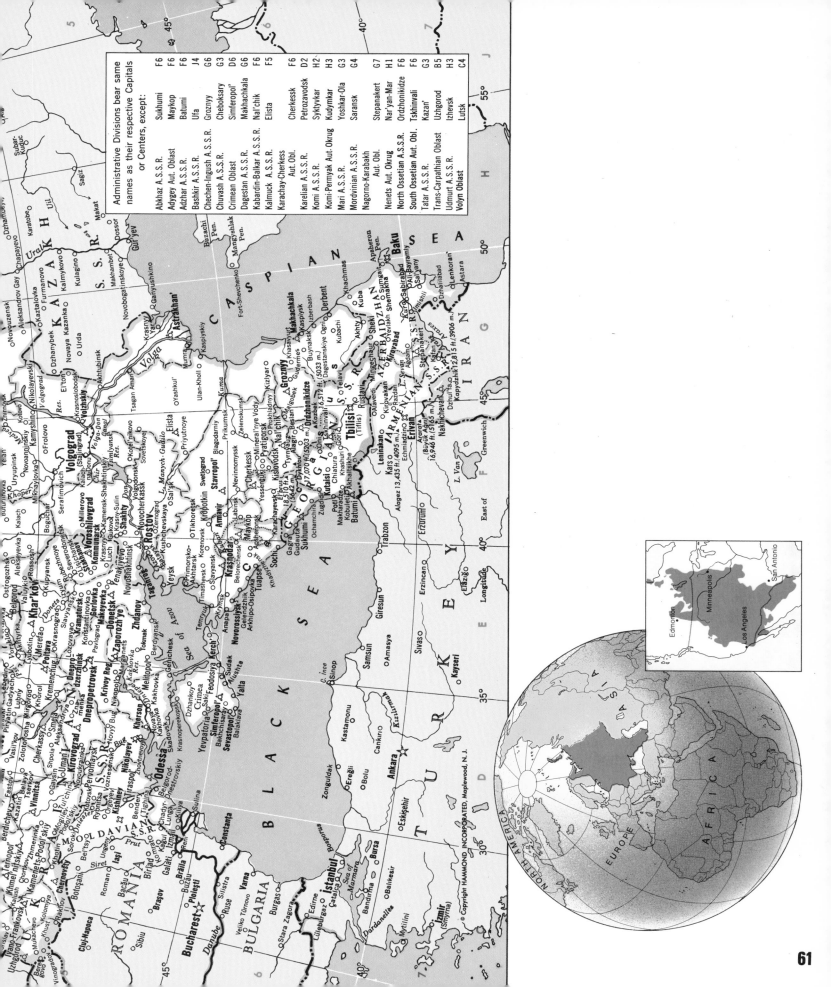

ASIA

LAMBERT AZIMUTHAL EQUAL-AREA PROJECTION

SCALE OF MILES

0   150   300   600   900   1200

SCALE OF KILOMETERS

0   300   600   900   1200

Capitals of Countries....☆   Canals........

International Boundaries........

Scale 1:50,000,000

® Copyright HAMMOND INCORPORATED, Maplewood, N.J.

63

On this map Chinese place-names have been rendered according to the Pinyin spelling system within the area controlled by the People's Republic of China. Alphabetically listed below are selected Chinese place-names spelled in the traditional manner, followed by the equivalent Pinyin form.

Amoy (Hsiamen)	Xiamen	Kirin	Jilin	Sian	Xi'an
Anhwei	Anhui	Kiukiang	Jiujiang	Siangtan	Xiangtan
Canton		Kwangsi	Guangxi	Sining	Xining
(Kwangchow)	Guangzhou	Chuang	Zhuangzu	Sinkiang-	
Chefoo (Yentai)	Yantai	Kwangtung	Guangdong	Uighur	Xinjiang Uygur
Chekiang	Zhejiang	Kweichow	Guizhou	Soochow	Suzhou
Chengchow	Zhengzhou	Kweilin	Guilin	Süchow	Xuzhou
Chengtu	Chengdu	Kweiyang	Guiyang	Swatow	Shantou
Chinchow	Jinzhou	Lanchow	Lanzhou	Szechuan	Sichuan
Chungking	Chongqing	Liuchow	Liuzhou	Tachai	Dazhai
Foochow	Fuzhou	Loyang	Luoyang	Tatung	Datong
Fukien	Fujian	Lüta	Lüda	Tibet	Xizang
Hangchow	Hangzhou	Mutankiang	Mudanjiang	Tientsin	Tianjin
Heilungkiang	Heilongjiang	Nanking	Nanjing	Tsinan	Jinan
Hofei	Hefei	Ningpo	Ningbo	Tsinghai	Qinghai
Honan	Henan	Ningsia Hui	Ningxia Huizu	Tsingtao	Qingdao
Hopei	Hebei	Paoting	Baoding	Tsining	Jining
Huhehot	Hohhot	Paotow	Baotou	Tsitsihar	Qiqihar
Hupeh	Hubei	Penki	Benxi	Tsunyi	Zunyi
Hwainan	Huainan	Peking	Beijing	Tzepo	Zibo
Inner Mongolia	Nei Monggol	Pengpu	Bengbu	Tungchwan	Tongchuan
Kansu	Gansu	Shansi	Shanxi	Urumchi	Ürümqi
Kiangsi	Jiangxi	Shantung	Shandong	Wusih	Wuxi
Kiangsu	Jiangsu	Shensi	Shaanxi	Yenan	Yan'an
Kingtehchen	Jingdezhen	Shihkiachwang	Shijiazhuang	Yinchwan	Yinchuan

For map coverage of Hainan Island and Leizhau Peninsula see page 68.

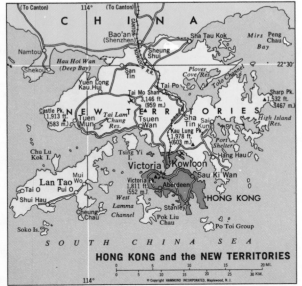

HONG KONG and the NEW TERRITORIES

© Copyright HAMMOND INCORPORATED, Maplewood, N.J.

64

CHINA and MONGOLIA

SCALE OF MILES
0   100   200   300   400   500

SCALE OF KILOMETERS
0   100   200   300   400   500

Capitals of Countries ⊛   International Boundaries ——
Provincial Capitals ⊙   Provincial Boundaries ——
Canals ——   Walls ~~~~~~

Scale 1:14,000,000

© Copyright HAMMOND INCORPORATED, Maplewood, N.J.

65

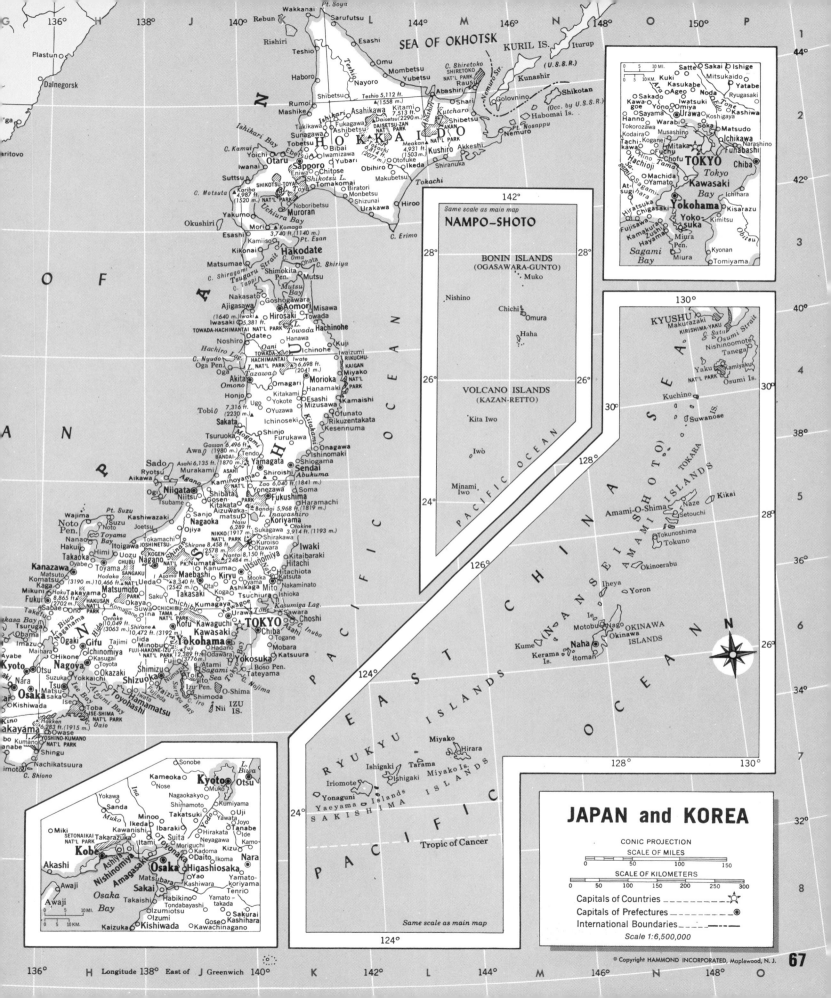

JAPAN and KOREA

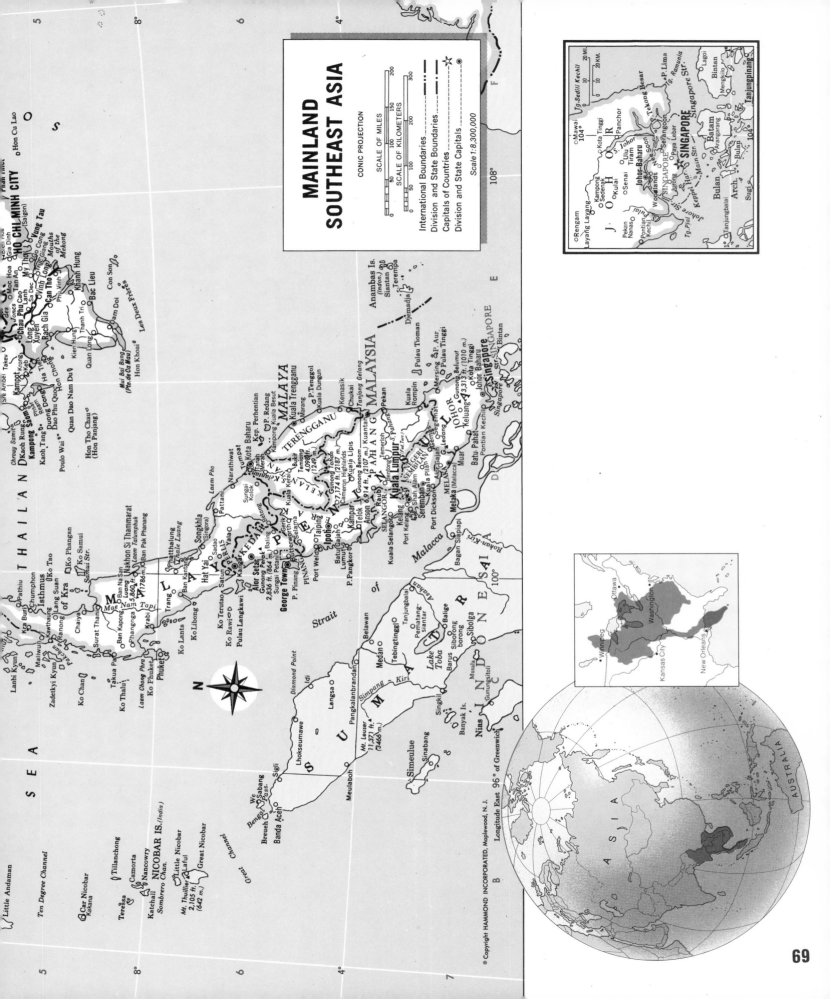

© Copyright HAMMOND INCORPORATED, Maplewood, N.J.

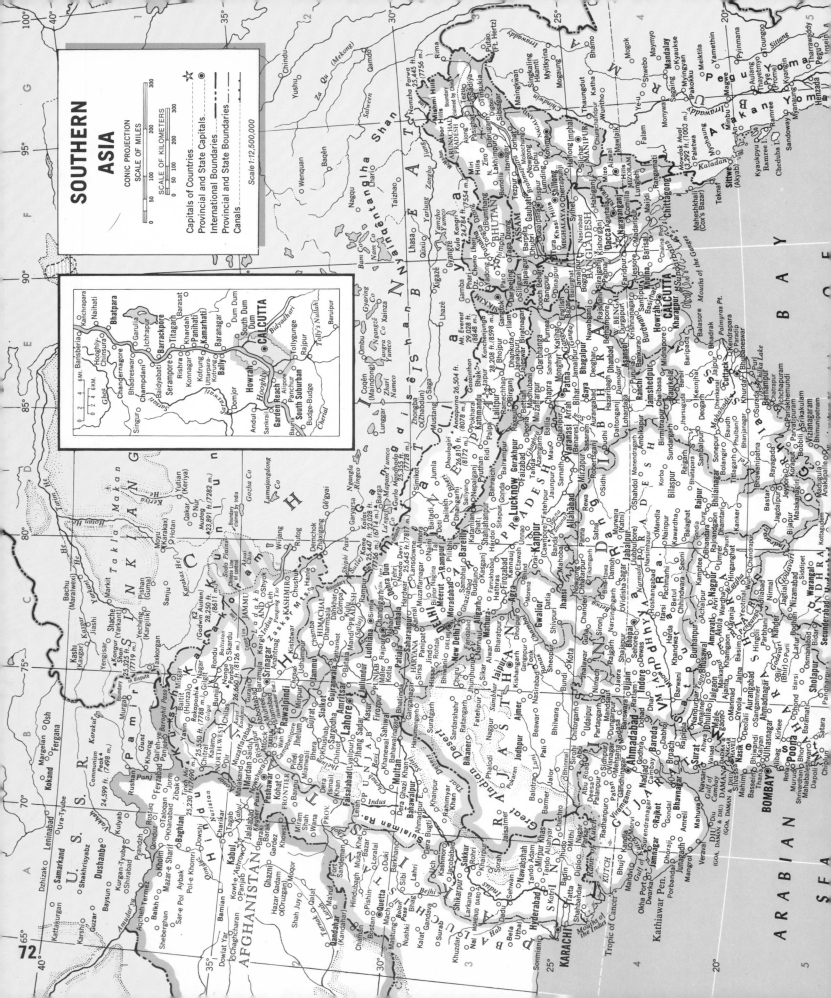

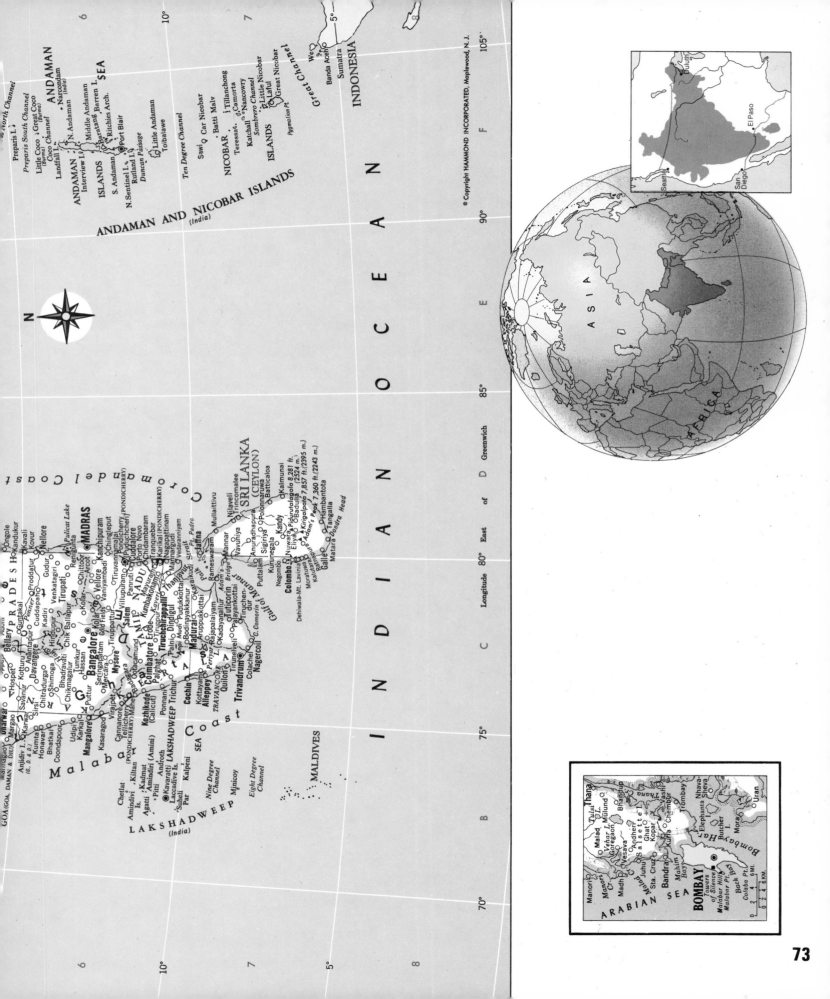

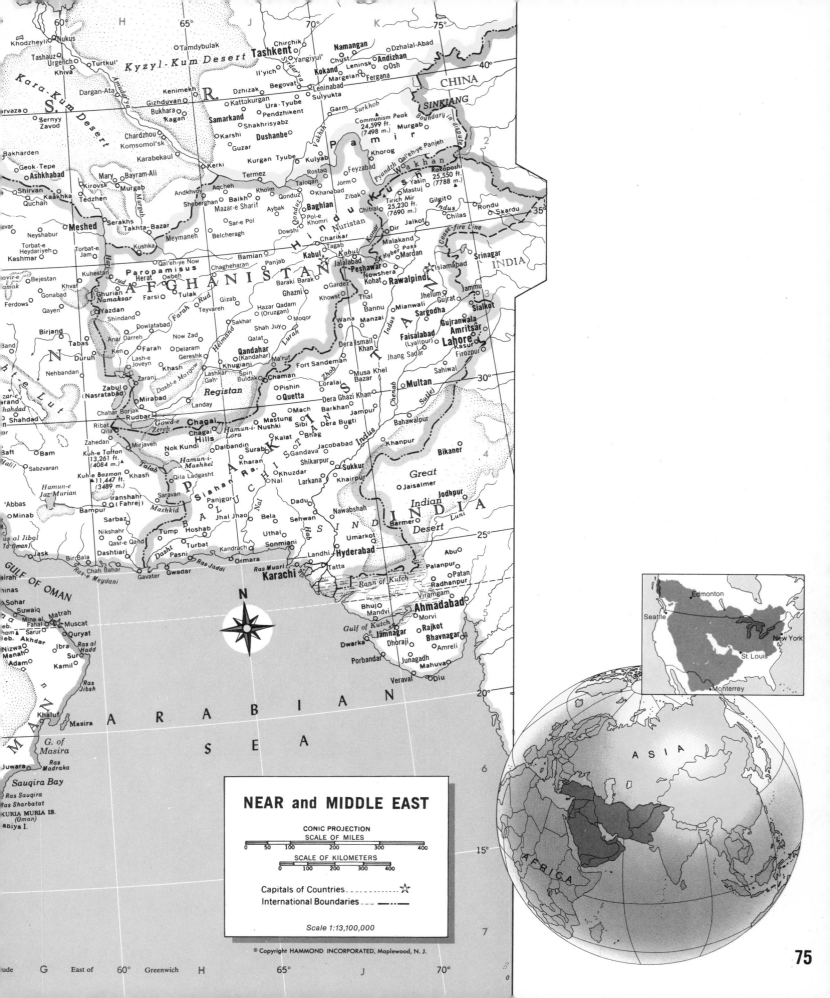

NEAR and MIDDLE EAST

CONIC PROJECTION
SCALE OF MILES

0 50 100   200   300   400

SCALE OF KILOMETERS

0   100   200   300   400

Capitals of Countries .... ★
International Boundaries ___ ___ ___

Scale 1:13,100,000

© Copyright HAMMOND INCORPORATED, Maplewood, N.J.

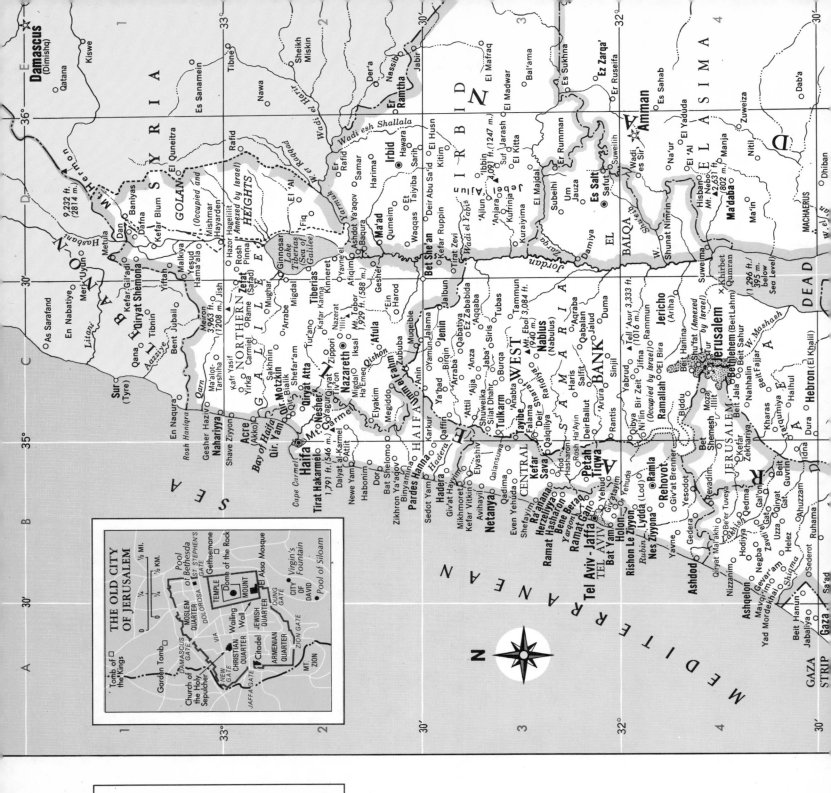
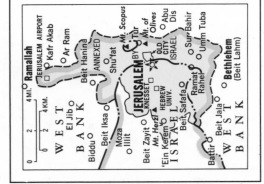

ISRAEL and JORDAN
CYLINDRICAL PROJECTION

SCALE OF MILES
5   10   15   20   25   30

SCALE OF KILOMETERS
0   5   10   15   20   25   30

Capitals of Countries........★
Internal Capitals...........◉
International Boundaries.....—··—
Internal Boundaries.........—·—

Scale 1:1,050,000

© Copyright HAMMOND INCORPORATED, Maplewood, N.J.

EL KARAK

El Qatrana
Wadi el Hafiri
El Manzil
El Karak ◉
El Karak
Rabba
Mazra
Sakka
Dhira
Mazra
El Lisan
Newe Zohar
Safi
El Ghor
Salt Pans
El Pans
Sedom
Hemar

Dhat Ras
Wadi el Hasa
TANNUR
Et Tafila
Abur
Buseira
Dana
Esh Shaubak
Shamakh
Uneiza
Jurf ad Darawish

O R O F

MA'AN
Ma'an ◉
Udhruh
Bir el Lasan
Ra's en Naqb

El Jafr
Qa el Jafr
El Jafr
Musawwal

Qa el Jinz

FEINAN
PETRA
Wadi Musa
Gharandal
El Quweira

Jebel Ramm
5,755 ft.
(1754 m.)

'Aqaba

Arad
Borot Kidod
Beer Ef'e
▲ Mt. Dimona 2,238 ft. (682 m.)
Dimona
Sedom
Oron
Yeroham
▲ Mt. Hatira 2,349 ft. (716 m.)

S O U T H E R N   N E G E V

Omer
Nevatim
Beersheba
(Be'er Sheva)
Beer Sheva
Revivim
Mash 'Abbe Sade
SUBEITA
Sede Boqer
AVDAT
Beer Hafir
Mizpe Ramon
Makhtesh Ramon

Hatseva
Yahav
Paran
Beer 'Ada
Beer Menuha
Gerofit
Yotvata

Hiyyon
Paran

▲ Mt. Ramon 3,396 ft. (1035 m.)

Biq'at 'Uvda
TIMNA
Beer Ora
Elat (Elath)
'Ein Netafim
Taba
Fara'un (Coral I.)

Gulf of 'Aqaba

Ofaqim
Urim
Magen
Nir Yitzhaq
Mivtahim
Rafah
Ze'elim
Besor

E G Y P T
Wadi Quraiya
Wadi el Arish
KADESH BARNEA
El Qusaima
Wadi Azariq

S I N A I

El Auja
El Kuntilla
El Thamad

Longitude East of Greenwich

31°
30'
5
6
30'
7
30'
8
30'
9
36°
35°

EUROPE
ASIA
AFRICA

Boston
Burlington
Albany
New York

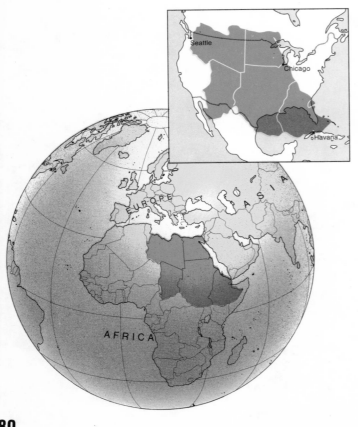

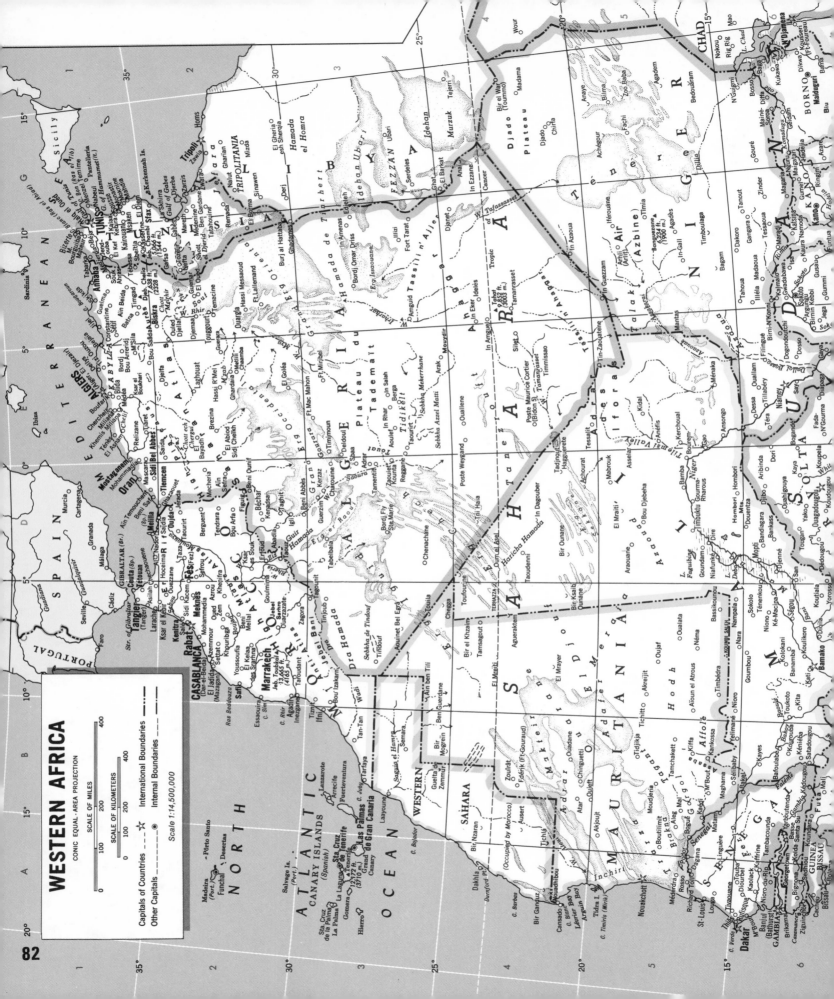

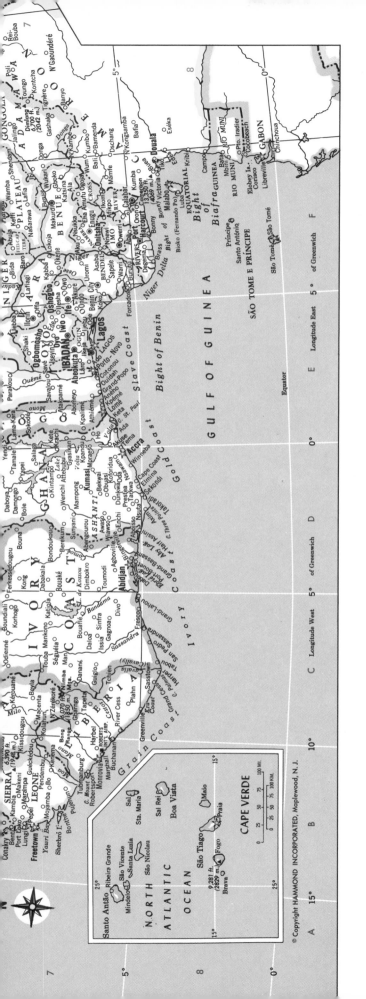

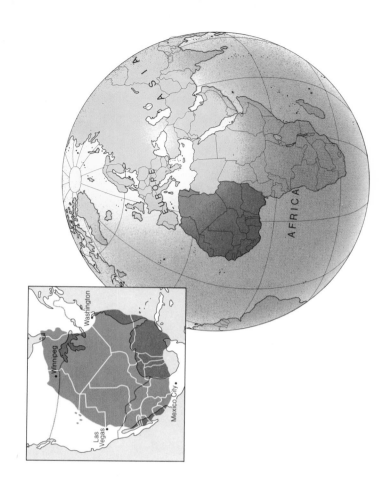

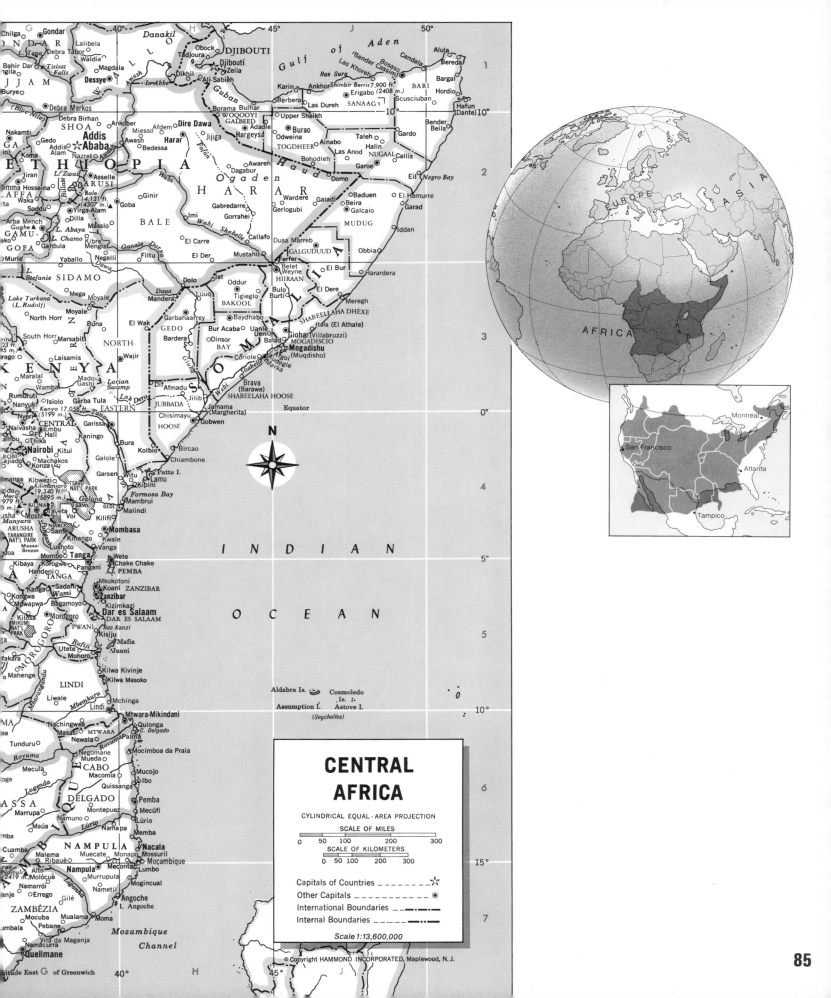

Gondar Chilga G Danakil H 40° I Obock 45° Gulf J of Aden 50° Alula
L. Tana Gondar Lalibela Tadjoura DJIBOUTI Candala Bereda
Bahir Dar Debra Tabor Waldia Magdala Djibouti Bender Cassim) Bosaso Alula
Tisisat Falls Dessye Ali-Sabieh Zeila Karin Bargal Hordio
Burye (Blue Nile) Dikhil Borama Bulhar Berbera Las Khoreh Las Dureh Hafun (Dante)
Debra Markos Guban Upper Sheikh BARI Scusciuban 10°
Nakamti SHOA Ankober Afdem Dire Dawa WOQOOYI Odweina Burao Taleh Gardo Bender Beila
Addis Ababa Harar Jijiga Hargeysa TOGDHEER Ainabo Las Anod NUGAAL Halin Callis
GA Jiran Addis Alam Nazret Awash Bedessa Awareh Dagabur SANAAG Garoe Garad
AFFA Jimma Hossena Asselle ARUSI Ginir Gabredarre Gorrahei SOMALIA Domo Eil Negro Bay
Waka Soddu Dilla Goba Imi Wabi Shebelle El Carre Callafo MUDUG El Hamurre Iddan
Arba Mench GAMU-GOFA Yirga-Alam Mengist El Der Mustahil Dusa Mareb Obbia
Murle Yaballo Negelli Filtu GALGUDUUD Harardera
L. Stefanie SIDAMO Mega Dolo Luuq Oddur Belet Weyne HIIRAAN El Bur
Lake Turkana (L. Rudolf) Moyale Daua Mandera BAKOOL Bulo Burti El Dere Meregh
North Horr El Wak Garbahaarrey Baydhabo SHABEELLAHA DHEXE Itala (El Athale)
South Horr Marsabit NORTH- GEDO Bur Acaba Uanle Uen Giohar (Villabruzzi)
KENYA Buna Bardera DINSOR BAY Balad MOGADISCIO
Laisamis Wajir Diif Afmadu Jilib Brava (Barawa) Mogadishu (Muqdisho)
Rumuruti EASTERN Lak Dera JUBBADA SHABEELAHA HOOSE Marka
Nyeri Kenya 17,058 ft. HOOSE Chisimayu Gobwen Equator 0°
CENTRAL Embu Garissa
Nairobi Kitui Kolbio Bircao
Machakos Galole Chiambone
Kajiado Garsen Witu Patta I. Lamu
Kilimanjaro 19,340 ft. Kipini Formosa Bay INDIAN
TSAVO NAT'L PARK Mambrui
Moshi Voi Malindi
Mombasa Kilifi 4
ARUSHA Kwale Vanga
TARANGIRE NAT'L PARK Wete
Tanga Korogwe Chake Chake PEMBA OCEAN
TANGA Pangani Mkokotoni
Koani ZANZIBAR
Zanzibar Kizimkazi
Morogoro Dar es Salaam DAR ES SALAAM
PWANI Ras Kanzi 5
Mafia Juani
Kilwa Kivinje
LINDI Kilwa Masoko
Liwale Mbemkuru
Lindi Mchinga
Mtwara-Mikindani Aldabra Is. Cosmoledo Is.
Nachingwea Quionga Assumption I. Astove I.
MTWARA C. Delgado (Seychelles) 10°
Newala Palma
Negomano CABO Mocímboa da Praia
Mueda DELGADO Mucojo
Macomia Ibo
Pemba Quissanga
Montepuez Mecúfi
NAMPULA Namuno Lúrio
Maúa Namapa Memba
Marrupa NACALA Nampula
ZAMBÉZIA Malema Ribauè Monapo Mossuril Moçambique
Nampula Mecontą Lumbo
Murrupula Mogincual
Angoche I. Angoche
Mocuba Mualama Moma Mozambique Channel
Vila da Maganja Namacurra
Quelimane

CENTRAL
AFRICA

CYLINDRICAL EQUAL-AREA PROJECTION

SCALE OF MILES

0 50 100   200   300

SCALE OF KILOMETERS

0 50 100   200   300

Capitals of Countries _ _ _ _ _ _ _ ★
Other Capitals _ _ _ _ _ _ _ _ ◉
International Boundaries _ _ ∎_∎_∎
Internal Boundaries _ _ _ _ ∎_∎

Scale 1:13,600,000

© Copyright HAMMOND INCORPORATED, Maplewood, N.J.

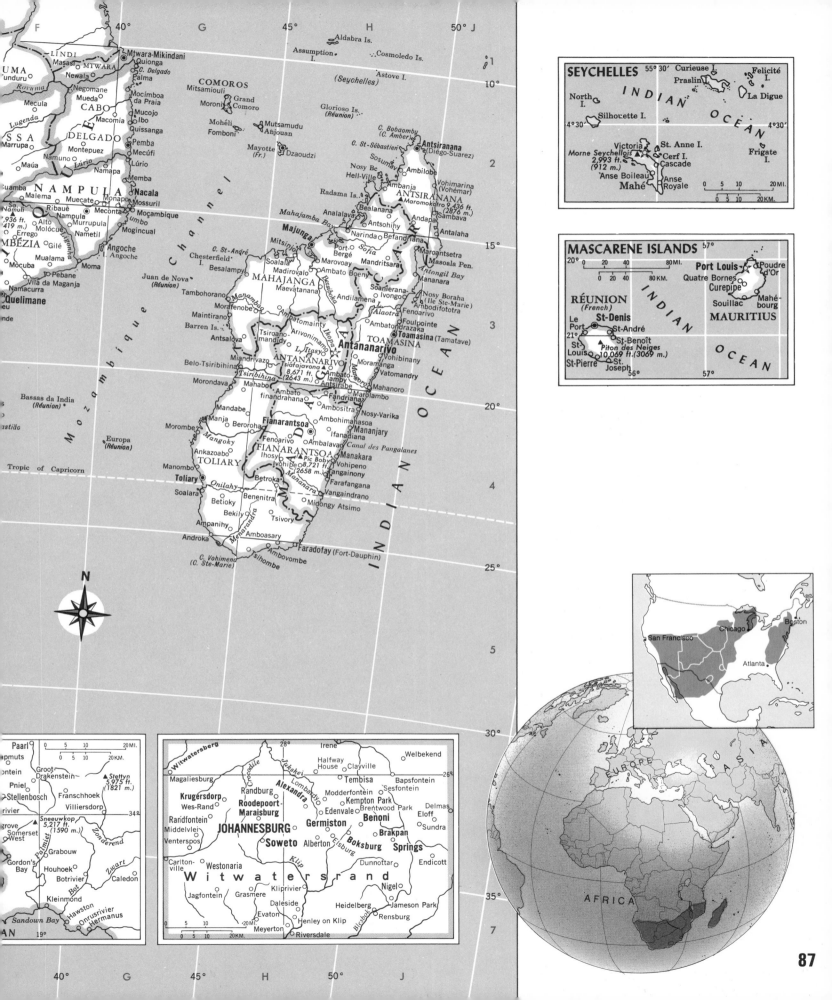

F
40° · G · 45° · H · 50° · J

LINDI
Mtwara-Mikindani
UMA · Masasi · Mtwara-Mikindani
unduru · Newala · Quionga
· Negomane · C. Delgado
Mecula · Mueda · Palma
· Mocímboa da Praia
· Macomia
CABO · Ibo
Marrupa · Montepuez · DELGADO · Quissanga
· Pemba
Maúa · Namuno · Lúrio · Mecúfi
· Namapa
NAMPULA · Memba
Malema · Muecate · Nacala
Namuli · Ribauê · Monapo · Mossuril
9,936 ft. · Nampula · Meconta · Moçambique
(419 m.) · Murrupula · Jumbo
BÉZIA · Gilé · Nametil · Mogincual
· Angoche
Mocuba · Mualama · Moma · I. Angoche
Namacurra · Vila da Maganja
Quelimane · Pebane

COMOROS
Mitsamiouli · Grand
Moroni · Comoro
Mohéli · Mutsamudu
Fomboni · Anjouan
Mayotte · Dzaoudzi
(Fr.)

Aldabra Is.
Assumption I. · Cosmoledo Is.
Astove I.
(Seychelles)
10°
Glorioso Is.
(Réunion)

C. Bobaomby
(C. Amber) · Antsiranana
C. St-Sébastien · (Diégo-Suarez)
Nosy Be · Sosumav · Ambilobe
Hell-Ville · Ambanja · Vohimarina
Radama Is. · (Vohémar)
ANTSIRANANA
Analalava · Bealanana · Andapa
Antsohihy · Antalaha
Narinda · Befandriana
Port · Sofia · Maroantsetra
Bergé · Masoala Pen.
Marovoay · Mandritsara
Soalala · Ambato Boeny · Antongil Bay
Mananara
Soanierana- · Nosy Boraha
Ivongo · (Ile Ste-Marie)
Ambodifototra
L. Alaotra · Foulpointe
Ambatondrazaka · Fenoarivo
Moramanga · Toamasina
Vohibinany · (Tamatave)
Vatomandry

Mahajamba Bay
Majunga
Mitsinjo
MAHAJANGA
C. St-André · Maevatanana
Chesterfield I. · Besalampy
Juan de Nova · Tamborohano
(Réunion) · Morafenobe
Maintirano
Barren Is.
Antsalova
Belo-Tsiribihina · Miandrivazo
Morondava · Mahabo
Mandabe
Morombe · Manja · Beroroha
Ankazoabo
TOLIARY · Manombo
Toliary
Soalara · Betioky
Benenitra
Bekily
Ampanihy · Androka

Tsiroano- · Arivonimamo
mandidy · siafajavona
ANTANANARIVO · 8,671 ft.
(2643 m.)
Ambato- · Ilampy
finandrahana · Antsirabe
Ambositra
Ambohimahasoa
Fianarantsoa
Fenoarivo
FIANARANTSOA
Ambalavao · Manakara
Ihosy · Pic Boby
Ivohibe · 8,721 ft.
Betroka · (2658 m.) · Vohipeno
Vangaindrano
Midongy Atsimo
Tsivory
Amboasary
Menarandra · Faradofay (Fort-Dauphin)
C. Vohimena · Ambovombe
(C. Ste-Marie) · sihombe

MADAGASCAR

Mahanoro
Antananarivo · Ambato
Fandriana
Marolambo
Mananjary
Ifanadiana
Canal des Pangalanes
Farafangana

2
15°
3
20°
Tropic of Capricorn
4
5
25°
30°

INDIAN OCEAN

Mozambique Channel

Bassas da India
(Réunion)
Europa
(Réunion)

N

SEYCHELLES
55° 30′ · Curieuse I. · Felicité I.
Praslin
North I. · INDIAN
4° 30′ · Silhouette I. · OCEAN · 4° 30′
La Digue
Victoria · St. Anne I.
Morne Seychellois · Cerf I.
2,993 ft. · Cascade
(912 m.)
Anse Boileau · Anse
Mahé · Royale · Frigate I.
0 · 5 · 10 · 20 MI.
0 · 5 · 10 · 20 KM.

MASCARENE ISLANDS
57°
20° · 0 · 20 · 40 · 80 MI.
0 · 20 · 40 · 80 KM.
Port Louis · Poudre d'Or
Quatre Bornes
RÉUNION · Curepipe
(French) · Souillac · Mahé-
bourg
Le · St-Denis · MAURITIUS
Port · St-André
21° · St-Benoît
St- · Piton des Neiges
Louis · 10,069 ft. (3069 m.)
St-Pierre · St.
Joseph
56° · 57°
INDIAN OCEAN

Paarl
0 · 5 · 10 · 20 MI.
0 · 5 · 10 · 20 KM.
Groot- · Stettyn
Drakenstein · 5,975 ft.
Pniel · (1821 m.)
Stellenbosch · Franschhoek
Villiersdorp
Sneeuwkop
5,217 ft.
grove · (1590 m.)
Somerset
West · Grabouw
Gordon's · Houhoek
Bay · Botrivier
Kleinmond · Caledon
Hawston
Onrusrivier · Hermanus
Sandown Bay
19°

Witwatersberg
28°
Irene · Welbekend
Halfway
Magaliesburg · House · Clayville
26°
Randburg · Tembisa · Bapsfontein
Alexandra · Sesfontein
Krugersdorp · Modderfontein
Roodepoort- · Kempton Park
Maraisburg · Edenvale · Delmas
Randfontein · Brentwood Park · Eloff
JOHANNESBURG · Germiston · Benoni · Sundra
Middelvlei
Soweto · Alberton · Brakpan
Venterspos · Boksburg · Springs
Carltonville · Dunnottar · Endicott
Westonaria
Witwatersrand · Nigel
Jagfontein · Kliprivier
Grasmere
Daleside · Heidelberg · Jameson Park
Evaton · Rensburg
Henley on Klip
Meyerton · Riversdale
0 · 5 · 10 · 20 MI.
0 · 5 · 10 · 20 KM.
30°
35°
7

EUROPE · ASIA
AFRICA

San Francisco · Chicago · Boston
Atlanta

40° · G · 45° · H · 50° · J

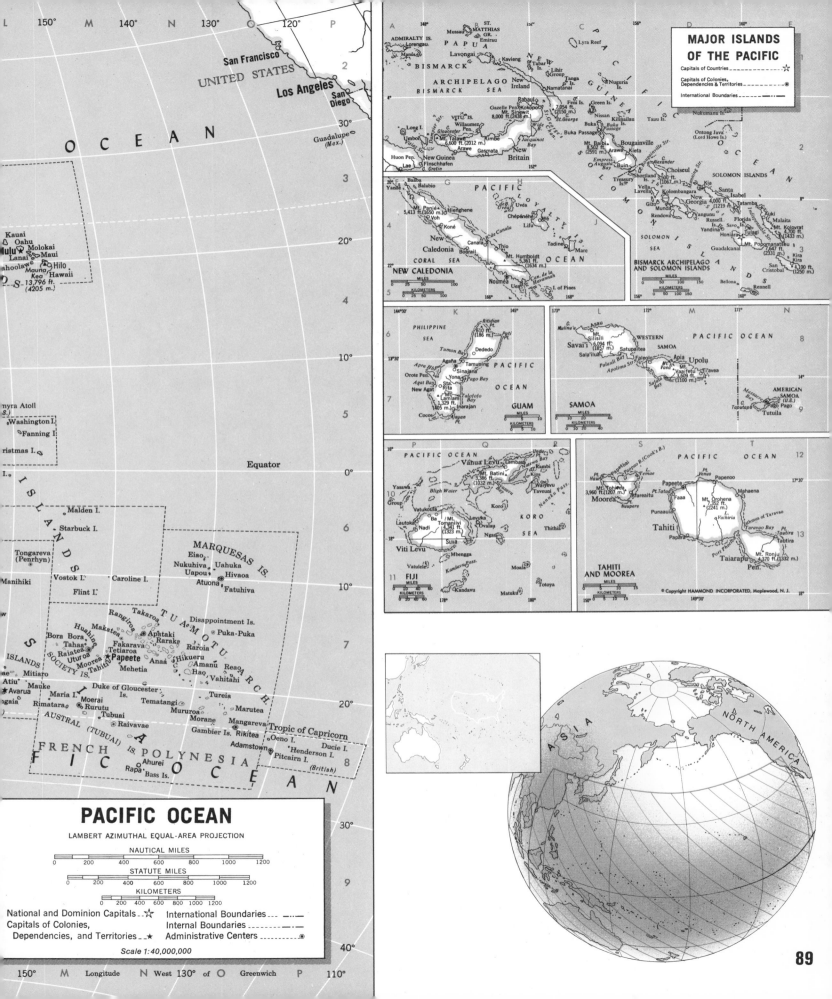

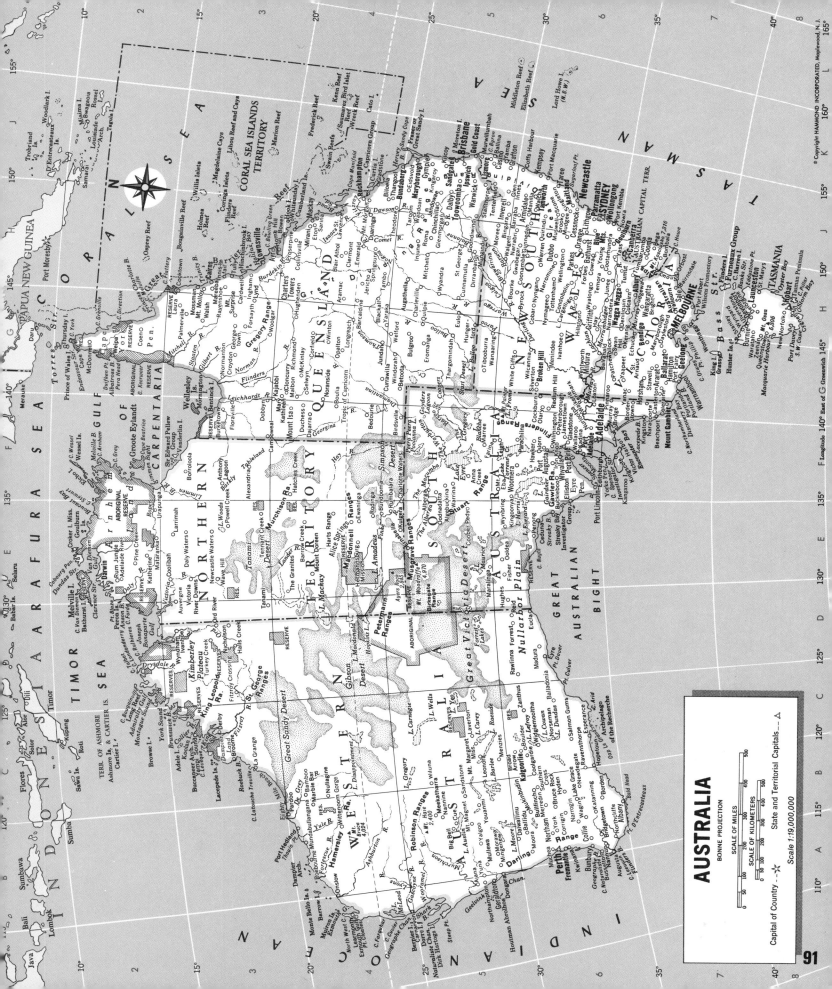

AUSTRALIA

BONNE PROJECTION

SCALE OF MILES

SCALE OF KILOMETERS

Scale 1:19,000,000

Capital of Country -- ☆   State and Territorial Capitals -- △

91

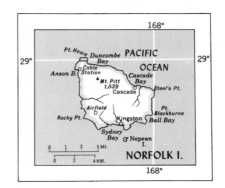

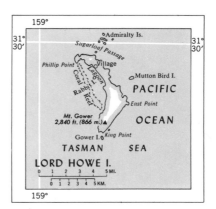

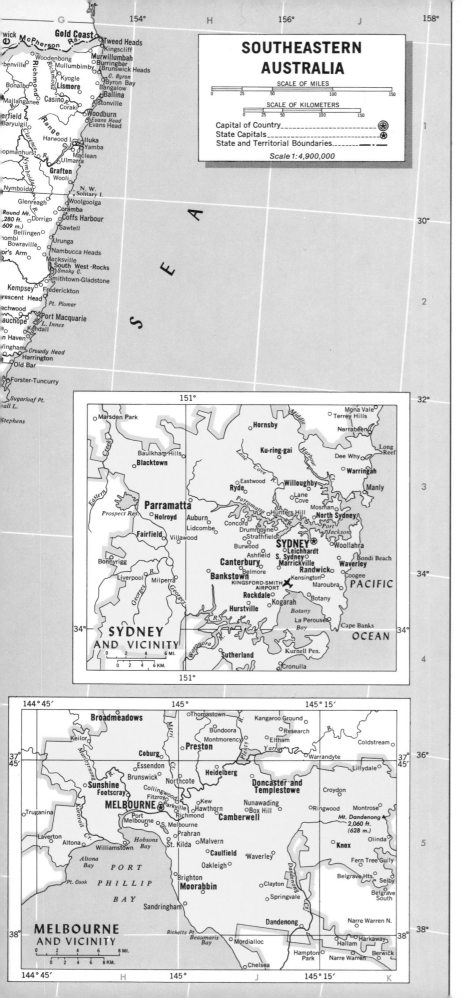

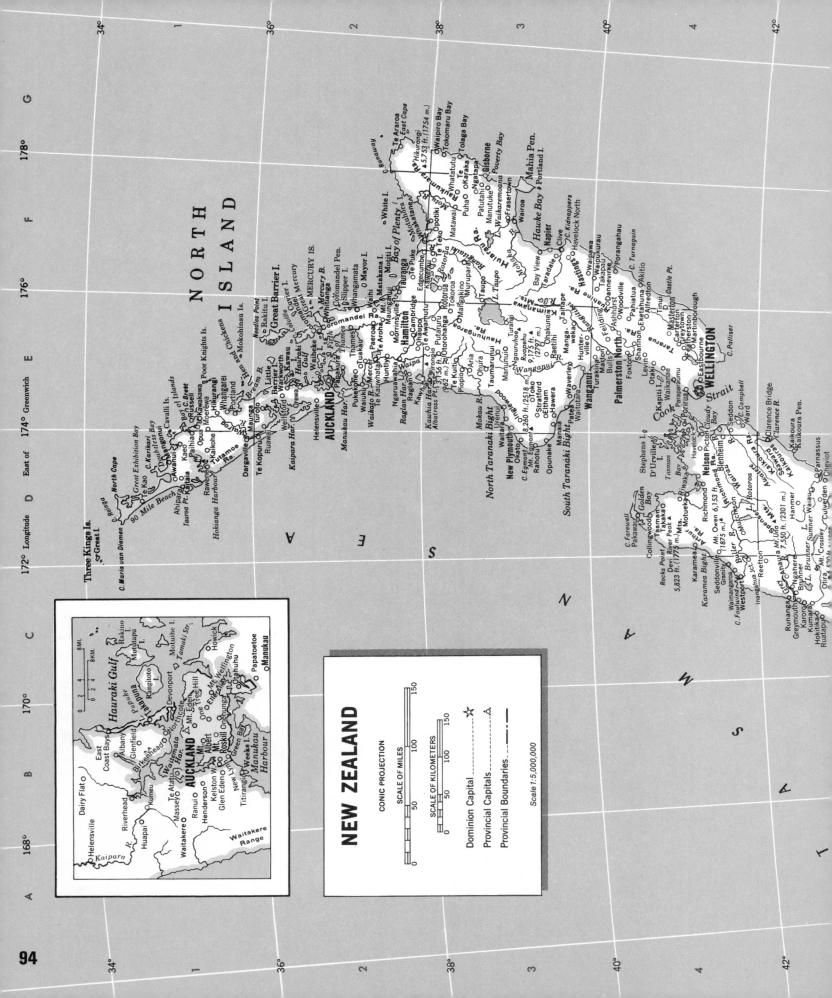

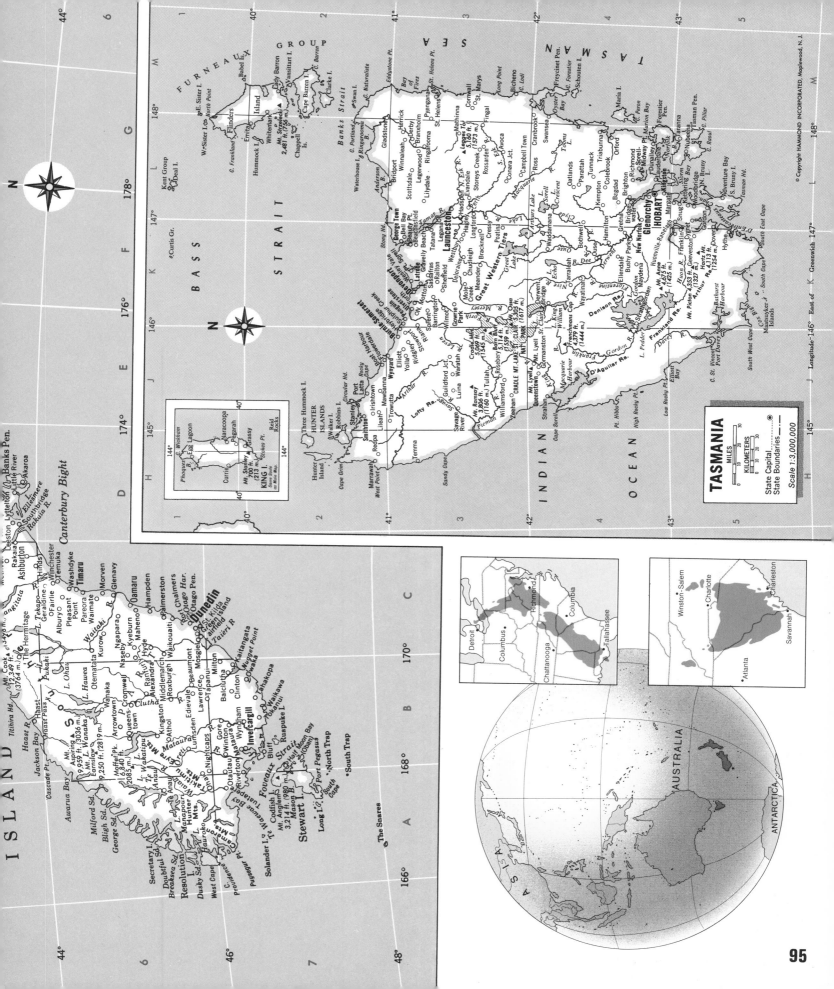

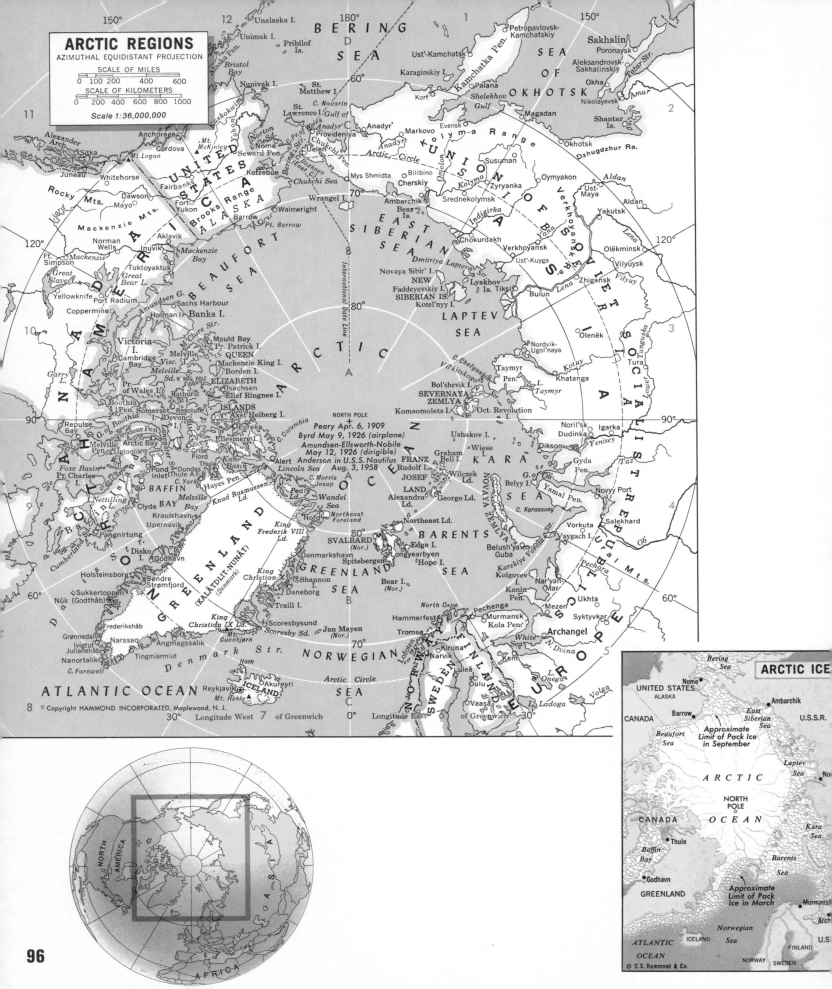

ARCTIC REGIONS
AZIMUTHAL EQUIDISTANT PROJECTION

SCALE OF MILES
0 100 200   400   600

SCALE OF KILOMETERS
0   200 400 600 800 1000

Scale 1:36,000,000

NORTH POLE
Peary Apr. 6, 1909
Byrd May 9, 1926 (airplane)
Amundsen-Ellsworth-Nobile
May 12, 1926 (dirigible)
Anderson in U.S.S. Nautilus
Aug. 3, 1958

© Copyright HAMMOND INCORPORATED, Maplewood, N.J.

30° Longitude West 7 of Greenwich 0° Longitude East of Greenwich 30°

ATLANTIC OCEAN

ARCTIC ICE

UNITED STATES
ALASKA

Bering Sea
Nome

Barrow

Ambarchik

East Siberian Sea

CANADA

U.S.S.R.

Beaufort Sea

Approximate Limit of Pack Ice in September

Laptev Sea

ARCTIC

NORTH POLE

OCEAN

CANADA

Thule

Kara Sea

Baffin Bay

Barents Sea

GREENLAND

Godhavn

Approximate Limit of Pack Ice in March

Murmans

© C.S. Hammond & Co.

Norwegian Sea

ATLANTIC OCEAN

ICELAND

NORWAY   SWEDEN   FINLAND

96

EARTH'S DIMENSIONS

Distance in:	Miles	Kilometers
Equatorial circumference	24,902	40,076
Meridional circumference	24,860	40,008
Equatorial diameter	7,927	12,757
Polar diameter	7,900	12,714
Mean distance from the Sun	93,000,000	150,000,000

Area in:	Sq. Miles	Sq. Kilometers
Total surface area	196,950,000	510,100,500
Land surface	57,609,000	149,208,000
Water surface	139,341,000	360,892,500

THE CONTINENTS

	Area in: Sq. Miles	Area in: Sq. Km.	Percent of World's Land
Asia	17,128,500	44,362,800	29.7
Africa	11,707,000	30,321,100	20.3
North America	9,363,000	24,250,200	16.3
South America	6,875,000	17,806,250	12.0
Antarctica	5,500,000	14,245,000	9.5
Europe	4,057,000	10,507,600	7.0
Australia	2,966,100	7,682,200	5.1

OCEANS AND MAJOR SEAS

	Area in: Sq. Miles	Area in: Sq. Km.	Greatest Depth in: Feet	Greatest Depth in: Meters
Pacific Ocean	64,186,000	166,241,700	36,198	11,033
Atlantic Ocean	31,862,000	82,522,600	28,374	8,648
Indian Ocean	28,350,000	73,426,500	25,344	7,725
Arctic Ocean	5,427,000	14,056,000	17,880	5,450
Caribbean Sea	970,000	2,512,300	24,720	7,535
Mediterranean Sea	969,000	2,509,700	16,896	5,150
South China Sea	895,000	2,318,000	15,000	4,600
Bering Sea	875,000	2,266,250	15,800	4,800
Gulf of Mexico	600,000	1,554,000	12,300	3,750
Sea of Okhotsk	590,000	1,528,100	11,070	3,370
East China Sea	482,000	1,248,380	9,500	2,900
Yellow Sea	480,000	1,243,200	350	107
Sea of Japan	389,000	1,007,500	12,280	3,740
Hudson Bay	317,500	822,300	846	258
North Sea	222,000	575,000	2,200	670
Black Sea	185,000	479,150	7,365	2,245
Red Sea	169,000	437,700	7,200	2,195
Baltic Sea	163,000	422,170	1,500	460

HIGHEST MOUNTAINS

	Height in: Feet	Meters
AFRICA		
Kilimanjaro, Tanzania	19,340	5,895
Kenya, Kenya	17,058	5,199
Margherita, Uganda-Zaire	16,795	5,119
Ras Dashan, Ethiopia	15,157	4,620
Toubkal, Morocco	13,665	4,165
Cameroon, Cameroon	13,350	4,069
ANTARCTICA		
Vinson Massif	16,864	5,140
Tyree	16,289	4,965
Kirkpatrick	14,856	4,528
Elizabeth	14,698	4,480
Markham	14,272	4,354
ASIA		
Everest, Nepal-China	29,028	8,848
Godwin Austen (K2), China-Pakistan	28,250	8,611
Kanchenjunga, Nepal-India	28,208	8,598
Makalu, Nepal-China	27,824	8,481
Dhaulagiri, Nepal	26,810	8,172
Nanga Parbat, Pakistan	26,660	8,126
Annapurna, Nepal	26,504	8,078
AUSTRALIA & OCEANIA		
Wilhelm, Papua New Guinea	15,400	4,694
Mauna Kea, Hawaii	13,796	4,205
Mauna Loa, Hawaii	13,677	4,169
Cook, New Zealand	12,349	3,764
Kosciusko, Australia	7,310	2,228
EUROPE		
El'brus, U.S.S.R.	18,510	5,642
Dykhtau, U.S.S.R.	17,070	5,203
Kazbek, U.S.S.R.	16,512	5,033
Mont Blanc, France	15,771	4,807
Monte Rosa, Italy-Switzerland	15,203	4,634
Matterhorn, Switzerland	14,691	4,478
NORTH AMERICA		
McKinley, Alaska	20,320	6,194
Logan, Yukon	19,524	5,951
Citlaltépetl, Mexico	18,855	5,747
St. Elias, Alaska-Yukon	18,008	5,489
Popocatépetl, Mexico	17,887	5,452
SOUTH AMERICA		
Aconcagua, Argentina	22,831	6,959
Ojos del Salado, Argentina	22,572	6,880
Bonete, Chile-Argentina	22,541	6,870
Tupungato, Chile-Argentina	22,310	6,800
Pissis, Argentina	22,241	6,779

RIVERS

	Length in: Miles	Km.
Nile, Africa	4,145	6,671
Amazon, S. Amer.	3,915	6,300
Chang Jiang (Yangtze), China	3,900	6,276
Mississippi-Missouri, U.S.A.	3,710	5,971
Ob'-Irtysh-Black Irtysh, U.S.S.R.	3,362	5,411
Yenisey-Angara, U.S.S.R.	3,100	4,989
Huang He (Yellow), China	2,877	4,630
Amur-Shilka-Onon, Asia	2,744	4,416
Lena, U.S.S.R.	2,734	4,400
Congo (Zaire), Africa	2,718	4,374
Mackenzie-Peace-Finlay, Canada	2,635	4,241
Mekong, Asia	2,610	4,200
Niger, Africa	2,548	4,101
Paraná-La Plata, S. Amer.	2,450	3,943
Murray-Darling, Australia	2,310	3,718
Volga, U.S.S.R.	2,194	3,531
Madeira, S. Amer.	2,013	3,240
Purus, S. Amer.	1,995	3,211
Yukon, Alaska-Canada	1,979	3,185
St. Lawrence, Canada-U.S.A.	1,900	3,058
Rio Grande, Mexico-U.S.A.	1,885	3,034
Syrdar'ya-Naryn, U.S.S.R.	1,859	2,992

LAKES

	Area in: Sq. Miles	Sq. Km.	Max. Depth in: Feet	Meters
Caspian Sea, Asia	143,240	371,000	3,264	995
Lake Superior, N.A.	31,700	82,100	1,301	397
Lake Victoria, Africa	26,720	69,200	270	82
Aral Sea, U.S.S.R.	25,675	66,500	256	78
Lake Huron, N.A.	23,000	59,600	748	228
Lake Michigan, U.S.	22,300	57,750	923	281
L. Tanganyika, Afr.	12,650	32,760	4,700	1,433
L. Baykal, U.S.S.R.	12,160	31,500	5,316	1,620
Great Bear Lake, Can.	12,100	31,330	1,356	413
Lake Nyasa, Africa	11,555	29,930	2,320	707
Great Slave Lake, Can.	11,270	29,190	2,015	614
Lake Erie, N.A.	9,910	25,670	209	64
Lake Winnipeg, Can.	9,420	24,390	60	18
Lake Ontario, N.A.	7,340	19,010	775	236
L. Ladoga, U.S.S.R.	7,105	18,400	738	225
L. Balkhash, U.S.S.R.	7,030	18,200	87	27
L. Maracaibo, Ven.	5,120	13,260	100	31
Lake Chad, Africa	4-10,000	10-26,000	25	8
L. Onega, U.S.S.R.	3,710	9,610	377	115
Lake Eyre, Australia	3,500-0	9,065-0	—	—
Lake Titicaca, S.A.	3,200	8,290	1,000	305
L. Nicaragua, N.A.	3,100	8,030	230	70

ISLANDS

	Area in: Sq. Mi.	Sq. Km.
Greenland	840,000	2,175,600
New Guinea	305,000	789,950
Borneo	290,000	751,100
Madagascar	226,400	586,370
Baffin, Canada	195,930	507,450
Sumatra, Indon.	164,000	424,760
Great Britain	88,765	229,900
Honshu, Japan	88,000	227,920
Victoria, Canada	83,900	217,300
Ellesmere, Canada	75,760	196,230
Celebes, Indon.	72,985	189,030
South I., N.Z.	58,390	151,240
Java, Indon.	48,840	126,500
North I., N.Z.	44,190	114,440
Newfoundland	42,030	108,860
Cuba	40,530	104,980
Luzon, Phil.	40,420	104,688
Iceland	39,770	103,000
Mindanao, Phil.	36,540	94,630
Novaya Zemlya	31,900	82,620
Ireland	31,740	82,210
Sakhalin, U.S.S.R.	29,500	76,400

Country	Area in: Sq. Miles	Sq. Km.	Population	Capital or Chief Town	Page Ref.
*Afghanistan	250,775	649,507	15,540,000	Kabul	75
Africa	11,707,000	30,321,100	469,000,000	......	79
Alabama, U.S.	51,705	133,916	3,444,165	Montgomery	15
Alaska, U.S.	591,004	1,530,700	401,851	Juneau	14
*Albania	11,100	28,749	2,590,000	Tiranë	56
Alberta, Canada	255,285	661,185	2,207,856	Edmonton	24
*Algeria	919,591	2,381,740	17,422,000	Algiers	82
American Samoa	76	197	32,395	Pago Pago	89
Andorra	175	453	31,000	Andorra	53
*Angola	481,351	1,246,700	7,078,000	Luanda	84
Anguilla	35	91	6,519	The Valley	28
Antarctica	5,500,000	14,245,000	......	......	35
*Antigua & Barbuda	171	443	72,000	St. John's	29
*Argentina	1,072,070	2,776,661	27,862,771	Buenos Aires	34
Arizona, U.S.	114,000	295,260	2,718,215	Phoenix	14
Arkansas, U.S.	53,187	137,754	2,286,435	Little Rock	15
Asia	17,128,500	44,362,800	2,633,000,000	......	63
*Australia	2,966,100	7,682,200	13,548,448	Canberra	91
*Austria	32,374	83,849	7,507,000	Vienna	48
*Bahamas	5,382	13,939	223,455	Nassau	28
*Bahrain	255	660	358,857	Manama	74
*Bangladesh	55,126	142,776	87,052,024	Dacca	72
*Barbados	166	430	249,000	Bridgetown	29
Belau (Palau)	188	487	12,177	Koror	88
*Belgium	11,781	30,513	9,855,110	Brussels	43
*Belize	8,867	22,965	144,857	Belmopan	27
*Benin	43,483	112,620	3,338,240	Porto-Novo	83
Bermuda	21	54	67,761	Hamilton	29
*Bhutan	18,147	47,000	1,298,000	Thimphu	72
*Bolivia	424,163	1,098,582	5,600,000	La Paz, Sucre	32
*Botswana	219,815	569,321	819,000	Gaborone	86
*Brazil	3,284,426	8,506,663	119,024,600	Brasília	33
British Columbia, Can.	366,253	948,596	2,716,301	Victoria	24
Brunei	2,226	5,765	191,765	Bandar Seri Begawan	71
*Bulgaria	42,823	110,912	8,862,000	Sofia	56
*Burma	261,789	678,034	32,913,000	Rangoon	68
*Burundi	10,747	27,835	4,021,910	Bujumbura	84
California, U.S.	158,706	411,049	23,667,902	Sacramento	14
*Cambodia	69,898	181,036	5,200,000	Phnom Penh	69
*Cameroon	183,568	475,441	8,503,000	Yaoundé	84
*Canada	3,851,787	9,976,139	24,105,163	Ottawa	24
*Cape Verde	1,557	4,033	324,000	Praia	83
Cayman Islands	100	259	16,677	Georgetown	28
*Central African Rep.	242,000	626,780	2,284,000	Bangui	84
*Chad	495,752	1,283,998	4,309,000	N'Djamena	80
Channel Islands	75	194	130,000	......	41
*Chile	292,257	756,946	11,198,789	Santiago	34
*China, People's Rep.	3,691,000	9,559,690	958,090,000	Peking	65
China, Rep. of, see Taiwan					
*Colombia	439,513	1,138,339	27,520,000	Bogotá	32
Colorado, U.S.	104,091	269,596	2,889,735	Denver	14
*Comoros	719	1,862	290,000	Moroni	87
*Congo	132,046	342,000	1,537,000	Brazzaville	84
Connecticut, U.S.	5,018	12,997	3,107,576	Hartford	15
Cook Islands	93	241	18,128	Avarua	88
*Costa Rica	19,575	50,700	2,245,000	San José	27
*Cuba	44,206	114,494	9,706,369	Havana	28
*Cyprus	3,572	9,251	629,000	Nicosia	74
*Czechoslovakia	49,373	127,876	15,276,799	Prague	48
Delaware, U.S.	2,044	5,294	594,317	Dover	15
*Denmark	16,629	43,069	5,124,000	Copenhagen	39
Dist. of Columbia, U.S.	67	173	638,333	Washington	15
*Djibouti	8,880	23,000	386,000	Djibouti	81
*Dominica	290	751	74,089	Roseau	29
*Dominican Republic	18,704	48,443	5,431,000	Sto. Domingo	28
*Ecuador	109,483	283,561	8,354,000	Quito	32
*Egypt	386,659	1,001,447	41,572,000	Cairo	81
*El Salvador	8,260	21,393	4,813,000	San Salvador	27
England, U.K.	50,516	130,836	46,220,955	London	41
*Equatorial Guinea	10,831	28,052	244,000	Malabo	84
*Ethiopia	471,776	1,221,900	31,065,000	Addis Ababa	81
Europe	4,057,000	10,507,600	676,000,000	......	37

Country	Area in: Sq. Miles	Sq. Km.	Population	Capital or Chief Town	Page Ref.
Faeroe Islands	540	1,399	42,000	Tórshavn	37
Falkland Islands	4,618	11,961	1,812	Stanley	34
*Fiji	7,055	18,272	588,068	Suva	88
*Finland	130,128	337,031	4,788,000	Helsinki	39
Florida, U.S.	58,664	151,940	9,746,342	Tallahassee	15
*France	210,038	543,998	53,788,000	Paris	44
French Guiana	35,135	91,000	64,000	Cayenne	32
French Polynesia	1,544	3,999	137,382	Papeete	89
*Gabon	103,346	267,666	551,000	Libreville	84
*Gambia	4,127	10,689	601,000	Banjul	82
Georgia, U.S.	58,910	152,577	5,463,105	Atlanta	15
*Germany, East (Dem. Rep.)	41,768	108,179	16,737,000	Berlin	47
*Germany, West (Fed. Rep.)	95,985	248,601	61,658,000	Bonn	47
*Ghana	92,099	238,536	11,450,000	Accra	83
Gibraltar	2	6	29,760	Gibraltar	53
*Greece	50,944	131,945	9,599,000	Athens	55
Greenland	840,000	2,175,600	49,773	Nûk	13
*Grenada	133	344	110,000	St. George's	29
Guadeloupe	687	1,779	319,000	Basse-Terre	29
Guam	212	549	105,821	Agaña	88
*Guatemala	42,042	108,889	7,262,419	Guatemala	27
*Guinea	94,925	245,856	5,143,284	Conakry	82
*Guinea-Bissau	13,948	36,125	777,214	Bissau	82
*Guyana	83,000	214,970	820,000	Georgetown	32
*Haiti	10,694	27,697	5,009,000	Port-au-Prince	28
Hawaii, U.S.	6,471	16,760	964,691	Honolulu	14
*Honduras	43,277	112,087	3,691,000	Tegucigalpa	27
Hong Kong	403	1,044	5,022,000	Victoria	64
*Hungary	35,919	93,030	10,709,536	Budapest	49
*Iceland	39,768	102,999	228,785	Reykjavík	38
Idaho, U.S.	83,564	216,431	944,038	Boise	14
Illinois, U.S.	56,345	145,934	11,426,518	Springfield	15
*India	1,269,339	3,287,588	683,810,051	New Delhi	72
Indiana, U.S.	36,185	93,719	5,490,224	Indianapolis	15
*Indonesia	788,430	2,042,034	147,383,075	Jakarta	71
Iowa, U.S.	56,275	145,752	2,913,808	Des Moines	15
*Iran	636,293	1,648,000	37,447,000	Tehran	74
*Iraq	172,476	446,713	12,767,000	Baghdad	74
*Ireland	27,136	70,282	3,440,427	Dublin	41
*Israel	7,847	20,324	3,878,000	Jerusalem	76
*Italy	116,303	301,225	57,140,000	Rome	54
*Ivory Coast	124,504	322,465	7,920,000	Abidjan	83
*Jamaica	4,411	11,424	2,161,000	Kingston	28
*Japan	145,730	377,441	117,057,485	Tokyo	67
*Jordan	35,000	90,650	2,152,273	Amman	76
Kansas, U.S.	82,277	213,097	2,364,236	Topeka	15
Kentucky, U.S.	40,409	104,659	3,660,777	Frankfort	15
*Kenya	224,960	582,646	15,327,000	Nairobi	85
Kiribati	290	754	56,213	Bairiki	88
Korea, North	46,540	120,539	17,914,000	P'yŏngyang	66
Korea, South	38,175	98,873	37,448,836	Seoul	66
*Kuwait	6,532	16,918	1,355,827	Al Kuwait	74
*Laos	91,428	236,800	3,721,000	Vientiane	68
*Lebanon	4,015	10,399	3,161,000	Beirut	74
*Lesotho	11,720	30,355	1,339,000	Maseru	86
*Liberia	43,000	111,370	1,873,000	Monrovia	83
*Libya	679,358	1,759,537	2,856,000	Tripoli	80
Liechtenstein	61	158	25,220	Vaduz	50
Louisiana, U.S.	47,752	123,678	4,205,900	Baton Rouge	15
*Luxembourg	999	2,587	364,000	Luxembourg	43
Macau	6	16	271,000	Macau	65
*Madagascar	226,657	587,041	8,742,000	Antananarivo	87
Maine, U.S.	33,265	86,156	1,125,027	Augusta	15
*Malawi	45,747	118,485	5,968,000	Lilongwe	86
Malaya, Malaysia	50,670	131,235	11,138,227	Kuala Lumpur	69
*Malaysia	128,308	332,318	13,435,588	Kuala Lumpur	70
*Maldives	115	298	143,046	Male	63
*Mali	464,873	1,204,021	6,906,000	Bamako	82
*Malta	122	316	343,970	Valletta	55
Manitoba, Canada	250,999	650,087	1,017,323	Winnipeg	24
Marianas, Northern	183	474	16,758	Capitol Hill	88

*Members of the United Nations

Country	Area in: Sq. Miles	Sq. Km.	Population	Capital or Chief Town	Page Ref.
Marshall Islands	70	181	31,042	Majuro	88
Martinique	425	1,101	308,000	Fort-de-France	29
Maryland, U.S.	10,460	27,091	4,216,975	Annapolis	15
Massachusetts, U.S.	8,284	21,456	5,737,037	Boston	15
*Mauritania	419,229	1,085,803	1,634,000	Nouakchott	82
*Mauritius	790	2,046	959,000	Port Louis	87
Mayotte	144	373	47,300	Dzaoudzi	87
*Mexico	761,601	1,972,547	67,395,826	Mexico City	26
Michigan, U.S.	58,527	151,585	9,262,078	Lansing	15
Micronesia, Fed. States of	266	689	73,755	Kolonia	88
Minnesota, U.S.	84,402	218,601	4,075,970	St. Paul	15
Mississippi, U.S.	47,689	123,515	2,520,638	Jackson	15
Missouri, U.S.	69,697	180,515	4,916,686	Jefferson City	15
Monaco	0.7	2	25,029	Monaco	45
*Mongolia	606,163	1,569,962	1,594,800	Ulaanbaatar	65
Montana, U.S.	147,046	380,849	786,690	Helena	14
Montserrat	40	104	12,073	Plymouth	29
*Morocco	172,414	446,550	20,242,000	Rabat	82
*Mozambique	303,769	786,762	12,130,000	Maputo	86
Namibia	317,827	823,172	1,200,000	Windhoek	86
Nauru	8	20	7,254	Yaren dist.	88
Nebraska, U.S.	77,355	200,349	1,569,825	Lincoln	15
*Nepal	54,663	141,577	14,179,301	Kathmandu	72
*Netherlands	15,892	41,160	14,227,000	Amsterdam, The Hague	42
Netherlands Antilles	390	1,010	246,000	Willemstad	28
Nevada, U.S.	110,561	286,353	800,493	Carson City	14
New Brunswick, Can.	28,354	73,437	688,926	Fredericton	25
New Caledonia & Dep.	7,335	18,998	133,233	Nouméa	88
Newfoundland, Can.	156,184	404,517	561,996	St. John's	25
New Hampshire, U.S.	9,279	24,033	920,610	Concord	15
New Jersey, U.S.	7,787	20,168	7,364,823	Trenton	15
New Mexico, U.S.	121,593	314,926	1,302,981	Santa Fe	14
New York, U.S.	49,108	127,190	17,558,072	Albany	15
*New Zealand	103,736	268,676	3,167,357	Wellington	94
*Nicaragua	45,698	118,358	2,703,000	Managua	27
*Niger	489,189	1,267,000	5,098,427	Niamey	82
*Nigeria	357,000	924,630	82,643,000	Lagos	83
North America	9,363,000	24,250,200	370,000,000	......	13
North Carolina, U.S.	52,669	136,413	5,881,766	Raleigh	15
North Dakota, U.S.	70,702	183,118	652,717	Bismarck	15
Northern Ireland, U.K.	5,452	14,121	1,543,000	Belfast	41
Northwest Terr., Can.	1,304,896	3,379,683	44,684	Yellowknife	24
*Norway	125,053	323,887	4,092,000	Oslo	39
Nova Scotia, Canada	21,425	55,491	837,789	Halifax	25
Ohio, U.S.	41,330	107,045	10,797,624	Columbus	15
Oklahoma, U.S.	69,956	181,186	3,025,290	Oklahoma Cty.	15
*Oman	120,000	310,800	891,000	Muscat	75
Ontario, Canada	412,580	1,068,582	8,551,733	Toronto	24
Oregon, U.S.	97,073	251,419	2,633,149	Salem	14
Pacific Islands, Terr. of the	707	1,831	133,732	Saipan	88
*Pakistan	310,403	803,944	83,782,000	Islamabad	75
*Panama	29,761	77,082	1,830,175	Panamá	27
*Papua New Guinea	183,540	475,369	3,006,799	Port Moresby	88
*Paraguay	157,047	406,752	2,973,000	Asunción	34
Pennsylvania, U.S.	45,308	117,348	11,863,895	Harrisburg	15
*Peru	496,222	1,285,215	17,031,221	Lima	32
*Philippines	115,707	299,681	47,914,017	Manila	71
*Poland	120,725	312,678	35,815,000	Warsaw	51
*Portugal	35,549	92,072	9,933,000	Lisbon	52
Pr. Edward Island, Can.	2,184	5,657	121,328	Charlottetown	25
Puerto Rico	3,515	9,104	3,186,076	San Juan	29
*Qatar	4,247	11,000	220,000	Doha	74
Québec, Canada	594,857	1,540,680	6,377,518	Québec	25
Réunion	969	2,510	491,000	St-Denis	87
Rhode Island, U.S.	1,212	3,139	947,154	Providence	15
*Romania	91,699	237,500	22,048,305	Bucharest	56
*Rwanda	10,169	26,337	4,819,317	Kigali	84
Sabah, Malaysia	29,388	76,115	1,002,608	Kota Kinabalu	71
St. Christopher-Nevis	104	269	44,404	Basseterre	29
*St. Lucia	238	616	115,783	Castries	29
St-Pierre & Miquelon	93	242	6,000	St-Pierre	25
*St. Vincent & Grenadines	150	388	124,000	Kingstown	29
San Marino	23	61	19,149	San Marino	54
*São Tomé e Príncipe	372	963	85,000	São Tomé	83
Sarawak, Malaysia	48,250	124,967	1,294,753	Kuching	70
Saskatchewan, Can.	251,699	651,900	957,025	Regina	24
*Saudi Arabia	829,995	2,149,687	8,367,000	Riyadh	74
Scotland, U.K.	30,414	78,772	5,117,146	Edinburgh	40
*Senegal	75,954	196,720	5,508,000	Dakar	82
*Seychelles	145	375	63,000	Victoria	87
*Sierra Leone	27,925	72,325	3,470,000	Freetown	83
*Singapore	226	585	2,413,945	Singapore	69
*Solomon Islands	11,500	29,785	221,000	Honiara	88
*Somalia	246,200	637,658	3,645,000	Mogadishu	85
*South Africa	455,318	1,179,274	23,771,970	Cape Town, Pretoria	86
South America	6,875,000	17,806,250	245,000,000	......	31
South Carolina, U.S.	31,113	80,583	3,121,833	Columbia	15
South Dakota, U.S.	77,116	199,730	690,768	Pierre	15
*Spain	194,881	504,742	37,430,000	Madrid	53
*Sri Lanka (Ceylon)	25,332	65,610	14,850,001	Colombo	73
*Sudan	967,494	2,505,809	18,691,000	Khartoum	81
*Suriname	55,144	142,823	352,041	Paramaribo	32
*Swaziland	6,705	17,366	547,000	Mbabane	86
*Sweden	173,665	449,792	8,320,000	Stockholm	39
Switzerland	15,943	41,292	6,329,000	Bern	50
*Syria	71,498	185,180	8,979,000	Damascus	74
Taiwan	13,971	36,185	16,609,961	Taipei	65
*Tanzania	363,708	942,003	17,527,560	Dar es Salaam	85
Tennessee, U.S.	42,144	109,153	4,591,120	Nashville	15
Texas, U.S.	266,807	691,030	14,229,191	Austin	15
*Thailand	198,455	513,998	46,455,000	Bangkok	68
Togo	21,622	56,000	2,472,000	Lomé	83
Tonga	270	699	90,128	Nuku'alofa	88
*Trinidad and Tobago	1,980	5,128	1,067,108	Port of Spain	29
*Tunisia	63,378	164,149	6,367,000	Tunis	82
*Turkey	300,946	779,450	45,217,556	Ankara	74
Turks & Caicos Is.	166	430	7,436	Cockburn Twn.	28
Tuvalu	10	26	7,349	Fongafale	88
*Uganda	91,076	235,887	12,630,076	Kampala	84
*Ukrainian S.S.R., U.S.S.R.	233,089	603,700	49,755,000	Kiev	61
*Union of Soviet Socialist Republics	8,649,490	22,402,179	262,436,227	Moscow	58
*United Arab Emirates	32,278	83,600	1,040,275	Abu Dhabi	74
*United Kingdom	94,399	244,493	55,672,000	London	41
*United States	3,623,420	9,384,658	226,504,825	Washington	14
*Upper Volta	105,869	274,200	6,908,000	Ouagadougou	82
*Uruguay	72,172	186,925	2,899,000	Montevideo	34
Utah, U.S.	84,899	219,888	1,461,037	Salt Lake City	14
*Vanuatu	5,700	14,763	112,596	Vila	88
Vatican City	0.2	0.4	728	......	55
*Venezuela	352,143	912,050	13,913,000	Caracas	32
Vermont, U.S.	9,614	24,900	511,456	Montpelier	15
Vietnam	128,405	332,569	52,741,766	Hanoi	68
Virginia, U.S.	40,767	105,587	5,346,818	Richmond	15
Virgin Is., British	59	153	12,000	Road Town	29
Virgin Is., U.S.	133	344	95,591	Charlotte Amalie	29
Wales, U.K.	8,017	20,764	2,790,462	Cardiff	41
Washington, U.S.	68,139	176,480	4,132,180	Olympia	14
Western Sahara	102,703	266,000	76,425	......	82
*Western Samoa	1,133	2,934	151,983	Apia	88
West Virginia, U.S.	24,231	62,758	1,950,279	Charleston	15
*White Russian S.S.R. (Byelorussia), U.S.S.R.	80,154	207,599	9,560,000	Minsk	60
Wisconsin, U.S.	56,153	145,436	4,705,767	Madison	15
World	57,609,000	149,208,000	4,415,000,000	......	8,9
Wyoming, U.S.	97,809	253,325	469,557	Cheyenne	14
*Yemen Arab Republic	77,220	200,000	6,456,189	San'a	74
*Yemen, People's Dem. Rep.	111,101	287,752	1,969,000	Aden	74
*Yugoslavia	98,766	255,804	22,471,000	Belgrade	56
Yukon Terr., Canada	207,075	536,324	22,684	Whitehorse	24
*Zaire	905,063	2,344,113	28,291,000	Kinshasa	84
*Zambia	290,586	752,618	5,679,808	Lusaka	84
*Zimbabwe	150,803	390,580	7,360,000	Salisbury	86

The following index, arranged in strict alphabetical order, includes more than 7,000 place names that appear on the maps of this atlas. The name of the country, town, or physical feature is followed by the name of the political division (country) in which it is located. Next, appearing in boldface type, is the page number of the map on which it will be found, and the key reference, a letter-number combination, necessary for finding its location on the map. Page references for maps covering more than one page are usually given for the page on which the major portion of the map appears. Entries are generally indexed to the map or inset having the largest scale.

NAME FORMS With few exceptions, the names throughout the index, as on the maps, match the local official spelling. However, conventional Anglicized spellings are used for major geographical divisions and for cities and topographical features for which English forms exist, that is, "Spain" instead of "España" or "Munich" instead of "München." Names of this type are sometimes followed by the local official spelling in parentheses. As an aid to the user, the index is cross-referenced for most current and former spellings of such names.

ALPHABETIZATION Names in the index are alphabetized in the normal order of the English alphabet. Diacritical marks and foreign alphabet characters are disregarded in the alphabetization. Where abbreviations form parts of names, they are alphabetized as if they were fully spelled out. Physical features are usually listed under their proper names and not according to their generic term; that is, the Sea of Marmara will be listed as "Marmara (sea)," and Rio das Mortes will be found under "Mortes (river)" and not under "Rio." Exceptions are such familiar names as Rio Grande. Where an article forms an integral part of a name, the name appears in its normal order, alphabetized with the article. Thus, we find Le Havre after Leghorn and El Karnak before Elk City.

INDEX KEY REFERENCES In order to locate an unfamiliar place, first find the entry in the index and note the page number and the key reference, a letter-number combination. Turn to the map and you will find its position within the square formed by the latitude and longitude lines for those coordinates, that is, the letters and figures printed in red along the map margin. Note that inset maps continue the sequence of letter-number coordinates from the main map. The diagram below illustrates the system of indexing. The index entry for Limoges, France, reads "44/D5." Limoges will be found on page 44 at key reference square D5.

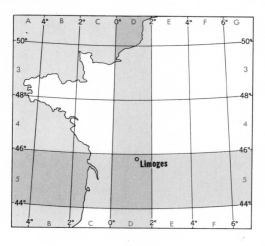

LIST OF ABBREVIATIONS

Afghan.	Afghanistan	Del.	Delaware	Iv. Coast	Ivory Coast	Nor.	Norway	S. Korea	South Korea
Afr.	Africa	Dem.	Democratic	Jam.	Jamaica	N.P.	National Park	S. Leone	Sierra Leone
Ala.	Alabama	Den.	Denmark	Jct.	Junction	N.S.	Nova Scotia	Sol. Is.	Solomon Islands
Alb.	Albania	Depr.	depression	Kans.	Kansas	N.W.T.	Northwest Territories	Sp.	Spain, Spanish
Alg.	Algeria	Des.	desert	Km.	Kilometer		(Canada)	Spr., Sprs.	Spring, Springs
Alta.	Alberta	Dist.	district	Ky.	Kentucky	N.Y.	New York	S.S.R.	Soviet Socialist
Amer.	America,	Dom. Rep.	Dominican Republic	L.	lac, lago, lake, loch,	N.Z.	New Zealand		Republic
	American	E.	East, Eastern		lough	Obl.	Oblast	St., Ste.	Saint, Sainte
Ant. & Bar.	Antigua &	Ecua.	Ecuador	La.	Louisiana	Okla.	Oklahoma	Sta.	Santa
	Barbuda	E. Ger.	East Germany	Leb.	Lebanon	Ont.	Ontario	St. Chris.-	St. Christopher-
Antarc.	Antarctica	El Sal.	El Salvador	Les.	Lesotho	Oreg.	Oregon	Nevis	Nevis
Arch.	archipelago	Eng.	England	Lib.	Liberia	Pa.	Pennsylvania	Sto.	Santo
Arg.	Argentina	Equat.	Equatorial	Liecht.	Liechtenstein	Pak.	Pakistan	Str.	strait
Ariz.	Arizona	Guin.	Guinea	Lux.	Luxembourg	Pan.	Panama	St. Vinc. &	Saint Vincent &
Ark.	Arkansas	Est.	estuary	Madag.	Madagascar	Papua N.G.	Papua New Guinea	Grens.	The Grenadines
A.S.S.R.	Autonomous Soviet	Eth.	Ethiopia	Man.	Manitoba	Par.	Paraguay	Sur.	Suriname
	Socialist Republic	Falk. Is.	Falkland Islands	Mart.	Martinique	P.D.R.	People's Democratic	Swaz.	Swaziland
Austr.,	Australia,	Fed.	Federal, Federated	Mass.	Massachusetts	Yemen	Republic of Yemen	Switz.	Switzerland
Austral.	Australian	Fin.	Finland	Maur.	Mauritania	P.E.I.	Prince Edward Island	Tanz.	Tanzania
Aut.	autonomous	Fla.	Florida	Md.	Maryland	Pen.	peninsula	Tenn.	Tennessee
B.	bay	For.	forest	Mex.	Mexico	Phil.	Philippines	Terr.	territory
Bah.	Bahamas	Fr.	France, French	Mich.	Michigan	Pk.	Park	Tex.	Texas
Bang.	Bangladesh	Fr. Gui.	French Guiana	Minn.	Minnesota	Plat.	plateau	Thai.	Thailand
Barb.	Barbados	Fr. Poly.	French Polynesia	Miss.	Mississippi	Pol.	Poland	Trin. & Tob.	Trinidad & Tobago
Bch.	beach	Ft.	Fort	Mo.	Missouri	Port.	Portugal, Portuguese	Tun.	Tunisia
Belg.	Belgium	G.	gulf	Mong.	Mongolia	P. Rico	Puerto Rico	U.A.E.	United Arab Emirates
Bol.	Bolivia	Ga.	Georgia	Mont.	Montana	Prom.	promontory	U.K.	United Kingdom
Bots.	Botswana	Ger.	Germany	Mor.	Morocco	Prov.	province, provincial	Upp. Volta	Upper Volta
Braz.	Brazil	Greenl.	Greenland	Moz.	Mozambique	Pt., Pte.	Point, Pointe	Urug.	Uruguay
Br., Brit.	British	Gt.	Great	Mt., mtn.	mount, mountain	Que.	Québec	U.S.	United States
Br. Col.	British Columbia	Guad.	Guadeloupe	Mts.	mountains	R.	river	U.S.S.R.	Union of Soviet
Br. Ind.	British Indian	Guat.	Guatemala	N.	North, Northern	Ra.	range		Socialist Republics
Oc. Terr.	Ocean Territory	Guin.-Biss.	Guinea-Bissau	N. Amer.	North America	Reg.	region	Va.	Virginia
Bulg.	Bulgaria	Guy.	Guyana	Nat'l Pk.	National Park	Rep.	Republic	Ven., Venez.	Venezuela
C.	cape	Har., harb.	harbor	N. Br.	New Brunswick	Res.	reservoir	V.I. (Br.)	Virgin Islands (British)
Calif.	California	Hd.	head	N.C.	North Carolina	R.I.	Rhode Island	V.I. (U.S.)	Virgin Islands (U.S.)
Camb.	Cambodia	Highl.	highland, highlands	N. Dak.	North Dakota	Riv.	river	Viet.	Vietnam
Can.	Canada	Hond.	Honduras	Nebr.	Nebraska	Rom.	Romania	Vill.	Village
Cap.	capital	Hts.	heights	Neth.	Netherlands	S.	South, Southern	Vol.	volcano
Cent. Afr.	Central African	Hung.	Hungary	Neth. Ant.	Netherlands Antilles	Sa.	serra, sierra	Vt.	Vermont
Rep.	Republic	I.	island, isle	Nev.	Nevada	S. Africa	South Africa	W.	Wadi
Cent. Amer.	Central America	Icel.	Iceland	New Cal.	New Caledonia	S. Amer.	South America	W.	West, Western
Chan.	channel	Ill.	Illinois	Newf.	Newfoundland	São T. & Pr.	São Tomé & Príncipe	Wash.	Washington
Chan. Is.	Channel Islands	Ind.	Indiana	New Hebr.	New Hebrides	Sask.	Saskatchewan	W. Ger.	West Germany
Col.	Colombia	Indon.	Indonesia	N.H.	New Hampshire	S.C.	South Carolina	W. Indies	West Indies
Colo.	Colorado	Int'l	International	Nic.	Nicaragua	Scot.	Scotland	Wis.	Wisconsin
Conn.	Connecticut	Ire.	Ireland	N. Ire.	Northern Ireland	Sd.	sound	W. Samoa	Western Samoa
C. Rica	Costa Rica	Is., isls.	islands	N.J.	New Jersey	S. Dak.	South Dakota	W. Va.	West Virginia
Ctr.	Center	Isl.	island, isle	N. Korea	North Korea	Sen.	Senegal	Wyo.	Wyoming
C. Verde	Cape Verde	Isr.	Israel	N. Mex.	New Mexico	Seych.	Seychelles	Yugo.	Yugoslavia
Czech.	Czechoslovakia	Isth.	isthmus	No.	Northern	Sing.	Singapore	Zim.	Zimbabwe

A

Aachen, W. Ger., 47/A3
Aarau, Switz., 50/D1
Aare (riv.), Switz., 50/D2
Aba, Nigeria, 83/F7
Abadan, Iran, 74/E3
Abbeville, France, 44/D2
Abbeville, La., 19/K7
Abbottabad, Pak., 75/K3
Abéché, Chad, 80/D5
Abenra, Den., 39/F9
Abeokuta, Nigeria, 83/E7
Aberdare, Wales, 41/D4
Aberystwyth, Wales, 41/D4
Abha, Saudi Arabia, 74/D6
Abidjan (cap.), Iv. Coast, 83/D7
Abilene, Kans., 18/J5
Abilene, Tex., 19/J6
Abingdon, Eng., 41/F5
Abingdon, Va., 21/N5
Abitibi (lake), Ont., 25/H6
Abitibi (riv.), Ont., 25/H5
Abomey, Benin, 83/E7
Abruzzi (reg.), Italy, 54/D3
Abu Dhabi (cap.), U.A.E., 74/F5
Abunã (riv.), S. Amer., 32/G6
Abu Road, India, 72/C4
Acadia Nat'l Pk., Maine, 20/R3
Acámbaro, Mex., 26/E4
Acapulco, Mex., 26/E5
Accra (cap.), Ghana, 83/D7
Acklins (isl.), Bah., 28/C2
Aconcagua (mt.), Arg., 34/F10
Acre (riv.), Braz., 32/G6
Acre, Isr., 76/C2
Ada, Minn., 18/J3
Ada, Okla., 19/J6
Adak (isl.), Alaska, 22/E5
Adamawa (reg.), Afr., 84/B2
Adam's Bridge (shoals), Asia, 73/D7
Adamstown (cap.), Pitcairn I., 89/N8
Adana, Turkey, 74/C2
Adapazari, Turkey, 74/B1
Addis Ababa (cap.), Eth., 81/G6
Addo Nat'l Pk., S. Africa, 86/D6
Adelaide, Austr., 91/F6
Aden (cap.), P.D.R. Yemen, 74/E7
Adige (riv.), Italy, 54/C1
Adirondack (mts.), N.Y., 20/P3
Adjuntas, P. Rico, see detailed map p. 29
Admiralty (inlet), N.W.T., 24/H1
Admiralty (isl.), Alaska, 22/F4
Admiralty (isls.), Papua N.G., 88/E6
Ado, Nigeria, 83/E7
Adrar, Alg., 82/D3
Adrar (reg.), Maur., 82/B4
Adrar des Iforas (plat.), Afr., 82/E5
Adrian, Mich., 20/N4
Adriatic (sea), Europe, 37/F4
Adwa, Eth., 81/G5
Aegean (sea), 56-57/G6
Afars & Issas, see Djibouti
Afghanistan, 75/H3
Afognak (isl.), Alaska, 22/D4
Africa, 78-79
Afyonkarahisar, Turkey, 74/B2
Agadès, Niger, 82/F5
Agaña (cap.), Guam, 88/E4
Agattu (isl.), Alaska, 22/D4
Agra, India, 72/D3
Aguascalientes, Mex., 26/D4
Aguilar, Colo., 18/G5
Agulhas (cape), S. Africa, 86/B7
Ahaggar (mts.), Alg., 82/E-F4
Ahmadabad, India, 72/C4
Ahvaz (Ahwaz), Iran, 75/E3
Aiea, Hawaii, 23/C4
Aiken, S.C., 21/N6
Aina Haina, Hawaii, 23/C4
Aïn Beïda, Alg., 82/F1
Aïoun el Atrous, Maur., 82/C5
Air (mts.), Niger, 82/F5
Aisne (riv.), France, 44/E3
Aix, France, 44/F6
Ajaccio, France, 44/B7
Ajdabia, Libya, 80/D1
Ajmer, India, 72/C3
Akimiski (isl.), N.W.T., 25/H5
Akita, Japan, 67/J4
Aklavik, N.W.T., 24/C2
Akko (Acre), Isr., 76/C2
Akron, Ohio, 20/N4
Aksum, Eth., 81/G5
Alabama (riv.), Ala., 19/M7
Alabama (state), U.S., 15/J4
Alajuela, C. Rica, 27/C3
Alakanuk, Alaska, 22/C3
Alamogordo, N. Mex., 17/G6
Aland (isls.), Fin., 39/L6
Alaska (gulf), Alaska, 22/E4
Alaska (state), U.S., 22

Albacete, Spain, 53/E3
Albania, 56/D4
Albany, Ga., 21/M7
Albany (cap.), N.Y., 20/P4
Albany, Oreg., 16/C3
Albert (Mobutu Sese Seko) (lake), Afr., 84/F3
Alberta (prov.), Can., 24/E5
Albert Lea, Minn., 18/K4
Albertville, Ala., 21/M6
Albion, Mich., 20/M4
Albuquerque, N. Mex., 17/G6
Aldabra (isls.), Seychelles, 87/H1
Alderney (isl.), Chan. Is., 41/E6
Aleknagik, Alaska, 22/D4
Alençon, France, 44/D3
Aleppo, Syria, 74/C2
Alert, N.W.T., 25/N3
Alessandria, Italy, 54/B2
Alesund, Nor., 39/D5
Aleutian (isls.), Alaska, 22/A5
Alexander (arch.), Alaska, 22/F4
Alexandra, S. Africa, 86/H6
Alexandra Fiord, N.W.T., 25/N3
Alexandria, Egypt, 81/E1
Alexandria, La., 19/K7
Alexandria, Minn., 18/K3
Alexandria, Va., 20/O5
Algeciras, Spain, 53/D4
Alger (cap.), Alg., see Algiers
Algeria, 82/D3
Algiers (cap.), Alg., 82/E1
Algona, Iowa, 18/K4
Alicante, Spain, 53/F3
Alice, Tex., 19/J9
Alice Sprs., Austr., 91/E4
Aligarh, India, 72/D3
Ali Sabieh, Djibouti, 81/H5
Al Kuwait (cap.), Kuwait, 74/E4
Allahabad, India, 72/D3
Allentown, Pa., 20/O4
Alliance, Nebr., 18/H4
Alliance, Ohio, 20/N4
Allier (riv.), France, 44/E5
Alma, Mich., 20/M4
Alma-Ata, U.S.S.R., 58/H5
Almería, Spain, 53/E4
Alofi (cap.), Niue, 88/K7
Alor Setar, Malaysia, 69/D6
Alpena, Mich., 20/M3
Alpine, Tex., 19/H7
Alps (mts.), Europe, 37/E-F4
Altay (mts.), Asia, 64/C2
Alton, Ill., 18/L5
Altoona, Pa., 20/O4
Altun Shan (Altyn Tagh) (mts.), China, 64/C4
Alturas, Calif., 16/C4
Altus, Okla., 19/J6
Alva, Okla., 19/J5
Amadjuak, N.W.T., 25/J3
Amagasaki, Japan, 67/H8
Amami (isls.), Japan, 67/N5
Amapala, Hond., 27/B2
'Amara, Iraq, 75/E3
Amarillo, Tex., 19/H6
Amazon (riv.), S. Amer., 32/J4
Ambato, Ecua., 32/E4
Amber (Bobaomby) (cape), Madag., 87/H2
Amboina, Indon., 71/H6
Ambriz, Angola, 84/B5
Amchitka (isl.), Alaska, 22/E5
Ameca, Mex., 26/D4
American Falls, Idaho, 16/E4
American Falls (res.), Idaho, 16/E4
American Fork, Utah, 16/E4
American Samoa, 89/N9
Amersfoort, Neth., 42/G4
Ames, Iowa, 18/K4
Amherst, N.S., 25/K7
Amiens, France, 44/D3
Amman (cap.), Jordan, 76/D4
Amos, Que., 25/J7
Amoy, China, see Xiamen
Amravati, India, 72/D4
Amritsar, India, 72/C2
Amsterdam (cap.), Neth., 43/G4
Amsterdam, N.Y., 20/P4
Amudar'ya (riv.), Asia, 75/H1
Amund Ringnes (isl.), N.W.T., 25/M3
Amundsen (sea), Antarc., 35/B9
Amur (riv.), Asia, 59/N4
Anaconda, Mont., 16/E3
Anacortes, Wash., 16/C2
Anadarko, Okla., 19/J6
Anadyr', U.S.S.R., 59/S3
Anaheim, Calif., 17/C6
Anchorage, Alaska, 22/E3
Ancona, Italy, 54/D3
Andalusia, Ala., 21/M7
Andalusia (reg.), Spain, 53/C-E4
Andaman (isls.), India, 73/G5
Anderson, Ind., 20/M4
Anderson, S.C., 21/N6
Andes (mts.), S. Amer., 34/F9-11
Andorra, 53/G1
Andorra la Vella (cap.), Andorra, 53/G1
Andreanof (isls.), Alaska, 22/F5
Andrews, Tex., 19/H6
Andros (isl.), Bah., 28/B1
Angara (riv.), U.S.S.R., 58/L4

Angel (fall), Ven., 32/H2
Angers, France, 44/C4
Angkor Wat (ruins), Camb., 68/D4
Angoche, Moz., 86/G3
Angola, 84/C6
Angoulême, France, 44/D5
Anguilla (isl.), St. Chris.-Nevis, 29/F3
Anjouan (isl.), Comoros, 87/G2
Ankara (cap.), Turkey, 74/B1
Anking, China, see Anqing
An Najaf, Iraq, 74/D3
Annaba, Alg., 82/F1
Annapolis (cap.), Md., 20/O5
Annapurna (mt.), Nepal, 72/E3
Ann Arbor, Mich., 20/N4
An Nasiriya, Iraq, 74/E3
Anniston, Ala., 21/M6
Annobón (isl.), Equat. Guin., 79/C5
Anoka, Minn., 18/K3
Anqing, China, 65/J5
Anshan, China, 65/K3
Antakya, Turkey, 74/C2
Antalya (gulf), Turkey, 74/B2
Antananarivo (cap.), Madag., 87/H3
Antarctica, 35
Antibes, France, 44/G6
Anticosti (isl.), Que., 25/K6
Antigo, Wis., 18/L3
Antigua, 29/G3
Antigua, Guat., 27/B2
Antigua & Barbuda, 29/G3
Antilles (isls.), W. Indies, 28-29/B-F 2-4
Antioch (Antakya), Turkey, 74/C2
Antlers, Okla., 19/K6
Antofagasta, Chile, 34/F8
Antrim, N. Ire., 40/D3
Antsirabe, Madag., 87/H3
Antsiranana (Diégo-Suarez), Madag., 87/H2
Antwerp, Belg., 42/E6
Aomori, Japan, 67/K3
Aosta, Italy, 54/A2
Apalachee (bay), Fla., 21/M7
Apalachicola, Fla., 21/M7
Apeldoorn, Neth., 42/H4
Apennines (mts.), Italy, 54/B-F 2-5
Apia (cap.), W. Samoa, 89/M8
Appalachian (mts.), U.S., 15/J-N 2-4
Appleton, Wis., 18/L3
Appleton City, Mo., 18/K5
Apurímac (riv.), Peru, 32/F6
'Aqaba (gulf), Asia, 74/C4
'Aqaba, Jordan, 76/C8
'Araba (wadi), Jordan, 77/E5
Arabia (pen.), Asia, 63/H7
Arabian (sea), Asia, 63/K8
Arabian (des.), Egypt, 81/F2
Aracaju, Braz., 33/N6
Arad, Rom., 56/E2
Arafura (sea), 91/D-F1
Aragón (reg.), Spain, 53/F2
Arak, Iran, 75/E3
Araks (riv.), Asia, 74/E2
Aral (sea), U.S.S.R., 58/F-G5
Aran (isls.), Ire., 41/B4
Aransas Pass, Tex., 19/J8
Ararat (mt.), Turkey, 74/D1
Aras (Araks) (riv.), Asia, 74/E2
Arcachon, France, 44/C5
Arcadia, Fla., 21/N8
Arcata, Calif., 16/B4
Archangel, U.S.S.R., 60/F2
Arco, Idaho, 16/E4
Arctic Circle, 96/C7
Arctic Ocean, 96
Arctic Red River, N.W.T., 24/C2
Arctic Village, Alaska, 22/E2
Ardabil, Iran, 75/E2
Ardennes (plat.), Belg., 43/F-J 8-9
Ardmore, Okla., 19/J6
Arecibo, P. Rico, see detailed map p. 29
Arezzo, Italy, 54/C3
Argenteuil, France, 44/A1
Argentina, 34
Arges (riv.), Rom., 56/G3
Árgos, Greece, 57/F7
Arguello (pt.), Calif., 17/C6
Arhus, Den., 39/F8
Arica, Chile, 32/F7
'Arish, el (wadi), Egypt, 77/A6
Arizona (state), U.S., 14/D4
Arkadelphia, Ark., 19/K6
Arkangel'sk (Archangel), U.S.S.R., 60/F2
Arkansas (riv.), U.S., 15/H3
Arkansas (state), U.S., 15/H3
Arkansas City, Kans., 19/J5
Arles, France, 44/F6
Arlington, Oreg., 16/C3
Arlington, Tex., 19/J6
Armagh, N. Ire., 40/D3
Armavir, U.S.S.R., 60/F5
Armenian S.S.R., U.S.S.R., 60/F6
Armentières, France, 44/E2
Armidale, Austr., 92/F2
Arnhem, Neth., 42/H4

Arno (riv.), Italy, 54/C3
Arran (isl.), Scot., 40/D3
Arras, France, 44/E2
Artesia, N. Mex., 19/G6
Artigas, Urug., 34/J10
Arua, Uganda, 84/F3
Aruba (isl.), Neth. Ant., 28/E4
Arusha, Tanz., 85/G4
Arvika, Sweden, 39/H7
Arvin, Calif., 17/D6
Asahikawa, Japan, 67/L2
Ascension (isl.), St. Helena, 79/A5
Ashanti (reg.), Ghana, 83/D7
Ashdod, Isr., 76/B4
Asheville, N.C., 21/N6
Ash Fork, Ariz., 17/E6
Ashkhabad, U.S.S.R., 58/F6
Ashland, Kans., 19/J5
Ashland, Ky., 20/N5
Ashland, Oreg., 16/C4
Ashland, Wis., 18/L2
Ashley, N. Dak., 18/J3
Ashqelon, Isr., 76/A4
Ashtabula, Ohio, 20/N4
Asi (riv.), Syria, 74/C2
Asia, 63
Asmara, Eth., 81/G4
Assab, Eth., 81/H5
Assam (state), India, 72/G3
Asselle, Eth., 81/G6
Asterabad (Gorgan), Iran, 74/F2
Asti, Italy, 54/B2
Astoria, Oreg., 16/C3
Astrakhan', U.S.S.R., 60/G5
Asturias (reg.), Spain, 53/C-D1
Asunción (cap.), Par., 34/J9
Aswân, Egypt, 81/A4
Asyût, Egypt, 81/A4
Atacama (des.), Chile, 32, 34/G8
Atakpamé, Togo, 83/E7
Atbara, Sudan, 81/F4
Atchison, Kans., 18/K5
Athabasca, Alta., 24/E5
Athabasca (lake), Can., 24/F4
Athens, Ala., 21/M6
Athens, Ga., 21/N6
Athens (cap.), Greece, 57/F7
Athens, Ohio, 20/N5
Athens, Tenn., 21/M6
Athos (mt.), Greece, 56/G5
Atikokan, Ont., 24/G6
Atitlán (lake), Guat., 27/B2
Atka (isl.), Alaska, 22/F5
Atlanta (cap.), Ga., 21/M6
Atlantic, Iowa, 18/K4
Atlantic City, N.J., 21/P5
Atlantic Ocean, 8/H3-8
Atlas (mts.), Afr., 79/B-C1
Atmore, Ala., 21/M7
Attalla, Ala., 21/M6
Attu (isl.), Alaska, 22/D4
Auburn, Ala., 21/M6
Auburn, Calif., 16/C5
Auburn, Maine, 20/R4
Auburn, Mo., 18/K4
Auburn, N.Y., 20/O4
Auckland, N.Z., 94/E2
Augsburg, W. Ger., 47/D4
Augusta, Ga., 21/N6
Augusta (cap.), Maine, 20/R3
Aurora, Colo., 18/G5
Aurora, Ill., 18/L4
Auschwitz, see Oswiecim
Austin, Minn., 18/K4
Austin (cap.), Tex., 19/J7
Austral (isls.), Fr. Poly., 89/L8
Australia, 91
Australian Alps (mts.), Austr., 92/D-E5
Austria, 48
Auvergne (mts.), France, 44/E5
Avignon, France, 44/F6
Ávila, Spain, 53/D2
Avon (riv.), Eng., 41/F4
Axel Heiberg (isl.), N.W.T., 25/N3
Ayacucho, Peru, 32/F6
Ayers Rock (mt.), Austr., 91/D5
Ayr, Scot., 40/D3
Ayutthaya, Thai., 68/D4
Azerbaidzhan S.S.R., U.S.S.R., 60/G6
Azbine (Air) (mts.), Niger, 82/F5
Azores (isls.), Port., see detailed map p. 52
Azov (sea), U.S.S.R., 60/E5
Aztec, N. Mex., 17/G5

B

Babanusa, Sudan, 81/E5
Bab el Mandeb (str.), 74/D7
Babylon, N.Y., 20/P4
Bacău, Rom., 56/H2
Bac Lieu, Viet., 68/E5
Bacolod, Phil., 71/G3
Badajoz, Spain, 53/C3
Bad Axe, Mich., 20/N4
Baden-Baden, W. Ger., 47/B4
Badgastein, Austria, 48/B3
Bad Kissingen, W. Ger., 47/D3
Badlands Nat'l Pk., S. Dak., 18/H4

Baffin (bay), 24-25/J-K1
Baffin (isl.), N.W.T., 24-25/J-K 2-3
Bafoussam, Cameroon, 84/B2
Baghdad (cap.), Iraq, 74/D3
Baghlan, Afghan., 75/J2
Bahamas, 28/C1
Bahawalpur, Pak., 75/K4
Bahia (Salvador), Braz., 33/N6
Bahía Blanca, Arg., 34/H11
Bahir Dar, Eth., 81/G5
Bahrain, 74/F4
Baida, Libya, 80/D1
Baie-St-Paul, Que., 25/J6
Bainbridge, Ga., 21/M7
Bairiki (cap.), Kiribati, 88/H5
Baja California Norte (state), Mex., 26/A1
Baja California Sur (state), Mex., 26/B3
Baker, Mont., 18/G3
Baker, Oreg., 16/D3
Baker (mt.), Wash., 16/C2
Baker Lake, N.W.T., 24/G3
Bakersfield, Calif., 17/C6
Baku, U.S.S.R., 60/H6
Balaton (lake), Hung., 49/D3
Bali (isl.), Indon., 71/E7
Balkan (mts.), Bulg., 56/F4
Balkh, Afghan., 75/J2
Balkhash (lake), U.S.S.R., 58/H5
Ballarat, Austr., 92/B5
Ballina, Austr., 92/G1
Ballina, Ire., 41/B3
Balmoral Castle, Scot., 40/E2
Baltic (sea), Europe, 37/F3
Baltimore, Ire., 41/B5
Baltimore, Md., 20/O5
Baltistan (reg.), Pak., 72/D1
Baluchistan (reg.), Pak., 72/B3
Bamako (cap.), Mali, 82/C6
Bamberg, W. Ger., 47/D4
Bamenda, Cameroon, 84/B2
Banaba (isl.), Pacific, 88/G6
Banda (isls.), Indon., 71/H7
Bandar 'Abbas, Iran, 75/G4
Bandar-e Pahlavi (Enzeli), Iran, 74/E2
Bandar Khomeini (Bandar Shahpur), Iran, 74/E3
Bandar Seri Begawan (cap.), Brunei, 71/E4
Bandiagara, Mali, 82/D6
Bandundu, Zaire, 84/C4
Bandung, Indon., 70/D7
Banff, Alta., 24/E5
Banff, Scot., 40/E2
Banff Nat'l Pk., Alta., 24/E5
Banfora, Upp. Volta, 83/D6
Bangalore, India, 72/D6
Bangassou, Cent. Afr. Rep., 84/D3
Bangkok (cap.), Thai., 68/D4
Bangladesh, 72/F4
Bangor, Maine, 20/R3
Bangui (cap.), Cent. Afr. Rep., 84/C3
Bangweulu (lake), Zambia, 84/F6
Banjarmasin, Indon., 71/E6
Banjul (cap.), Gambia, 82/A6
Banks (isl.), N.W.T., 24/D1
Banning, Calif., 17/D6
Baraboo, Wis., 18/L4
Barbados, 29/G4
Barbers (pt.), Hawaii, 23/B4
Barberton, Ohio, 20/N4
Barbuda, Ant. & Bar., 29/G3
Barcelona, Spain, 53/H2
Barcelona, Ven., 32/G2
Bareilly, India, 72/D3
Barents (sea), Europe, 37/D2
Bar Harbor, Maine, 20/R3
Bari, Italy, 54/F4
Barnaul, U.S.S.R., 58/J4
Barnwell, S.C., 21/N6
Baroda, India, 72/C4
Barotseland (reg.), Zambia, 84/D7
Barqa (Cyrenaica) (reg.), Libya, 80/D1
Barquisimeto, Ven., 32/F2
Barranquilla, Col., 32/F1
Barre, Vt., 20/P3
Barrow (pt.), Alaska, 22/D1
Barrow (str.), N.W.T., 24/G1
Barstow, Calif., 17/D6
Bartlesville, Okla., 19/K5
Bartow, Fla., 21/N8
Baskatong (lake), Que., 25/J6
Basra, Iraq, 74/E3
Bassas da India (isl.), Réunion, 86/F4
Bassein, Burma, 68/B3
Basse-Terre (cap.), Guad., 29/F4
Basseterre (cap.), St. Chris.-Nevis, 29/F3
Bastogne, Belg., 43/H9
Bastrop, La., 19/L6
Basutoland, Afr., see Lesotho
Bata, Equat. Guin., 84/B3
Batavia, N.Y., 20/O4
Batdambang, Camb., 68/D4

Batesville, Ark., 19/K6
Bath, Eng., 41/E5
Bath, Maine, 20/R4
Bathurst, Austr., 92/E3
Bathurst (Banjul) (cap.), Gambia, 82/A6
Bathurst, N.Br., 25/K6
Bathurst (isl.), N.W.T., 25/M3
Batna, Alg., 82/F1
Baton Rouge (cap.), La., 19/L7
Battambang, Camb., see Batdambang
Battle Creek, Mich., 20/M4
Battleford, Sask., 24/E5
Battle Harbour, Newf., 25/L5
Batumi, U.S.S.R., 60/F6
Bat Yam, Isr., 76/B4
Bauchi, Nigeria, 83/F6
Bauld (cape), Newf., 25/L5
Bavaria (state), W. Ger., 47/D4
Bay City, Mich., 20/N4
Bay City, Tex., 19/K7
Baydhabo, Somalia, 85/H3
Bayeux, France, 44/C3
Baykal (lake), U.S.S.R., 59/L4
Baykonur, U.S.S.R., 58/G5
Bay Minette, Ala., 21/M7
Bayonne, France, 44/C6
Bayreuth, W. Ger., 47/D4
Bayrūt, Leb., see Beirut
Bay St. Louis, Miss., 19/L7
Baytown, Tex., 19/K7
Bear (lake), U.S., 16/F4
Bearpaw (mts.), Mont., 16/F2
Beatrice, Nebr., 18/J4
Beaufort (sea), N. Amer., 13/D-E2
Beaufort, S.C., 21/N6
Beaumaris, Wales, 41/D4
Beaumont, Tex., 19/K7
Beauvais, France, 44/E3
Beaver Dam, Wis., 18/L4
Beaverhead (mts.), Idaho, 16/E3
Béchar, Alg., 81/D2
Bechuanaland, see Botswana
Beckley, W. Va., 20/N5
Bedford, Eng., 41/F4
Bedford, Ind., 20/M5
Beersheba, Isr., 76/D4
Beeville, Tex., 19/J7
Beijing (Peking) (cap.), People's Rep. of China, 65/J3
Beira, Moz., 86/F3
Beirut (cap.), Leb., 74/B3
Beja, Tun., 82/F1
Bejaïa, Alg., 82/F1
Belau (isls.), 88/D5
Belcher (isl.), Ont., 24/H4
Belém, Braz., 33/L4
Belet Weyne, Somalia, 85/J3
Belfast, Maine, 20/R3
Belfast (cap.), N. Ire., 40/D3
Belfort, France, 44/G4
Belgian Congo, see Zaire
Belgium, 43
Belgrade (cap.), Yugo., 56/E3
Belize, 27/B1
Belize City, Belize, 27/B1
Bellary, India, 72/D5
Belle Fourche, S. Dak., 18/H3
Belle Glade, Fla., 21/N8
Belle Isle (str.), Canada, 25/L5
Belleville, Ill., 18/L5
Bellingham, Wash., 16/C2
Bellingshausen (sea), Antarc., 35/C9-10
Bellot (str.), N.W.T., 24/G1
Belmopan (cap.), Belize, 27/B1
Belo Horizonte, Braz., 33/M7
Beloit, Wis., 18/L4
Belton, Tex., 19/J7
Bemidji, Minn., 18/K3
Benares (Varanasi), India, 72/E3
Bend, Oreg., 16/C3
Bendigo, Austr., 92/C5
Benevento, Italy, 54/E4
Bengal (bay), Asia, 63/M-N8
Benghazi, Libya, 80/C1
Benguela, Angola, 84/B6
Beni Mellal, Mor., 82/C2
Benin, 83/E6-7
Benin City, Nigeria, 83/F7
Beni Saf, Alg., 82/D1
Beni Suef, Egypt, 81/J3
Benkelman, Nebr., 18/H4
Bennettsville, S.C., 21/N6
Bennington, Vt., 20/P4
Benoni, S. Africa, 86/J6
Bentiu, Sudan, 81/E6
Benton, Ark., 19/K6
Benton Harbor, Mich., 20/M4
Benue (riv.), Afr., 79/C4
Beograd (Belgrade), Yugo., 56/E3
Berber, Sudan, 81/F4
Berberati, Cent. Afr. Rep., 84/C3
Berchtesgaden, W. Ger., 47/E5
Berens River, Man., 24/G5
Bergen, Nor., 39/D6
Bergerac, France, 44/D5
Bering (sea), 96/D12
Bering (str.), 96/C12
Bering Land Bridge Nat'l Pk., Alaska, 22/C2
Berkeley, Calif., 16/C5
Berlin, N.H., 20/R3
Berlin, East (cap.), E. Ger., 47/F4
Berlin, West, W. Ger. 47/E4

Bermuda, *see detailed map p. 29*
Bern (cap.), Switz., 50/C2
Bernalillo, N. Mex., 17/G6
Berthold, N. Dak., 18/H2
Berwick-on-Tweed, Eng., 41/F3
Besançon, France, 44/G4
Bessemer, Ala., 21/M6
Bessemer, Mich., 18/L3
Bethlehem, Pa., 20/P4
Bethlehem, West Bank, 76/C4
Bet She'an, Isr., 76/D3
Bettles Field, Alaska, 22/D2
Bhagalpur, India 72/F4
Bhatpara, India, 72/F1
Bhavnagar, India, 72/C4
Bhopal, India, 72/D4
Bhutan, 72/G3
Bialystok, Pol., 51/F2
Biarritz, France, 44/C6
Biddeford, Maine, 20/R4
Bié, Angola, 84/C6
Bien Hoa, Viet., 68/E4
Big Bend Nat'l Pk., Tex., 19/G7
Bighorn (mts.), Wyo., 16/G3-4
Bighorn (riv.), U.S., 14/E1
Big Rapids, Mich, 20/M4
Big Shady, Mont., 16/F2
Big Spring, Tex., 19/H6
Big Stone Gap, Va., 21/N5
Bikini (atoll), Marshall Is., 88/G4
Bilbao, Spain, 53/E1
Billings, Mont., 16/F3
Bilma, Niger, 82/G6
Biloxi, Miss., 19/L7
Biminis, The (isls.), Bah., 28/B1
Bingerville, Iv. Coast, 83/D7
Binghamton, N.Y., 20/P4
Bioko (isl.), Equat. Guin., 84/A3
Birkenhead, Eng., 41/E4
Birmingham, Ala., 21/M6
Birmingham, Eng., 41/E4
Bir Mogreïn, Maur., 82/B3
Birni-N'Konni, Niger, 82/E6
Bisbee, Ariz., 17/F7
Biscay (bay), Europe, 37/D4
Biscayne Nat'l Park, Fla., 21/N8
Bisho, S. Africa, 86/D6
Biskra, Alg., 82/F2
Bismarck (cap.), N. Dak., 18/H3
Bismarck (arch.), Papua N.G., 89/B1
Bissau (cap.), Guin.-Biss., 82/A6
Bitterroot (range), U.S., 14/D1
Bizerte, Tun., 82/F1
Black (sea), 37/H4
Black (for.), W. Ger., 47/B5
Blackfoot, Idaho, 16/E4
Black Hills (mts.), U.S., 18/H3
Blackpool, Eng., 41/E4
Black Volta (riv.), Afr., 83/D6
Blackwell, Okla., 19/J5
Blagoveshchensk, U.S.S.R., 59/N4
Blair, Nebr., 18/J4
Blakely, Ga., 21/M7
Blanc (mt.), Europe, 37/E4
Blanca (peak), Colo., 18/G5
Blanding, Utah, 17/F5
Blantyre, Malawi, 86/E3
Blarney, Ire., 41/B5
Blida, Alg., 82/E1
Blind River, Ont., 25/H6
Bloemfontein, S. Africa, 86/C5
Blois, France, 44/D4
Bloomington, Ill., 18/L5
Bloomington, Ind., 20/M5
Bloomington, Minn., 18/K3
Blue (mts.), Oreg., 16/D3
Blue Earth, Minn., 18/K4
Bluefield, W. Va., 21/N5
Bluefields, Nic., 27/C3
Blue Mountains, Austr., 92/F3
Blue Nile (riv.), Afr., 81/F5
Blythe, Calif., 17/E6
Blytheville, Ark., 19/L6
Bo, Sierra Leone, 83/B7
Boa Vista (isl.), Cape Verde, 83/B8
Bobaomby (cape), Madag., 87/H2
Bobo Dioulasso, Upp. Volta, 83/D6
Bodensee (Constance) (lake), Europe, 50/E1
Bogalusa, La., 19/L7
Bogotá (cap.), Col., 32/F3
Bohemian-Moravian Heights (hills), Czech., 48/C2
Boise (cap.), Idaho, 16/D4
Boksburg, S. Africa, 86/J6
Bol, Chad, 80/B5
Bolama, Guin.-Biss., 82/A6
Bollvar (mt.), Ven., 32/F2
Bolivia, 32/G-J7
Bologna, Italy, 54/C2
Boma, Zaire, 84/B5
Bombay, India, *see detailed map p. 73*
Bon (cape), Tun., 82/G1
Bonaire (isl.), Neth. Ant., 28/E4
Bône, Alg., *see Annaba*
Bonifacio (str.), Europe, 54/B4
Bonin (isls.), Japan, 67/M3
Bonn (cap.), W. Ger., 47/B3
Bonners Ferry, Idaho, 16/D2
Bonneville (dam), U.S., 16/C3
Boone, Iowa, 18/K4

Boothia (gulf), N.W.T., 24/H2
Boothia (isth.), N.W.T., 24/G2
Boothia (pen.), N.W.T., 24/G1
Bophuthatswana (aut. rep.), S. Africa, 86/C5
Borabora (isl.), Fr. Poly., 89/L7
Borah (peak), Idaho, 16/E3
Boras, Sweden, 39/H8
Bordeaux, France, 44/C5
Bordj Bou Arreridj, Alg., 82/E1
Borger, Tex., 19/H6
Borneo (isl.), Asia, 71/E5
Bornholm (isl.), Den., 39/J9
Borujird, Iran, 75/E3
Bosaso, Somalia, 85/J1
Bosnia-Hercegovina (rep.), Yugo., 56/C3
Bosporus (str.), Turkey, 74/A1
Bossangoa, Cent. Afr. Rep., 84/C2
Bossier City, La., 19/K6
Boston, Eng., 41/F4
Boston (cap.), Mass., 20/R4
Botany (bay), Austr., 92/M4
Bothnia (gulf), Europe, 39/K-O 4-6
Botswana, 86/C4
Bottineau, N. Dak., 18/H2
Bouaké, Iv. Coast, 83/D7
Bougainville (isl.), Papua N.G., 89/C2
Boulder, Colo., 18/G4
Boulder City, Nev., 17/E6
Boulogne, France, 44/D2
Bountiful, Utah, 16/F4
Bourg, France, 44/F4
Bourges, France, 44/E4
Boutilimit, Maur., 82/B5
Bowie, Tex., 19/J6
Bowling Green, Ky., 21/M5
Bowling Green, Mo., 18/L5
Boyama (Stanley) (falls), Zaire, 84/E3
Bozeman, Mont., 16/E3
Bradenton, Fla., 21/N8
Bradford, Eng., 41/E4
Bradford, Pa., 20/O4
Brady, Tex., 19/J7
Braemar, Scot., 40/E2
Braga, Port., 52/B2
Bragança, Port., 52/C2
Brahmaputra (riv.), Asia, 72/G3
Brăila, Rom., 56/H3
Brainerd, Minn., 18/K3
Brakpan, S. Africa, 86/J6
Brandberg (mt.), Namibia, 86/A4
Brandenburg (reg.), E. Ger., 47/E2
Brandon, Man., 24/F4
Brasília (cap.), Braz., 33/L7
Braşov, Rom., 56/G3
Bratislava, Czech., 48/D2
Brawley, Calif., 17/E6
Brazil, 33-34
Brazos (riv.), Tex., 19/J7
Brazzaville (cap.), Congo, 84/B4
Breckenridge, Tex., 19/J6
Breda, Neth., 42/F5
Bredasdorp Nat'l Pk., S. Africa, 86/C6
Bremen, W. Ger., 47/C2
Bremerhaven, W. Ger., 47/C2
Bremerton, Wash., 16/C3
Brenham, Tex., 19/J7
Brenner (pass), Europe, 48/A3
Breslau (Wrocław), Pol., 51/C3
Brest, France, 44/A3
Breton (sound), La., 19/L7
Brewton, Ala., 21/M7
Bridgeport, Conn., 20/P4
Bridgeton, N.J., 20/P5
Bridgetown (cap.), Barb., 29/G4
Brigham City, Utah, 16/F4
Brighton, Colo., 18/G5
Brighton, Eng., 41/F5
Brikama, Gambia, 82/A6
Brindisi, Italy, 54/G4
Brisbane (cap.), Austr., 91/J5
Bristol (bay), Alaska, 22/C4
Bristol, Eng., 41/E5
Bristol (chan.), U.K., 41/E5
Bristol, Va., 21/N5
British Columbia (prov.), Can., 24/D5
British Honduras, *see Belize*
British Indian Ocean Terr., 63/L10
Brno, Czech., 48/D2
Brodeur (pen.), N.W.T., 24/H1
Broken Bow, Nebr., 18/J4
Broken Hill, Austr., 92/A3
Brookfield, Mo., 18/K5
Brookhaven, Miss., 19/L7
Brookings, S. Dak., 18/J3
Brooks (range), Alaska, 22/D2
Brownfield, Tex., 19/H6
Browning, Mont., 16/E2
Brownsville, Tex., 19/J8
Brownwood, Tex., 19/J7
Bruges, Belg., 43/C6
Brunei, 71/E5
Brunswick, Ga., 21/N7
Brunswick, W. Ger., 47/D2
Brussels (cap.), Belg., 43/E7
Bryan, Ohio, 20/M4
Bryan, Tex., 19/J7
Bryce Canyon Nat'l Pk., Utah, 17/E5

Bucaramanga, Col., 32/F2
Buchanan, Lib., 83/B7
Bucharest (cap.), Rom., 56/G3
Budapest (cap.), Hung., 49/E3
Buea, Cameroon, 84/A3
Buenaventura, Col., 32/E3
Buenos Aires (cap.), Arg., 34/H10
Buffalo, N.Y., 20/O4
Buffalo, Wyo., 16/G3
Bug (riv.), Europe, 51/F2
Bujumbura (cap.), Burundi, 84/E4
Bukavu, Zaire, 84/E4
Bukhara, U.S.S.R., 58/G5
Bukoba, Tanz., 84/F4
Bulawayo, Zim., 86/D3
Bulgaria, 56/F-H4
Buraida, Saudi Arabia, 74/D4
Burao, Somalia, 85/J2
Burbank, Calif., 17/D6
Burgas, Bulg., 56/H4
Burgos, Spain, 53/E1
Burley, Idaho, 16/E4
Burlington, Iowa, 18/K4
Burlington, N.C., 21/O5
Burlington, Vt., 20/P3
Burma, 68/D2
Bursa, Turkey, 74/A1
Burundi, 84/E4
Bushehr, Iran, 74/F4
Butiaba, Uganda, 84/F3
Butler, Pa., 20/N4
Butte, Mont., 16/E3
Bydgoszcz, Pol., 51/C2
Byelorussia, U.S.S.R., *see White Russian S.S.R.*

C

Caatingas (reg.), Braz., 33/L6
Cabot (str.), Canada, 25/K-L6
Cáceres, Spain, 53/C3
Cacheu, Guin.-Biss., 82/A6
Cadillac, Mich., 20/M3
Cádiz, Spain, 53/C4
Caen, France, 44/C3
Caernarfon, Wales, 41/D4
Cagayan de Oro, Phil., 71/G4
Cagliari, Italy, 54/B5
Caguas, P. Rico, *see detailed map p. 29*
Caicos (isls.), Turks & Caicos Is., 28/D2
Cairns, Austr., 91/H3
Cairo (cap.), Egypt, 81/F2
Cairo, Ill., 18/L5
Calabar, Nigeria, 83/F7
Calabria (reg.), Italy, 54/F5
Calais, France, 44/D2
Calais, Maine, 20/S3
Calcutta, India, 72/F1
Caldwell, Idaho, 16/D4
Calexico, Calif., 17/D6
Calgary, Alta., 24/E5
Cali, Col., 32/E3
Calicut (Kozhikode), India, 72/D6
California (gulf), Mex., 26/B2
California (state), U.S., 14/B3
Calipatria, Calif., 17/E6
Callander, Ont., 25/H6
Callao, Peru, 32/E6
Cambay (gulf), India, 72/C4
Cambodia, 68/D4
Cambrai, France, 44/E2
Cambridge, Eng., 41/G4
Cambridge, Md., 20/O5
Camden, Ark., 19/K6
Camden, N.J., 20/P5
Camden, S.C., 21/N6
Cameron, Tex., 19/J7
Cameroon, 84/B2
Campbellton, N. Br., 25/K6
Campeche (bay), Mex., 26/F4
Campinas, Braz., 34/L8
Campos (reg.), Braz., 33/M6
Cam Ranh (bay), Viet., 68/F5
Camrose, Alta., 24/E5
Canada, 24-25
Canadian, Tex., 19/H6
Canadian (riv.), U.S., 15/J5
Çanakkale, Turkey, 74/A1
Canary (isls.), Spain, *see map p. 52*
Canaveral (cape), Fla., 21/N7
Canberra (cap.), Austr., 92/E4
Cancer, Tropic of, 8/G4
Canea (Khaniá), Greece, 57/G8
Cannes, France, 44/G6
Canon City, Colo., 18/G5
Cantabrian (mts.), Spain, 53/C1
Canterbury, Austr., 92/J3
Canterbury, Eng., 41/G5
Can Tho, Viet., 68/E5
Canton, China, 65/H7
Canton (isl.), Kiribati, 88/J6
Canton, Ill., 18/L4
Canton, Miss., 19/L6
Canton, Mo., 18/K4
Canton, Ohio, 20/N4
Canton, S. Dak., 18/J4
Canyon, Tex., 19/H6
Canyonlands Nat'l Pk., Utah, 14/E3
Cap-Chat, Que., 25/K6

Cape Breton (isl.), N.S., 25/K6
Cape Charles, Va., 20/P5
Cape Coast, Ghana, 83/D7
Cape Girardeau, Mo., 18/L5
Cape of Good Hope (prov.), S. Africa, 86/C6
Cape Town (cap.), S. Africa, 86/B6
Cape Verde, 82/A6
Cape York (pen.), Austr., 91/G2
Cap-Haïtien, Haiti, 28/D3
Capri (isl.), Italy, 54/E4
Capricorn, Tropic of, 8/J7
Caprivi Strip (reg.), Namibia, 86/C3
Captain Cook, Hawaii, 23/E4
Caracas (cap.), Ven., 32/G1
Carbondale, Ill., 18/L5
Carbondale, Pa., 20/O4
Carcassonne, France, 44/D6
Cárdenas, Cuba, 28/B2
Cardiff, Wales, 41/E5
Cardigan, Wales, 41/D4
Cardston, Alta., 24/E6
Caribbean (sea), 28
Caribou, Maine, 20/R3
Carlisle, Eng., 41/E3
Carlisle, Pa., 20/O4
Carlsbad, N. Mex., 19/G6
Carlsbad Caverns Nat'l Pk., N. Mex., 19/G6
Carmarthen, Wales, 41/D5
Carmel (mt.), Isr., 76/C2
Carnot, Cent. Afr. Rep., 84/C3
Caroline (isls.), Micronesia, 88/E-F5
Carpathians (mts.), Europe, 37/H3
Carpentaria (gulf), Austr., 91/F2
Carrara, Italy, 54/C2
Carrick, Ire., 41/C4
Carrington, N. Dak., 18/H3
Carrizo (mts.), Ariz., 17/F5
Carrizo Springs, Tex., 19/J7
Carrizozo, N. Mex., 17/G6
Carroll, Iowa, 18/K4
Carrollton, Ga., 21/M6
Carrollton, Ky., 20/M5
Carrollton, Mo., 18/K5
Carson (sink), Nev., 16/D5
Carson City (cap.), Nev., 16/D5
Cartagena, Col., 32/E1
Cartagena, Spain, 53/F4
Cartago, C. Rica, 27/D3
Cartersville, Ga., 21/M6
Carthage, Mo., 18/K5
Carthage, N.Y., 20/P3
Cartwright, Newf., 25/L5
Casablanca, Mor., 82/C2
Casa Grande, Ariz., 17/F6
Cascade, Idaho, 16/D3
Cascade (range), U.S., 14/B2
Casper, Wyo., 16/G4
Caspian (sea), 58/F6
Castel Gandolfo, Italy, 54/D4
Castellammare, Italy, 54/D5
Castellón de la Plana, Spain, 53/G2
Castelo Branco, Port., 52/C3
Castile (reg.), Spain, 53/E3
Cat (isl.), Bah., 28/C1
Catalonia (reg.), Spain, 53/G2
Catamarca, Arg., 34/G9
Catania, Italy, 54/E6
Catanzaro, Italy, 54/F5
Catletsburg, Ky., 20/N5
Catskill (mts.), N.Y., 20/P4
Cauca (riv.), Col., 32/E2
Caucasus (mts.), U.S.S.R., 60/F6
Cavan, Ire., 41/C4
Cawnpore (Kanpur), India, 72/E3
Caxias, Braz., 33/M4
Caxito, Angola, 84/B5
Cayenne (cap.), Fr. Guiana, 32/K2
Cayman Islands, 28/B3
Ceará (Fortaleza), Braz., 33/N4
Cebu, Phil., 71/G3
Cedar City, Utah, 17/E5
Cedar Falls, Iowa, 18/K4
Cedar Rapids, Iowa, 18/K4
Cedartown, Ga., 21/M6
Cegléd, Hung., 49/E3
Celebes (sea), Asia, 71/G5
Celebes (isl.), Indon., 71/G6
Centerville, Iowa, 18/K4
Central African Republic, 84/D2
Central America, 27
Central City, Nebr., 18/J4
Centralia, Ill., 18/L5
Centralia, Wash., 16/C3
Cephalonia (Kefallinía) (isl.), Greece, 57/E6
Ceram (isl.), Indon., 71/H6
Cerro de Pasco, Peru, 32/E6
Cessnock, Austr., 92/F3
Ceuta, Spain, 53/D5
Ceylon (Sri Lanka), 73/E7
Chaco, Gran (reg.), S. Amer., 34/H9
Chad, 80/C4
Chad (lake), Afr., 80/B5
Chadron, Nebr., 18/H4
Chagos (arch.), Br. Ind. Oc. Terr., 63/L10
Challis, Idaho, 16/E3
Châlons, France, 44/F3

Chamberlain, S. Dak., 18/H4
Chambersburg, Pa., 20/O4
Chamonix, France, 44/G5
Champaign, Ill., 18/L5
Champasak, Laos, 68/E4
Champlain (lake), N. Amer., 20/P3
Chandigarh, India, 72/D2
Changchun, China, 65/K3
Chang Jiang (riv.), China, 65/K5
Changsha, China, 65/H6
Channel Islands, 41/E6
Channel Is. Nat'l Pk., Calif., 17/D6
Channel-Port aux Basques, Newf., 25/L6
Chanute, Kans., 18/K5
Chao Phraya (riv.), Thai., 68/D4
Chapleau, Ont., 24/H6
Chardzhou, U.S.S.R., 58/G6
Charente (riv.), France, 44/C5
Chariton, Iowa, 18/K4
Charleroi, Belg., 43/E8
Charles City, Iowa, 18/K4
Charleston, S.C., 21/O6
Charleston (cap.), W. Va., 20/N5
Charlotte (hbr.), Fla., 21/N8
Charlotte, Mich., 20/M4
Charlotte, N.C., 21/N6
Charlotte Amalie (cap.), V.I. (U.S.), *see detailed map p. 29*
Charlottesville, Va., 20/O5
Charlottetown (cap.), P.E.I., 25/K6
Chartres, France, 44/D3
Châteaudun, France, 44/D3
Château-Thierry, France, 44/E3
Chatham, N. Br., 25/K6
Chattahoochee, Fla., 21/M7
Chattahoochee (riv.), U.S., 15/J4
Chattanooga, Tenn., 21/M6
Cheboygan, Mich., 20/M3
Chefoo, China, *see Yantai*
Chehalis, Wash., 16/C3
Cheju (isl.), S. Korea, 66/C7
Chelan, Wash., 16/C3
Chelan (lake), Wash., 16/C2
Chelyabinsk, U.S.S.R., 58/G4
Chelyuskin (cape), U.S.S.R., 58/L2
Chemnitz (Karl-Marx-Stadt), E. Ger., 47/E3
Chengchow, China, *see Zhengzhou*
Chengdu (Chengtu), China, 65/F5
Cher (riv.), France, 44/D4
Cherbourg, France, 44/C3
Cherkessk, U.S.S.R., 60/F6
Chernovtsy, U.S.S.R., 60/C5
Cherokee, Iowa, 18/K4
Cherrapunji, India, 72/G3
Chesapeake (bay), U.S., 15/L3
Chester, Eng., 41/E4
Chester, Pa., 20/P4
Chesterfield, Eng., 41/F4
Chesterfield (inlet), N.W.T., 24/G-H3
Chesterfield Inlet, N.W.T., 24/G3
Chetumal, Mex., 26/H4
Chewelah, Wash., 16/C3
Cheyenne (riv.), U.S., 18/H3
Cheyenne (cap.), Wyo., 18/G4
Cheyenne Wells, Colo., 18/H5
Chiang Mai, Thai., 86/C3
Chiba, Japan, 67/P2
Chibougamau, Que., 25/J6
Chicago, Ill., 18/L4
Chichén-Itzá (ruins), Mex., 26/H4
Chicoutimi, Que., 25/J6
Chidley (cape), Newf., 25/K3
Chihuahua, Mex., 26/D2
Childress, Tex., 19/H5
Chile, 34/F8-13
Chililabombwe, Zambia, 84/E6
Chillicothe, Mo., 18/K5
Chillicothe, Ohio, 20/N5
Chilliwack, Br. Col., 24/D6
Chiloé (isl.), Chile, 34/E12
Chimborazo (mt.), Ecua., 32/E4
Chimoio, Moz., 86/E3
China, 65
Chincoteague, Va., 20/P5
Chinde, Moz., 86/F3
Chingola, Zambia, 84/E6
Chinguetti, Maur., 82/B4
Chipata, Zambia, 84/F6
Chippewa Falls, Wis., 18/L3
Chiquimula, Guat., 27/B2
Chiriquí (gulf), Pan., 27/D4
Chisholm, Minn., 18/K3
Chita, U.S.S.R., 59/M4
Chittagong, Bang., 72/G4
Choiseul Nat'l Pk., Bots., 86/D3
Ch'ŏngju, S. Korea, 66/C5
Chongqing, China, 65/G6
Choteau, Mont., 16/E3
Christchurch, N.Z., 94/D5
Christiansted, V.I. (U.S.), *see detailed map p. 29*
Christmas (isl.), Austr., 63/O11
Christmas (isl.), Kiribati, 89/K5
Chukchi (pen.), U.S.S.R., 59/T3
Chula Vista, Calif., 17/D6

Chungking, China, *see Chongqing*
Chur, Switz., 50/E2
Churchill, Man., 24/G4
Churchill (cape), Man., 24/G4
Churchill (riv.), Can., 24/F-G4
Churchill (riv.), Newf., 25/K5
Cimarron (riv.), U.S., 15/J5
Cincinnati, Ohio, 20/N5
Cisco, Tex., 19/J6
Ciskei (aut. rep.), S. Africa, 86/D6
Citlaltépetl (mt.), Mex., 26/F4
Ciudad Bolívar, Ven., 32/H2
Ciudad Guayana, Ven., 32/H2
Ciudad Juárez, Mex., 26/C1
Ciudad Obregón, Mex., 26/C2
Ciudad Real, Spain, 53/D3
Ciudad Victoria, Mex., 26/E3
Civitavecchia, Italy, 54/C3
Clanton, Ala., 21/M6
Claremont, N.H., 20/P4
Claremore, Okla., 19/K5
Clarinda, Iowa, 18/K4
Clarksburg, W. Va., 20/O5
Clarkston, Wash., 16/D3
Clarksdale, Miss., 19/L6
Clarksville, Tenn., 21/M5
Clear (cape), Ire., 41/B5
Clear (lake), Calif., 16/C5
Clearfield, Utah, 16/F4
Clearwater, Fla., 21/N8
Clearwater (mts.), Idaho, 16/D3
Cleburne, Tex., 19/J6
Cle Elum, Wash., 16/C3
Clermont-Ferrand, France, 44/E5
Cleveland, Miss., 19/L6
Cleveland, Ohio, 20/N4
Cleveland, Tenn., 21/M6
Cleveland Heights, Ohio, 20/N4
Clifton, Ariz., 17/F6
Clinton, Iowa, 18/L4
Clinton, Mo., 18/K5
Clinton, N.C., 21/O6
Clinton, Okla., 19/J6
Clonmel, Ire., 41/C4
Cloquet, Minn., 18/K3
Clovis, N. Mex., 19/H6
Cluj-Napoca, Rom., 56/F2
Clyde (riv.), Scot., 40/E3
Coalinga, Calif., 17/C5
Coast (mts.), Br. Col., 13/E-F4
Coast (range), U.S., 13/F5-6
Coatzacoalcos, Mex., 26/F4
Cobalt, Ont., 25/H6
Cobán, Guat., 27/B2
Cóbh, Ire., 41/B5
Coburg, W. Ger., 47/D3
Cochabamba, Bol., 32/G7
Cochin, India, 72/D6
Cochrane, Ont., 25/H6
Cocos (isls.), Austr., 63/N11
Cocos (isl.), C. Rica, 13/K9
Cod (cape), Mass., 20/R4
Cody, Wyo., 16/F3
Coeur d'Alene, Idaho, 16/D3
Coffeyville, Kans., 19/K5
Cognac, France, 44/C5
Cohoes, N.Y., 20/P4
Coimbatore, India, 72/D6
Coimbra, Port., 52/B2
Colchester, Eng., 41/G5
Coldstream, Scot., 40/F3
Coldwater, Mich., 20/M4
Coleman, Tex., 19/J7
Colima, Mex., 26/D4
College, Alaska, 22/E2
College Station, Tex., 19/J7
Cologne, W. Ger., 47/B3
Colombia, 32/E-G3
Colombo (cap.), Sri Lanka, 73/D7
Colón, Pan., 27/D3
Colonia, Urug., 34/J10
Colorado (riv.), Tex., 19/J7
Colorado (riv.), U.S., 14/C4
Colorado (state), U.S., 14/E3
Colorado City, Tex., 19/H6
Colorado Springs, Colo., 18/G5
Columbia, Miss., 19/L7
Columbia, Mo., 18/L5
Columbia, Tenn., 21/M6
Columbia (cap.), S.C., 21/N6
Columbia (riv.), U.S., 15/B1
Columbia Falls, Mont., 16/E2
Columbus, Ga., 21/M6
Columbus, Ind., 20/M5
Columbus, Miss., 21/L6
Columbus, Nebr., 18/J4
Columbus (cap.), Ohio, 20/N5
Colville (riv.), Alaska, 22/D2
Communism (peak), U.S.S.R., 58/H6
Como (lake), Italy, 54/B1
Comorin (cape), India, 72/D7
Comoros, 87/G2
Compiègne, France, 44/E3
Conakry (cap.), Guinea, 83/B7
Concepción, Chile, 34/F11
Concepción, Par., 34/J8
Conception (pt.), Calif., 17/C6
Concord (cap.), N.H., 20/R4
Concord, N.C., 21/N6
Concordia, Kans., 18/J5
Congo, 84/C4
Congo (riv.), Afr., 79/D5
Congo, Democratic Rep. of the, *see Zaire*

Connecticut (state), U.S., 15/M2
Conroe, Tex., 19/K7
Constance (lake), Europe, 50/E1
Constanţa, Rom., 56/J3
Constantine (lake), Alg., 82/F1
Constantinople, Turkey, see Istanbul
Conway, Ark., 19/K6
Conway, N.H., 20/R4
Conway, S.C., 21/O6
Cook (inlet), Alaska, 22/D3-4
Cook (mt.), N.Z., 94/K7
Cook (str.), N.Z., 94/L6
Cookeville, Tenn., 21/M5
Cook Islands, 89/L7
Coolidge, Ariz., 17/F6
Coos Bay, Oreg., 16/B4
Copenhagen (cap.), Den., 39/G9
Copiapó, Chile, 34/F9
Coppermine, N.W.T., 24/E2
Coquimbo, Chile, 34/F9
Coral (sea), 88/F7
Coral Gables, Fla., 21/N8
Coral Sea Is. (terr.), Austr., 91/J3
Corbin, Ky., 21/N5
Corcoran, Calif., 17/D6
Cordele, Ga., 21/N7
Córdoba, Arg., 34/G10
Córdoba, Spain, 53/D4
Cordova, Alaska, 22/E3
Corfu (Kérkira), Greece, 57/D6
Corinth, Greece, 57/F7
Corinth, Miss., 19/L6
Cork, Ire., 41/B5
Corner Brook, Newf., 25/L6
Corning, N.Y., 20/O4
Cornwall, Ont., 25/J7
Coro, Ven., 32/G1
Coromandel (coast), India, 72/E6
Corpus Christi, Tex., 19/J8
Corrientes, Arg., 34/J9
Corsica (isl.), France, 44/B6
Corsicana, Tex., 19/J6
Cortez, Colo., 17/F5
Cortina d'Ampezzo, Italy, 54/D1
Cortland, N.Y., 20/O4
Corvallis, Oreg., 16/C3
Cosenza, Italy, 54/F5
Cosmoledo (isls.), Seychelles, 87/H1
Costa Brava (reg.), Spain, 53/H2
Costa de Mosquitos, Cent. Amer., 27/D2
Costa Rica, 27/C3
Côte-d'Or (mts.), France, 44/F4
Cotentin (pen.), France, 44/C3
Cotonou, Benin, 83/E7
Cotopaxi (mt.), Ecua., 32/E4
Cottage Grove, Oreg., 16/C4
Cottbus, E. Ger., 47/F3
Council Bluffs, Iowa, 18/K4
Courantyne (riv.), S. Amer., 32/J3
Courtrai (Kortrijk), Belg., 43/C7
Coventry, Eng., 41/F4
Covington, Ga., 21/N6
Covington, Ky., 20/M5
Covington, La., 19/L7
Covington, Tenn., 19/L6
Covington, Va., 20/N5
Cozumel (isl.), Mex., 26/H4
Cracow, Pol., 51/E3
Cranbrook, Br. Col., 24/E5
Crater (lake), Oreg., 16/C4
Crater Lake Nat'l Pk., Oreg., 16/C4
Crawfordsville, Ind., 20/M4
Cremona, Italy, 54/B2
Crépy, France, 44/E3
Creston, Iowa, 18/K4
Crestview, Fla., 21/M7
Crete (isl.), Greece, 57/G8
Crimea (pen.), U.S.S.R., 60/D5
Crişul Alb (riv.), Rom., 56/F2
Croatia (rep.), Yugo., 56/C3
Crockett, Tex., 19/K7
Crookston, Minn., 18/J3
Crossett, Ark., 19/K6
Crotone, Italy, 54/F5
Crowley, La., 19/K7
Croydon, Eng., see detailed map p. 41
Crystal City, Tex., 19/J7
Csongrád, Hung., 49/F3
Cuanza (riv.), Angola, 84/C5
Cuba, 28/A-C2
Cubango (riv.), Afr., 79/D6
Cúcuta, Col., 32/F2
Cuenca, Ecua., 32/E4
Cuenca, Spain, 53/E2
Cuernavaca, Mex., 26/E4
Cuiabá, Braz., 32/J7
Culebra (isl.), P. Rico, see detailed map p. 29
Culiacán, Mex., 26/C3
Cullman, Ala., 21/M6
Cumaná, Ven., 32/H1
Cumberland, Md., 20/O5
Cumberland (pen.), N.W.T., 25/K2
Cupar, Scot., 40/E2
Curaçao (isl.), Neth. Ant., 28/E4
Curitiba, Braz., 34/L9
Cusco, Peru, 32/F6
Custer, S. Dak., 18/H4

Cut Bank, Mont., 16/E2
Cuttack, India, 72/F4
Cyclades (isls.), Greece, 57/G7
Cyprus, 74/B3
Cyrenaica (reg.), Libya, 80/D1
Czechoslovakia, 48
Czech Socialist Rep., Czech., 49/B1
Czestochowa, Pol., 51/D3

D

Dabou, Iv. Coast, 83/D7
Dacca (cap.), Bang., 72/G4
Dachau, W. Ger., 47/D4
Da Hingan (Gt. Khingan) (range), China, 65/J-K 2-3
Dahomey, see Benin
Dairen, China, see Lüta
Daito (isls.), Japan, 64/M6
Dakar (cap.), Sen., 82/A6
Dakhla, W. Sahara, 82/A4
Da Lat, Viet., 68/F5
Dalhart, Tex., 19/H5
Dallas, Oreg., 16/C3
Dallas, Tex., 19/J6
Dalles, The, Oreg., 16/C3
Dalton, Ga., 21/M6
Damamhur, Egypt, 81/J3
Damaraland (reg.), Namibia, 86/B4
Damascus (cap.), Syria, 74/C3
Damavand (mt.), Iran, 74/F2
Damietta, Egypt, 81/J3
Dammam, Saudi Arabia, 74/F4
Dan, Isr., 76/D5
Dana, Jordan, 76/E5
Da Nang, Viet., 68/E3
Danube (riv.), Europe, 37/G4
Danville, Ill., 18/L4
Danville, Ky., 20/M5
Danville, Va., 21/O5
Danzig, Pol., see Gdańsk
Danzig (gulf), Pol., 51/D1
Dardanelles (str.), Turkey, 74/A2
Dar es Salaam (cap.), Tanz., 85/G5
Darién (mts.), Pan., 27/E3
Darjeeling, India, 72/F3
Darlac (plat.), Viet., 68/F5
Darling (riv.), Austr., 92/G6
Darlington, S.C., 21/N6
Darmstadt, W. Ger., 47/C4
Dartmouth, N.S., 25/K7
Daru, Papua N.G., 88/B6
Darwin, Austr., 91/E2
Davao, Phil., 71/H4
Davenport, Iowa, 18/L4
David, Pan., 27/D3
Davis (sea), Antarc., 35/C3-4
Davis (str.), N. Amer., 13/N3
Davos, Switz., 50/D2
Dawson, Ga., 21/M7
Dawson, Yukon, 24/C3
Dawson Creek, Br. Col., 24/D4
Dayton, Ohio, 20/M5
Daytona Beach, Fla., 21/N7
Dead (sea), Asia, 76/C4
Deadwood, S. Dak., 18/G3
Death Valley (depr.), Calif., 17/D5
Deauville, France, 44/C3
Debra Markos, Eth., 81/G5
Debra Tabor, Eth., 81/G5
Debrecen, Hung., 49/F3
Decatur, Ala., 21/M6
Decatur, Ga., 21/M7
Decatur, Ill., 18/L5
Deccan (plat.), India, 72/D5-6
Decorah, Iowa, 18/K4
Dee (riv.), Scot., 40/E2
Deer Lodge, Mont., 16/E3
Defiance, Ohio, 20/M4
De Funiak Springs, Fla., 21/M7
Dehra Dun, India, 72/D2
Delagoa (bay), Moz., 86/E5
De Land, Fla., 21/N7
Delano, Calif., 17/D6
Delaware (bay), U.S., 15/M3
Delaware (state), U.S., 15/L3
Delft, Neth., 42/E4
Delgado (cape), Moz., 86/G2
Delhi, India, 72/D3
Deloraine, Man., 24/F6
Delray Beach, Fla., 21/O8
Del Rio, Tex., 19/H7
Deming, N. Mex., 17/F6
Demopolis, Ala., 21/M6
Denali Nat'l Pk., Alaska, 22/D3
Denbigh, Wales, 41/E4
Denison, Iowa, 18/K4
Denison, Tex., 19/J6
Denmark, 39/E9
Denmark (str.), 96/C7-8
Denton, Tex., 19/J6
Denver (cap.), Colo., 18/G5
Derby, Austr., 91/C3
Derby, Eng., 41/F4
De Ridder, La., 19/K7
Derna, Libya, 80/D1
Des Moines (cap.), Iowa, 18/K4
De Soto, Mo., 18/L5
Dessau, E. Ger., 47/E3
Dessye, Eth., 81/G5

Detroit, Mich., 20/M4
Detroit Lakes, Minn., 18/K3
Deva, Rom., 56/F3
Deventer, Neth., 42/J4
Devil's (isl.), Fr. Guiana, 32/K2
Devils Lake, N. Dak., 18/J2
Devon (isl.), N.W.T., 24/H1
Dexter, Mo., 19/L5
Dezful, Iran, 75/E3
Dezhnev (cape), U.S.S.R., 59/T3
Dhahran, Saudi Arabia, 74/E4
Dhaulagiri (mt.), Nepal, 72/E3
Dhiban, Jordan, 76/D5
Dhofar (reg.), Oman, 75/F6
Diamond (head), Hawaii, 23/C5
Diamond Coast (reg.), Afr., 86/A5
Dickinson, N. Dak., 18/H3
Dickson City, Pa., 20/O4
Didsbury, Alta., 24/D5
Diego Garcia (isls.), Br. Ind. Oc. Terr. 63/L10
Diégo-Suarez (Antsiranana), Madag., 87/H2
Dien Bien Phu, Viet., 68/D2
Dieppe, France, 44/D3
Dijon, France, 44/F4
Dili, Indon., 71/H7
Dillingham, Alaska, 22/D4
Dillon, Mont., 16/E3
Dimashq (Damascus) (cap.), Syria, 74/C3
Dimbokro, Iv. Coast, 83/D7
Dinaric Alps (mts.), Yugo., 56/B-C 3-4
Diomede (isls.), 22/C2
Diourbel, Sen., 82/A6
Dire Dawa, Eth., 81/H6
Disappointment (cape), Wash., 16/B3
District of Columbia, U.S., 15/L3
Divo, Iv. Coast, 83/C7
Dixon, Ill., 18/L4
Dixon Entrance (str.), N. Amer., 13/A4
Diyarbakir, Turkey, 74/D2
Djajapura, Indon., see Jayapura
Djakarta (cap.), Indon., see Jakarta
Djelfa, Alg., 82/E2
Djenné, Mali, 82/D6
Djerba (isl.), Tun., 82/G2
Djibouti, 81/H5
Djibouti (cap.), Djibouti, 81/H5
Djokjakarta, Indon., see Yogyakarta
Dnepropetrovsk, U.S.S.R., 60/D5
Dnieper (riv.), U.S.S.R., 60/D5
Dniester (riv.), U.S.S.R., 60/C5
Dodecanese (isls.), Greece, 57/H8
Dodge City, Kans., 18/H5
Dodoma, Tanz., 85/F5
Doha (cap.), Qatar, 74/F4
Dolgellau, Wales, 41/E4
Dolomite Alps (mts.), Italy, 54/C1
Dominica, 29/G4
Dominican Republic, 28/D3
Domrémy-la-Pucelle, France, 44/F3
Don (riv.), Eng., 41/F4
Don (riv.), Scot., 40/E2
Don (riv.), U.S.S.R., 60/F5
Doncaster, Eng., 41/F4
Dondra (head), Sri Lanka, 73/E7
Donegal, Ire., 41/B3
Donets (riv.), U.S.S.R., 60/E5
Donetsk, U.S.S.R., 60/E5
Dongola, Sudan, 81/F4
Doorn, Neth., 42/G4
Dordogne (riv.), France, 44/D5
Dordrecht, Neth., 42/F5
Dornbirn, Austria, 48/A3
Dortmund, W. Ger., 47/B3
Dothan, Ala., 21/M7
Douai, France, 44/E2
Douala, Cameroon, 84/B3
Douglas, Ariz., 17/F7
Douglas, Ga., 21/N7
Douglas (cap.), I. of Man, 40/D3
Dover (cap.), Del., 20/P5
Dover, Eng., 41/G5
Dover (str.), Europe, 41/G5
Dover, N.H., 20/R4
Dovrefjell (mts.), Nor., 39/F5
Downpatrick, N. Ire., 40/C3
Dragons Mouth (passage), 29/F5
Drake (passage), 35/C10
Drakensberg (range), Afr., 86/D-E 5-6
Dráma, Greece, 56/F5
Dráva (riv.), Europe, 49/D3
Dresden, E. Ger., 47/E3
Drobeta-Turnu Severin, Rom., 56/F3
Drumheller, Alta., 24/E5
Dubai, U.A.E., 74/F4
Dubbo, Austr., 92/G6
Dublin, Ga., 21/N6
Dublin (cap.), Ire., 41/C4
Du Bois, Pa., 20/O4
Dubrovnik, Yugo., 56/D4
Dubuque, Iowa, 18/L4
Duero (Douro) (riv.), Europe, 53/C2
Dufourspitze (mt.), Switz., 50/C3
Duisburg, W. Ger., 47/B3
Duluth, Minn., 18/K3

Dumas, Tex., 19/H6
Dumbarton, Scot., 40/D3
Dumfries, Scot., 40/E3
Duncan, Okla., 19/J6
Dundalk, Ire., 41/C4
Dundee, Scot., 40/E2
Dunedin, N.Z., 94/K7
Dunfermline, Scot., 40/D2
Dunkirk (Dunkerque), France, 44/E2
Dunkirk, N.Y., 20/O4
Dún Laoghaire, Ire., 41/C4
Durango, Colo., 17/G5
Durango, Mex., 26/D3
Durant, Okla., 19/J6
Durazno, Urug., 34/J10
Durban, S. Africa, 86/E5
Durgapur, India, 72/F4
Durham, Eng., 41/F3
Durham, N.C., 21/O5
Durrës, Alb., 56/D5
Dushanbe, U.S.S.R., 58/G6
Düsseldorf, W. Ger., 47/B3
Dutch Harbor, Alaska, 22/C5
Dvina, Northern (riv.), U.S.S.R., 60/F2
Dvina, Western (riv.), U.S.S.R., 60/C3
Dyersburg, Tenn., 19/L5
Dzaoudzi (cap.), Mayotte, 87/H2
Dzerzhinsk, U.S.S.R., 60/F3
Dzhambul, U.S.S.R., 58/H5
Dzungaria (reg.), China, see Junggar Pendi

E

Eagle Pass, Tex., 19/H7
Ealing, Eng., see detailed map p. 41
Easley, S.C., 21/N6
Eastbourne, Eng., 41/G5
East China (sea), Asia, 65/L6
Easter (isl.), Chile, 8/D7
Eastern Ghats (mts.), India, 72/D-F 4-6
East Frisian (isls.), W. Ger., 47/B2
East Grand Forks, Minn., 18/J2
East Korea (bay), N. Korea, 66/D4
East London, S. Africa, 86/D6
Eastmain, Que., 25/J5
East Pakistan, see Bangladesh
East Point, Ga., 21/M6
Eastport, Maine, 20/S3
East St. Louis, Ill., 18/L5
East Siberian (sea), U.S.S.R., 59/R2
Eau Claire, Wis., 18/L3
Eboli, Italy, 54/E4
Ebolowa, Cameroon, 84/B3
Ebro (riv.), Spain, 53/F2
Ecuador, 32/E4
Edam, Neth., 42/G4
Ed Damazin, Sudan, 81/F5
Ed Damer, Sudan, 81/F5
Ed Dueim, Sudan, 81/F5
Ede, Neth., 42/H4
Ede, Nigeria, 82/F7
Edenton, N.C., 21/O5
Edinburg, Tex., 19/J8
Edinburgh (cap.), Scot., 40/C1
Edirne, Turkey, 74/A1
Edmond, Okla., 19/J5
Edmonton (cap.), Alta., 24/E5
Edmundston, N. Br., 25/K6
Edward (lake), Afr., 79/E5
Edwards (plat.), Tex., 19/H7
Eel (riv.), Calif., 16/C4-5
Efate (isl.), Vanuatu, 88/G7
Effingham, Ill., 18/L5
Egmont (mt.), N.Z., 94/D3
Egypt, 81/E-F2
Eindhoven, Neth., 42/G6
El Agheila, Libya, 80/B1
El 'Alamein, Egypt, 81/E1
El Asnam, Alg., 82/E1
Elat (Elath), Isr., 76/B8
El Azizia, Libya, 80/B1
Elba (isl.), Italy, 54/C2
Elbe (riv.), Ger., 47/D2
Elbert (mt.), Colo., 18/G5
Elberton, Ga., 21/N6
El'brus (mt.), U.S.S.R., 37/J4
Elburz (mts.), Iran, 74/F2
El Cajon, Calif., 17/D6
El Campo, Tex., 19/J7
El Centro, Calif., 17/D6
El Dorado, Ark., 19/K6
El Dorado, Kans., 18/J5
Elephanta (isl.), India, see detailed map p. 73
Elephant Butte (res.), N. Mex., 17/G6
Eleuthera (isl.), Bah., 28/C1
El Faiyûm, Egypt, 81/F2
El Fasher, Sudan, 81/E5
El Geneina, Sudan, 81/D5
Elgin, Scot., 40/E2
Elgon (mt.), Afr., 79/F4

Elizabeth City, N.C., 21/P5
Elizabethton, Tenn., 21/N5
Elizabethtown, Ky., 21/M5
Elizabethville, Congo, see Lubumbashi, Zaire
Elk City, Okla., 19/J6
Elkhart, Ind., 20/M4
Elkins, W. Va., 20/N5
Elko, Nev., 16/E4
Ellef Ringnes (isl.), N.W.T., 25/M3
Ellensburg, Wash., 16/C3
Ellesmere (isl.), N.W.T., 25/N3
Ellice Is. (terr.), Pacific, see Tuvalu
El Mahalla el Kubra, Egypt, 81/J3
El Mansûra, Egypt, 81/J3
El Marj, Eth., 80/D1
El Minya, Egypt, 81/J4
Elmira, N.Y., 20/O4
El Obeid, Sudan, 81/E5
Eloy, Ariz., 17/F6
El Paso, Tex., 19/G7
El Puerto de Santa María, Spain, 53/C4
El Queneitra, Syria, 76/D1
El Rashid, Syria, 74/C2
El Reno, Okla., 19/J6
El Salvador, 27/B2
El Seibo, Dom. Rep., 28/E3
Elsiesrivier, S. Africa, 86/F6
Elwood, Ind., 20/M4
Ely, Eng., 41/G4
Ely, Nev., 16/E5
Elyria, Ohio, 20/N4
Embu, Kenya, 85/G4
Emden, W. Ger., 47/B2
Emerson, Man., 24/G6
Emporia, Kans., 18/J5
Emporia, Va., 21/O5
Ems (riv.), W. Ger., 47/B2
Enderbury (atoll), Kiribati, 89/K6
Endicott, N.Y., 20/O4
Enewetak (atoll), Marshall Is., 88/G4
Engadine (valley), Switz., 50/E2
England, 41/F4
English (chan.), Europe, 44/A-D 2-3
Enid, Okla., 19/J5
Enköping, Sweden, 39/K7
En Nahud, Sudan, 80/E5
Enns (riv.), Austria, 48/C3
Enschede, Neth., 42/J4
Ensenada, Mex., 26/A1
Entebbe, Uganda, 84/F4
Enterprise, Ala., 21/M7
Enugu, Nigeria, 83/F7
Enzeli, Iran, 74/E2
Ephrata, Wash., 16/D3
Epping, Eng., 41/G5
Equatorial Guinea, 84/A3
Erbil, Iraq, 74/D2
Erfurt, E. Ger., 47/D3
Erie (lake), N. Amer., 15/K2
Erie, Pa., 20/N4
Erivan, U.S.S.R., 60/F6
Erne (lake), N. Ire., 40/C3
Er Rahad, Sudan, 81/F5
Er Ramtha, Jordan, 76/E3
Er Roseires, Sudan, 81/F5
Erzgebirge (mts.), Europe, 47/E3
Erzurum, Turkey, 74/D2
Esbjerg, Den., 39/F9
Escalante (des.), Utah, 17/E5
Escanaba, Mich., 20/M3
Escondido, Calif., 17/D6
Escuintla, Guat., 27/B2
Esmeraldas, Ecua., 32/D3
Espíritu Santo (isl.), Vanuatu, 88/G7
Es Salt, Jordan, 76/D3
Essaouira, Mor., 82/B2
Essen, W. Ger., 47/B3
Essequibo (riv.), Guyana, 32/J2
Es Suweida, Syria, 74/C3
Estados (isl.), Arg., 34/H14
Este, Italy, 54/C2
Estevan, Sask., 24/F6
Estherville, Iowa, 18/K4
Estonian S.S.R., U.S.S.R., 60/C3
Estremadura (reg.), Spain, 53/C3
Esztergom, Hung., 49/E3
Ethiopia, 81/G-H5
Etna (vol.), Italy, 54/E6
Etosha (salt pan), Namibia, 86/B3
Et Tafila, Jordan, 77/D6
Euboea (Evvoia) (isl.), Greece, 57/G6
Eufaula, Ala., 21/M7
Eugene, Oreg., 16/C3
Eunice, La., 19/K7
Eupen, Belg., 43/J7
Euphrates (riv.), Asia, 74/E3
Eure (riv.), France, 44/D3
Eureka, Calif., 16/C4
Eureka, Kans., 18/J5
Europe, 36-37
Evans, Colo., 18/G5
Evanston, Ill., 18/M4
Evansville, Ind., 20/M5
Everest (mt.), Asia, 72/F3
Everett, Wash., 16/C3

Everglades Nat'l Pk., Fla., 21/N8
Evesham, Eng., 41/F4
Évora, Port., 52/C3
Evvoia (isl.), Greece, 57/G6
Ewa Beach, Hawaii, 23/B4
Excelsior Springs, Mo., 18/K5
Exeter, Eng., 41/E5
Exuma (sound), Bah., 28/C1
Eyre (lake), Austr., 91/F5

F

Fada-N'Gourma, Upp. Volta, 82/E6
Faenza, Italy, 54/D2
Faeroe (isls.), Den., 37/D2
Fagersta, Sweden, 39/J6
Fairbanks, Alaska, 22/E3
Fairbury, Nebr., 18/J4
Fairfield, Iowa, 18/L4
Fairmont, Minn., 18/K4
Fairmont, W. Va., 20/N5
Faizabad, India, 72/E3
Falaise, France, 44/C3
Falcon (res.), N. Amer., 19/J8
Falfurrias, Tex., 19/J8
Falkirk, Scot., 40/E3
Falkland Islands, 34/H14
Fall River, Mass., 20/R4
Falls City, Nebr., 18/K4
Falmouth, Eng., 41/D5
Falun, Sweden, 39/J6
Famagusta, Cyprus, 74/B3
Famatina (mts.), Arg., 34/G9
Fanning (isl.), Kiribati, 89/L5
Farewell (cape), Greenl., 96/D8
Fargo, N. Dak., 18/J3
Faribault, Minn., 18/K3
Farmington, Mo., 18/L5
Farmington, N. Mex., 17/F5
Faro, Port., 52/B4
Farrukhabad-cum Fatehgarh, India, 72/D3
Fatshan, China, see Foshan
Faya Largeau, Chad, 80/C4
Fayetteville, Ark., 19/K5
Fayetteville, N.C., 21/O6
Fayetteville, Tenn., 21/M6
F'derik, Maur., 82/B4
Fear (cape), N.C., 21/O6
Fehmarn (isl.), W. Ger., 47/D1
Feinan (ruins), Jordan, 76/C6
Feldkirch, Austria, 48/A3
Fenoarivo, Madag., 87/H3
Fergana, U.S.S.R., 58/H5
Fergus Falls, Minn., 18/K3
Ferkessédougou, Iv. Coast, 83/D7
Fernandina Beach, Fla., 21/N7
Fernando Po (Bioko) (isl.), Equat. Guin., 84/A3
Fernie, Br. Col., 24/E6
Ferrara, Italy, 54/C2
Ferrol del Caudillo, Spain, 52/B1
Fès, Mor., 82/D2
Feuilles (riv.), Que., 25/J4
Feyzabad, Afghan., 75/K2
Fez (Fès), Mor., 82/D2
Fezzan (reg.), Libya, 80/B2
Ffestiniog, Wales, 41/E4
Fianarantsoa, Madag., 87/H4
Fianga, Chad, 80/C6
Fichtelgebirge (mts.), W. Ger., 47/D3
Fifth Cataract (falls), Sudan, 81/F4
Fiji, 89/P11
Findlay, Ohio, 20/N4
Finisterre (cape), Spain, 52/B1
Finland, 39/O-P 2-6
Finland (gulf), Europe, 37/G3
Finlay (riv.), Br. Col., 24/D4
Finsteraarhorn (mt.), Switz., 50/D2
Firenze (Florence), Italy, 54/C3
Firozepore, India, 72/C2
Fitzgerald, Ga., 21/N7
Fiume (Rijeka), Yugo., 56/B3
Fiumicino, Italy, 54/C4
Flagstaff, Ariz., 17/F6
Flaming Gorge (res.), U.S., 16/F4
Flathead (lake), Mont., 16/E3
Flattery (cape), Wash., 16/B2
Flensburg, W. Ger., 47/C1
Flevoland (polders), Neth., 42/G4
Flin Flon, Man., 24/F4
Flint, Mich., 20/N4
Florence, Ala., 21/M6
Florence, Italy, 54/C3
Florence, S.C., 21/O6
Flores (isl.), Indon., 71/G7
Florianópolis, Braz., 34/L9
Florida (bay), Fla., 21/N8
Florida (straits), N. Amer., 13/K-L7
Florida (state), U.S., 15/K5
Florida, Urug., 34/J10
Floydada, Tex., 19/H6
Flushing, Neth., 42/C6
Fly (riv.), Papua N.G., 88/E6
Fodor, Sen., 83/B5
Foggia, Italy, 54/E4
Fogo (isl.), Newf., 25/L6
Foix, France, 44/D6
Folkestone, Eng., 41/G5

Fomboni, Comoros, 87/G2
Fond du Lac, Wis., 18/L4
Fongafale (cap.), Tuvalu, 88/H6
Fonseca (gulf), Cent. Amer., 27/C2
Fontainebleau, France, 44/E3
Foochow, China, see Fuzhou
Forfar, Scot., 40/E2
Forlì, Italy, 54/D2
Formosa, Arg., 34/J9
Formosa (Taiwan) (isl.), China, 65/K7
Forrest City, Ark., 19/L6
Fortaleza, Braz., 33/N4
Ft. Bragg, Calif., 16/B5
Ft-Chimo, Que., 25/K4
Ft. Chipewyan, Alta., 24/E4
Ft. Collins, Colo., 18/G4
Ft-de-France (cap.), Mart., 29/G4
Ft. Dodge, Iowa, 18/K4
Ft. Frances, Ont., 24/G6
Ft. Franklin, N.W.T., 24/D2
Ft-George, Que., 25/J5
Forth (firth), Scot., 40/E2
Ft. Kent, Maine, 20/R3
Ft-Lamy, Chad, see N'Djamena
Ft. Lauderdale, Fla., 21/O8
Ft. Liard, N.W.T., 24/D3
Ft. Lupton, Colo., 18/G4
Ft. Macleod, Alta., 24/E6
Ft. Madison, Iowa, 18/L4
Ft. McKay, Alta., 24/E4
Ft. McMurray, Alta., 24/E4
Ft. McPherson, N.W.T., 24/C2
Ft. Morgan, Colo., 18/G4
Ft. Myers, Fla., 21/N8
Ft. Nelson, Br. Col., 24/D4
Ft. Norman, N.W.T., 24/D3
Ft. Peck (lake), Mont., 16/G3
Ft. Pierce, Fla., 21/N8
Ft. Providence, N.W.T., 24/E3
Ft. Reliance, N.W.T., 24/F3
Ft. Resolution, N.W.T., 24/E3
Ft. St. James, Br. Col., 24/D5
Ft. St. John, Br. Col., 24/D4
Ft. Saskatchewan, Alta., 24/E5
Ft. Scott, Kans., 18/K5
Ft. Selkirk, Yukon, 24/C3
Ft. Simpson, N.W.T., 24/D3
Ft. Smith, Ark., 19/K6
Ft. Smith, N.W.T., 24/E3
Ft. Stockton, Tex., 19/H7
Ft. Sumner, N. Mex., 19/G6
Ft. Valley, Ga., 21/N6
Ft. Vermilion, Alta., 24/E4
Ft. Victoria, Zim., 86/E4
Ft. Walton Bch., Fla., 21/M7
Ft. Wayne, Ind., 20/M4
Ft. William, Scot., 40/D2
Ft. Worth, Tex., 19/J6
Ft. Yates, N. Dak., 18/H3
Foshan, China, 65/H7
Fossil, Oreg., 16/D3
Foumban, Cameroon, 84/B2
Fourth Cataract (falls), Sudan, 81/F4
Fox (isls.), Alaska, 22/C5
Foxe (basin), N.W.T., 24/J2
Foxe (chan.), N.W.T., 24/H-J3
Foxe (pen.), N.W.T., 25/J3
France, 44
Franceville, Gabon, 84/B4
Francis Case (lake), S. Dak., 18/H4
Francistown, Bots., 86/D4
Frankfort, Ind., 20/M4
Frankfort (cap.), Ky., 20/M5
Frankfort, Mich., 20/M3
Frankfurt-am-Main, W. Ger., 47/C3
Frankfurt-an-der-Oder, E. Ger., 47/F2
Franklin, N.H., 20/P4
Franklin (str.), N.W.T., 24/G1
Franklin, Pa., 20/O4
Franklin, Tenn., 21/M6
Franklin D. Roosevelt (lake), Wash., 16/D3
Franz Josef Land (isls.), U.S.S.R., 58/E-G1
Fraser (riv.), Br. Col., 24/D5
Fredericia, Den., 39/F9
Frederick, Okla., 19/J6
Fredericksburg, Tex., 19/J7
Fredericksburg, Va., 20/O5
Frederikshavn, Den., 39/G8
Fredericton (cap.), N. Br., 25/K6
Freeport, Ill., 18/L4
Freeport, Tex., 19/K7
Freetown (cap.), S. Leone, 83/B7
Freiburg im Breisgau, W. Ger., 47/B5
Freising, W. Ger., 47/D4
Fremantle, Austr., 90/A6
Fremont, Calif., 16/C5
Fremont, Nebr., 18/J4
French Guiana, 32/K3
Frenchman (riv.), N. Amer., 16/F2
French Polynesia, 89/L-N8
French Somaliland, see Djibouti
Fresno, Calif., 17/C5
Fribourg, Switz., 50/C2
Friedrichshafen, W. Ger., 47/C5
Frio (cape), Braz., 34/M8
Frobisher Bay, N.W.T., 25/K3
Front Royal, Va., 20/O5

Fruita, Colo., 16/F5
Frunze, U.S.S.R., 58/H5
Fuerteventura (isl.), Spain, see Canary Is. map p. 52
Fujairah, U.A.E., 75/G4
Fuji (mt.), Japan, 67/J6
Fujisawa, Japan, 67/O3
Fukui, Japan, 67/G5
Fukuoka, Japan, 66/E7
Fukushima, Japan, 67/K5
Fukuyama, Japan, 67/F6
Fulda, W. Ger., 47/C3
Fulton, Mo., 18/L5
Fulton, N.Y., 20/O4
Funabashi, Japan, 67/F2
Funchal, Port., see Madeira map p. 52
Fundy (bay), N. Amer., 25/K7
Fürstenfeldbruck, W. Ger., 47/D4
Fürth, W. Ger., 47/D4
Fushun, China, 65/K3
Füssen, W. Ger., 47/D5
Fuzhou, China, 65/J6

G

Gabès, Tun., 82/F2
Gabès (gulf), Tun., 82/G2
Gabon, 84/B4
Gaborone (cap.), Bots., 86/D4
Gadsden, Ala., 21/M6
Gaeta, Italy, 54/D4
Gafsa, Tun., 82/F2
Gagnoa, Iv. Coast, 83/C7
Gagnon, Que., 25/K5
Gainesville, Fla., 21/N7
Gainesville, Ga., 21/N6
Gainesville, Tex., 19/J6
Galápagos (isls.), Ecua., see detailed map p. 32
Galati, Rom., 56/H3
Galcaio, Somalia, 85/J2
Galesburg, Ill., 18/L4
Galicia (reg.), Spain, 52/B1
Galilee (reg.), Isr., 76/C2
Galle, Sri Lanka, 73/D7
Gallipoli, Turkey, 74/A1
Gällivare, Sweden, 38/M3
Gallup, N. Mex., 17/F6
Galveston, Tex., 19/K7
Galway, Ire., 41/B4
Gambia, 82/A6
Gambier (isls.), Fr. Poly., 89/N8
Gander, Newf., 25/L6
Ganges (riv.), Asia, 63/F3
Gangtok, India, 72/F3
Gao, Mali, 82/E5
Gap, France, 44/G5
Garamba Nat'l Pk., Zaire, 84/E3
Garanhuns, Braz., 33/N5
Garda (lake), Italy, 54/C2
Garden City, Kans., 18/H5
Garissa, Kenya, 85/G4
Garland, Tex., 19/J6
Garmisch-Partenkirchen, W. Ger., 47/D5
Garonne (riv.), France, 44/C5
Garoua, Cameroon, 84/B2
Garrison, N. Dak., 18/H3
Gary, Ind., 20/M4
Gaspé, Que., 25/K6
Gastonia, N.C., 21/N6
Gates of the Arctic Nat'l Pk., Alaska, 22/D2
Gatineau (riv.), Que., 25/J6
Gatooma, Zim., 86/D3
Gauhati, India, 72/G3
Gävle, Sweden, 39/K6
Gaya, India, 72/F4
Gaza, Gaza Strip, 74/B3
Gaza Strip, 76/A5
Gaziantep, Turkey, 74/C2
Gdańsk, Pol., 51/D1
Gdynia, Pol., 51/D1
Gedaref, Sudan, 81/G5
Geelong, Austr., 92/G6
Gelsenkirchen, W. Ger., 47/B3
Geneva (lake), Europe, 50/B2
Geneva, N.Y., 20/O4
Geneva, Switz., 50/B2
Genghis Khan Wall (ruins), Asia, 65/J2
Genoa (Genova), Italy, 54/B2
George (riv.), Que., 25/K5
Georgetown (cap.), Cayman Is., 28/A3
Georgetown (cap.), Guyana, 32/J2
George Town, Malaysia, 68/C6
Georgetown, S.C., 21/O6
Georgetown, Tex., 19/J7
Georgia (state), U.S., 15/K4
Georgian (bay), Ont., 25/H7
Georgian S.S.R., U.S.S.R., 60/F6
Gera, E. Ger., 47/E3
Geraldton, Austr., 91/A5
Geraldton, Ont., 24/H6
Gering, Nebr., 18/G4
Gerlachovka (mt.), Czech., 49/E2
Germany, 47
Germiston, S. Africa, 87/H6
Gerona, Spain, 53/H2
Gezira, El (reg.), Sudan, 81/F5
Ghadames, Libya, 80/A1

Ghana, 83/D7
Ghardaïa, Alg., 82/E2
Gharian, Libya, 80/B1
Ghazni, Afghan., 75/J3
Ghent, Belg., 42/D6
Gibraltar, 53/D4
Gibraltar (str.), 53/D5
Gibson (des.), Austr., 91/D4
Gifu, Japan, 67/H6
Gila (riv.), U.S., 14/D4
Gila Bend, Ariz., 17/E6
Gilbert Is., see Kiribati
Gillette, Wyo., 18/G3
Gironde (riv.), France, 44/C5
Gisborne, N.Z., 94/M6
Gitega, Burundi, 84/F4
Giuba (riv.), Somalia, 85/H3
Giza, Egypt, 81/B4
Gjoa Haven, N.W.T., 24/G2
Glace Bay, N.S., 25/L6
Glacier Bay Nat'l Pk., Alaska, 22/F4
Glacier Nat'l Pk., Br. Col., 24/E5
Glacier Nat'l Pk., Mont., 16/E2
Gladstone, Mich., 20/M3
Glama (riv.), Nor., 39/G6
Glasgow, Ky., 21/M5
Glasgow, Scot., 40/D3
Glendale, Ariz., 17/E6
Glendale, Calif., 17/D6
Glendive, Mont., 18/G3
Glens Falls, N.Y., 20/P4
Glenwood Sprs., Colo., 16/G5
Glittertinden (mt.), Nor., 39/F6
Globe, Ariz., 17/F6
Gloucester, Eng., 41/E5
Gloversville, N.Y., 20/P4
Goa (dist.), India, 72/C5
Gobabis, Namibia, 86/B4
Gobi (des.), Asia, 63/O5
Godavari (riv.), India, 72/D5
Godhavn, Greenl., 96/C4
Gods (lake), Man., 24/G4
Godthab (Nûk) (cap.), Greenl., 96/C8
Godwin Austen (K2) (mt.), Pak., 72/D1
Goiânia, Braz., 33/L7
Golan Heights, Syria, 76/D1
Golconda (ruins), India, 72/D5
Gold Coast, Austr., 91/J5
Gold Coast (reg.), Ghana, 83/D8
Goldfield, Nev., 17/D5
Goldsboro, N.C., 21/O6
Gómez Palacio, Mex., 26/D2
Gonâve (isl.), Haiti, 28/D3
Gondar, Eth., 81/G5
Gongga Shan (mt.), China, 65/F6
Gonzales, Tex., 19/J7
Good Hope (cape), S. Africa, 86/E7
Goodland, Kans., 18/H5
Goose (lake), U.S., 14/B2
Goose Bay, Newf., 25/K5
Gorakhpur, India, 72/E3
Gorgan, Iran, 74/F2
Gorizia, Italy, 54/D2
Gor'kiy, U.S.S.R., 60/F3
Görlitz, E. Ger., 47/F3
Gorongosa Nat'l Pk., Moz., 86/E3
Goslar, W. Ger., 47/D3
Göta (canal), Sweden, 39/J7
Göteborg, Sweden, 39/G8
Gotha, E. Ger., 47/D3
Gotland (isl.), Sweden, 39/L8
Göttingen, W. Ger., 47/D3
Gottwaldov, Czech., 49/D2
Gouda, Neth., 42/F4
Gouin (res.), Que., 25/J6
Goulburn, Austr., 92/E4
Goundam, Mali, 82/D5
Gouverneur, N.Y., 20/O3
Gozo (isl.), Malta, 55/E6
Grafton, Austr., 92/G1
Grafton, N. Dak., 18/J2
Graham (isl), N.W.T., 25/M3
Graham, Tex., 19/H6
Grahamstown, S. Africa, 86/D6
Graian Alps (mts.), Europe, 44/G5
Grain Coast, Afr., 83/B8
Granada, Nic., 27/C3
Granada, Spain, 53/E4
Gran Canaria (isl.), Spain, see Canary Is. map p. 52
Gran Chaco (reg.), S. Amer., 34/H9
Grand (canal), China, 65/J4
Grand Bahama (isl.), Bah., 28/B1
Grand-Bassam, Iv. Coast, 83/D7
Grand Canyon, Ariz., 17/E6
Grand Canyon Nat'l Pk., Ariz., 17/E5
Grand Cayman (isl.), Cayman Is., 28/B3
Grand Comoro (isl.), Comoros, 87/G2
Grand Coulee, Wash., 16/D3
Grande (bay), Arg., 34/G14
Grande (riv.), Bol., 32/H7
Grande Prairie, Alta., 24/E4
Grand Erg Occidental (des.), Alg., 82/D-E2
Grand Erg Oriental (des.), Alg., 82/F2
Grande-Rivière, La (riv.), Que., 25/J5

Grand Falls, Newf., 25/L6
Grand Forks, N. Dak., 18/J2
Grand Island, Nebr., 18/J4
Grand Junction, Colo., 17/F5
Grand Marais, Minn., 18/L3
Grand Rapids, Mich., 20/M4
Grand Rapids, Minn., 18/K3
Grand Teton Nat'l Pk., Wyo., 16/F4
Granite (peak), Mont., 16/F3
Granite Falls, Minn., 18/J3
Gran Paradiso (mt.), Italy, 54/A2
Grants, N. Mex., 17/G6
Grants Pass, Oreg., 16/C4
Granville, France, 44/C3
Grasse, France, 44/G6
Gravesend, Eng., 41/G5
Grayling, Mich., 20/M3
Graz, Austria, 49/C3
Great Abaco (isl.), Bah., 28/C1
Gt. Australian (bight), Austr., 91/D-E6
Gt. Barrier (reef), Austr., 91/H-J 2-3
Gt. Bear (lake), N.W.T., 24/D2
Great Bend, Kans., 18/J5
Great Britain, see United Kingdom
Gt. Dividing (range), Austr., 91/H-J 4-5
Gt. Exuma (isl.), Bah., 28/C2
Great Falls, Mont., 16/F3
Gt. Inagua (isl.), Bah., 28/D2
Gt. Indian (des.), Asia, 72/C3
Gt. Khingan (range), China, see Da Hingan
Gt. Namaland (reg.), Namibia, 86/B4-5
Gt. Ouse (riv.), Eng., 41/G4
Gt. Salt (lake), Utah, 16/E4
Gt. Sandy (des.), Austr., 91/C4
Gt. Slave (lake), N.W.T., 24/E3
Gt. Smoky Mts. Nat'l Pk., U.S., 21/N6
Gt. Victoria (des.), Austr., 91/D-E5
Gt. Wall (ruins), China, 65/H4
Great Yarmouth, Eng., 41/G4
Greece, 57/E-F 5-6
Greeley, Colo., 18/G4
Green (riv.), U.S., 14/E2
Green Bay, Wis., 18/M3
Greeneville, Tenn., 21/N5
Greenland, 96/B-C8
Greenland (sea), 96/B6-7
Greenock, Scot., 40/D3
Green River, Wyo., 16/F4
Greensboro, N.C., 21/O5
Greenville, Ala., 21/M7
Greenville, Lib., 83/C8
Greenville, Mich., 20/M4
Greenville, Miss., 19/L6
Greenville, N.C., 21/O6
Greenville, S.C., 21/N6
Greenville, Tex., 19/J6
Greenwich, Eng., see detailed map p. 41
Greenwood, Miss., 19/L6
Greenwood, S.C., 21/N6
Gregory (range), Austr., 91/G3
Greiz, E. Ger., 47/E3
Grenada, 29/G4
Grenada, Miss., 19/L6
Grenadines (isls.), W. Indies, 29/G4
Grenoble, France, 44/F5
Gretna, La., 19/L7
Gretna, Scot., 40/E3
Greybull, Wyo., 16/G3
Greymouth, N.Z., 94/C5
Griffin, Ga., 21/M6
Grimsby, Eng., 41/F4
Griqualand West (reg.), S. Africa, 86/C5
Grise Fjord, N.W.T., 25/N3
Grodno, U.S.S.R., 60/B4
Groningen, Neth., 42/K2
Groote Eylandt (isl.), Austr., 91/F2
Grootfontein, Namibia, 86/B3
Grosseto, Italy, 54/C3
Grossglockner (mt.), Austria, 48/B3
Grouard Mission, Alta., 24/E4
Groves, Tex., 19/K7
Groznyy, U.S.S.R., 60/G6
Grudziadz, Pol., 51/D2
Guadalajara, Mex., 26/D4
Guadalajara, Spain, 53/E2
Guadalcanal (isl.), Sol. Is., 88/F7
Guadalquivir (riv.), Spain, 53/C4
Guadalupe (mts.), U.S., 19/G7
Guadalupe Mts. Nat'l Pk., Tex., 19/G7
Guadarrama (mts.), Spain, 53/E2
Guadeloupe, 29/F3
Guadiana (riv.), Europe, 53/D3
Guainía (riv.), S. Amer., 32/G3
Guajira (pen.), S. Amer., 32/F1
Guam, 89/K7
Guanabacoa, Cuba, 28/A2
Guanajay, Cuba, 28/A2
Guanajuato, Mex., 26/E4
Guanare, Ven., 32/G2
Guangdong (prov.), China, 65/H7
Guangzhou (Canton), China, 65/H7

Guantánamo (bay), Cuba, 28/C3
Guaporé (riv.), S. Amer., 32/H6
Guarda, Port., 52/C2
Guatemala, 27/B2
Guatemala (cap.), Guat., 27/B2
Guaviare (riv.), Col., 32/F3
Guayama, P. Rico, see detailed map p. 29
Guayaquil, Ecua., 32/D4
Guaymas, Mex., 26/B2
Guben (Wilhelm-Pieck-Stadt), E. Ger., 47/F3
Guelma, Alg., 82/F1
Guelph, Ont., 25/H7
Guernsey (isl.), Chan. Is., 41/E6
Guildford, Eng., 41/F5
Guinea, 83/B6
Guinea (gulf), Afr., 83/E8
Guinea-Bissau, 82/A6
Güines, Cuba, 28/B2
Guise, France, 44/E3
Guiyang, China, 65/G6
Gulfport, Miss., 21/L7
Gulja (Yining), China, 65/B3
Guntur, India, 72/D5
Gur'yev, U.S.S.R., 58/F5
Guthrie, Okla., 19/J6
Guyana, 32/J2-3
Guymon, Okla., 19/H5
Gwalior, India, 72/D3
Gwelo, Zim., 86/D3
Gyor, Hung., 49/D3

H

Haarlem, Neth., 42/F4
Hachinohe, Japan, 67/K3
Hachioji, Japan, 67/O2
Hadramaut (reg.), P.D.R. Yemen, 74/E-F6
Hagen, W. Ger., 47/B3
Hagerstown, Md., 20/O5
Hague, The (cap.), Neth., 42/E4
Haguenau, France, 44/G3
Haifa, Isr., 76/B2
Hail, Saudi Arabia, 74/D4
Hailar, China, 65/J2
Haina, Hawaii, 23/F3
Hainan (isl.), China, 68/F3
Haines City, Fla., 21/N7
Haiphong, Viet., 68/E2
Haiti, 28/D3
Hakodate, Japan, 67/K3
Halawa, Hawaii, 23/F3
Halden, Nor., 39/G7
Haleakala Nat'l Pk., Hawaii, 23/E3
Haleb (Aleppo), Syria, 74/C2
Haleiwa, Hawaii, 23/B3
Halifax, Eng., 41/E4
Halifax (cap.), N.S., 25/K7
Hall (pen.), N.W.T., 25/K3
Halle, E. Ger., 47/D3
Hallein, Austria, 48/B3
Halmahera (isl.), Indon., 71/H5
Halmstad, Sweden, 39/H8
Halq el Oued, Tun., 82/G1
Hama, Syria, 74/C2
Hamadan, Iran, 74/E3
Hamamatsu, Japan, 67/H6
Hamburg, W. Ger., 47/D2
Hämeenlinna, Fin., 39/N6
Hameln, W. Ger., 47/C2
Hamersley (range), Austr., 91/B4
Hamhung, N. Korea, 66/C4
Hami, China, 65/D3
Hamilton (cap.), Bermuda, see detailed map p. 29
Hamilton (inlet), Newf., 25/L5
Hamilton, N.Z., 94/E2
Hamilton, Ohio, 20/M5
Hamilton, Ont., 25/H7
Hamilton, Tex., 19/H6
Hamlin, Tex., 19/H6
Hammamet (gulf), Tun., 82/G1
Hammerfest, Nor., 38/N1
Hammond, La., 19/L7
Hamun, S. Korea, 66/C6
Hana, Hawaii, 23/F3
Hanalei, Hawaii, 23/B1
Hanapepe, Hawaii, 23/B2
Hanau, W. Ger., 47/C3
Hancock, Mich., 18/L3
Hanford, Calif., 17/D5
Hangchow, China, see Hangzhou
Hangö, Fin., 39/N7
Hangzhou, China, 65/J5
Hannibal, Mo., 18/L5
Hannover, W. Ger., 47/C2
Hanoi (cap.), Viet., 68/E2
Harar, Eth., 81/H6
Harbel, Lib., 83/B7
Harbin, China, 65/L2
Harbour (isl.), Bah., 28/C1
Harbour Grace, Newf., 25/L6
Hardanger (fjord), Nor., 39/D7
Hargeysa, Somalia, 81/H6
Harlan, Iowa, 18/K4
Harlan, Ky., 21/N5
Harlingen, Tex., 19/J8
Harney (lake), Oreg., 16/D4
Harney (peak), S. Dak., 18/H4
Harper, Lib., 83/C8

Harriman, Tenn., 21/M5
Harris (dist.), Scot., 40/C2
Harrisburg, Ill., 18/L5
Harrisburg (cap.), Pa., 20/O4
Harrison, Ark., 19/K5
Harrisonburg, Va., 20/O5
Harrodsburg, Ky., 21/M5
Harrow, Eng., see detailed map p. 41
Harstad, Nor., 38/K2
Hartford (cap.), Conn., 20/P4
Harwich, Eng., 41/G5
Harz (mts.), Ger., 47/D3
Hasa (reg.), Saudi Arabia, 74/F4
Hastings, Nebr., 18/J4
Hastings, N.Z., 94/F3
Hatteras (cape), N.C., 21/P6
Hattiesburg, Miss., 19/L7
Haugesund, Nor., 39/D7
Havana (cap.), Cuba, 28/A2
Havasu (lake), U.S., 17/E6
Havel (riv.), E. Ger., 47/E2
Havre, Mont., 16/F3
Havre de Grace, Md., 20/P5
Havre-St-Pierre, Que., 25/K5
Hawaii (isl.), Hawaii, 23/F4
Hawaii (state), U.S., 23
Hawaii Volcanoes Nat'l Pk., Hawaii, 23/F4
Hawkinsville, Ga., 21/N6
Hay River, N.W.T., 24/E3
Hays, Kans., 18/J5
Hazard, Ky., 21/N5
Hazleton, Pa., 20/P4
Hearst, Ont., 24/H6
Heber Sprs., Ark., 19/K6
Hebrides (isls.), Scot., 40/C1-3
Hebron, West Bank, 76/C4
Hefei, China, 65/J5
Heidelberg, Austr., 93/J5
Heidelberg, W. Ger., 47/C4
Heilbronn, W. Ger., 47/C4
Hejaz (reg.), Saudi Arabia, 74/C4-5
Hekla (mt.), Icel., 38/W1
Helena (cap.), Mont., 16/E3
Helgoland (isl.), W. Ger., 47/C1
Heliopolis, Egypt, 81/J3
Hell-Ville, Madag., 87/H2
Helmand (riv.), Afghan., 75/J3
Helmond, Neth., 42/H6
Helsingborg, Sweden, 39/H8
Helsingor, Den., 39/H8
Helsinki (cap.), Fin., 39/O6
Henderson, Ky., 21/M5
Henderson, Nev., 17/E5
Henderson, N.C., 21/O5
Hendersonville, N.C., 21/N6
Henryetta, Okla., 19/K6
Henzada, Burma, 68/B3
Herat, Afghan., 75/H3
Herceg Novi, Yugo., 56/D4
Heredia, C. Rica, 27/D3
Hereford, Eng., 41/E4
Hereford, Tex., 19/H6
Hermon (mt.), Syria, 76/D1
Hermosillo, Mex., 26/B2
Herning, Den., 39/F8
Hertford, Eng., 41/G5
Hialeah, Fla., 21/N8
Hiawatha, Kans., 18/K5
Hibbing, Minn., 18/K3
Hickam Housing, Hawaii, 23/C4
Hickory, N.C., 21/N6
High Point, N.C., 21/N6
High River, Alta., 24/E5
Hilla, Iraq, 74/D3
Hillsboro, Tex., 19/J7
Hilo, Hawaii, 23/F4
Hilversum, Neth., 42/G4
Himalaya (mts.), Asia, 73/D-G 2-3
Hindu Kush (mts.), Asia, 73/B-C1
Hiroshima, Japan, 66/E6
Hispaniola (isl.), W. Indies, 28/D2
Hitachi, Japan, 67/K5
Hjorring, Den., 39/F8
Ho, Ghana, 83/E7
Hobart, Austr., 95/L4
Hobbs, N. Mex., 19/H6
Ho Chi Minh City, Viet., 68/E3
Hodeida, Yemen Arab Rep., 74/D7
Hof, W. Ger., 47/D3
Hofei, China, see Hefei
Hofuf, Saudi Arabia, 74/E4
Hokkaido (isl.), Japan, 67/K-M2
Holbaek, Den., 39/G9
Holdenville, Okla., 19/J6
Holdrege, Nebr., 18/J4
Holguín, Cuba, 28/C2
Hollam's Bird (isl.), Namibia, 86/A4
Holland, see Netherlands
Holland, Mich., 20/M4
Hollister, Calif., 16/C5
Holly Springs, Miss., 19/L6
Hollywood, Fla., 21/O8
Holon, Isr., 76/B3
Holstebro, Den., 39/F8
Holy Cross, Alaska, 22/D3
Holyhead, Wales, 41/D4
Homburg, W. Ger., 47/C3
Homer, La., 19/K6
Homewood, Ala., 21/M6
Homs, Libya, 80/B1

Homs, Syria, 74/C3
Hon, Libya, 80/C2
Hondo, Tex., 19/J7
Honduras, 27/C2
Honduras (gulf), Cent. Amer., 27/B1
Honfleur, France, 44/D3
Hon Gai, Viet., 68/E2
Hong Kong, 65/H7
Honiara (cap.), Sol. Is., 88/F6
Honolulu (cap.), Hawaii, 23/C4
Honshu (isl.), Japan, 66-67/F-K 3-6
Hood (mt.), Oreg., 16/C3
Hooper Bay, Alaska, 22/C3
Hoover (dam), U.S., 17/E6
Hope, Alaska, 22/D3
Hope, Ark., 19/K6
Hopewell, Va., 20/O5
Hopkinsville, Ky., 21/M5
Hoquiam, Wash., 16/B3
Hormuz (str.), Asia, 74/G4
Hornell, N.Y., 20/O4
Horn (cape), Chile, 34/G15
Horsens, Den., 39/F9
Horsham, Austr., 92/B5
Horten, Nor., 39/G7
Hospitalet, Spain, 53/H2
Hotan, China, 65/A4
Hot Springs, S. Dak., 18/H4
Hot Sprs. Nat'l Pk., Ark., 19/K6
Hottentot (bay), Namibia, 86/A5
Houghton, Mich., 18/L3
Houlton, Maine, 20/R3
Houma, La., 19/L7
Houston, Tex., 19/K7
Hovd, Mong., 65/D2
Howrah, India, 72/F2
Huambo, Angola, 84/C6
Huancayo, Peru, 32/E6
Huang He (riv.), China, 65/H5
Huánuco, Peru, 32/E6
Huascarán (mt.), Peru, 32/E5
Hubli-Dharwar, India, 72/C5
Huddersfield, Eng., 41/F4
Hudson (bay), Can., 24/H3
Hudson (str.), Can., 25/J3
Hue, Viet., 68/E3
Huelva, Spain, 52/C4
Huesca, Spain, 53/F1
Hugo, Okla., 19/K6
Hugoton, Kans., 18/H5
Huila (mt.), Col., 32/E3
Hull, Eng., 40/F4
Hull, Que., 25/J6
Humber (riv.), Eng., 41/G4
Humboldt, Nev., 16/D4
Humboldt (riv.), Nev., 16/D4
Humboldt, Sask., 24/F5
Humboldt, Tenn., 19/L6
Humphreys (peak), Ariz., 17/E6
Hungary, 49/D-F3
Hüngnam, N. Korea, 66/C4
Huntingdon, Eng., 41/F4
Huntington, Ind., 20/M4
Huntington, W. Va., 20/N5
Huntsville, Ala., 21/M6
Huntsville, Tex., 19/K7
Hunza (Baltit), Pak., 72/C1
Huon (gulf), Papua N.G., 88/E6
Huron (lake), N. Amer., 15/K2
Huron, S. Dak., 18/J3
Hurstville, Austr., 93/J4
Huslia, Alaska, 22/D2
Hutchinson, Kans., 18/J5
Hutchinson, Minn., 18/K4
Hwang Ho, China, see Huang He
Hyderabad, India, 72/D5
Hyderabad, Pak., 75/J4

I

Iaşi, Rom., 56/H2
Ibadan, Nigeria, 83/E7
Ibagué, Col., 32/E3
Ibarra, Ecua., 32/E3
Ibiza, Spain, 53/G3
Ibiza (isl.), Spain, 53/G3
Ica, Peru, 32/E6
Iceland, 38/W-X1
Idabel, Okla., 19/K6
Idaho (state), U.S., 14/D2
Idaho Falls, Idaho, 16/E4
Ife, Nigeria, 83/E7
Iférouane, Niger, 82/F5
Igloolik, N.W.T., 24/H2
Iguala, Mex., 26/E4
Iguaçú (falls), S. Amer., 34/K9
Iguidi, Erg (des.), Afr., 82/C-D3
IJsselmeer (lake), Neth., 42/G3
Ikaría (isl.), Greece, 57/G7
Ilebo, Zaire, 84/D4
Ilesha, Nigeria, 83/F7
Ilhavo, Port., 52/B2
Ilhéus, Braz., 33/N6
Ili (riv.), U.S.S.R., 58/H5
Iliamna (lake), Alaska, 22/D4
Illampu (mt.), Bol., 32/G7
Illinois (state), U.S., 15/J4
Iloilo, Phil., 71/G3
Ilorin, Nigeria, 83/E7
Imperia, Italy, 54/B3

Impfondo, Congo, 84/C3
Imphal, India, 72/G4
Inari (lake), Fin., 38/P2
Inch'ŏn, S. Korea, 66/C5
Independence, Kans., 18/K5
Independence, Mo., 18/K5
Independence (mts.), Nev., 16/D4
India, 72
Indiana (state), U.S., 15/J3
Indianapolis (cap.), Ind., 20/M5
Indian Ocean, 9/M-Q6
Indigirka (riv.), U.S.S.R., 59/P3
Indio, Calif., 17/D6
Indochina (reg.), Asia, 68
Indonesia, 70-71/C-K 6-7
Indore, India, 72/D4
Indre (riv.), France, 44/D4
Indus (riv.), Asia, 72/B3
Ingham, Austr., 91/H3
Ingolstadt, W. Ger., 47/D4
Inhambane, Moz., 86/F6
Inn (riv.), Europe, 48/B2
Innsbruck, Austria, 48/A3
Inoucdjouac, Que., 25/H4
Insein, Burma, 68/C3
Interlaken, Switz., 50/C2
International Falls, Minn., 18/K2
Inuvik, N.W.T., 24/C2
Inveraray, Scot., 40/D2
Invercargill, N.Z., 94/K7
Inverness, Scot., 40/D2
Inyokern, Calif., 17/D6
Ioánnina, Greece, 56/E6
Iola, Kans., 18/K5
Iona (isl.), Scot., 40/C2
Ionia, Mich., 20/M4
Ionian (sea), Europe, 57/D-E 7-8
Ionian (isls.), Greece, 57/D6
Íos (isl.), Greece, 57/G7
Iowa (state), U.S., 15/H2
Iowa City, Iowa, 18/K4
Iowa Falls, Iowa, 18/K4
Ipoh, Malaysia, 68/D6
Ipswich, Austr., 91/J5
Ipswich, Eng., 41/G4
Iquique, Chile, 32/F8
Iquitos, Peru, 32/F4
Iráklion, Greece, 57/G8
Iran, 74-75/F-G3
Irapuato, Mex., 26/D4
Iraq, 74/D3
Irbid, Jordan, 76/D2
Ireland, 41/B-C4
Irian Jaya (reg.), Indon., 71/J6
Iringa, Tanz., 85/G5
Irish (sea), Europe, 41/D4
Irkutsk, U.S.S.R., 58/L4
Iron Mountain, Mich., 18/L3
Iron River, Mich., 18/L3
Ironton, Ohio, 20/N5
Ironwood, Mich., 18/L3
Iroquois Falls, Ont., 25/H6
Irrawaddy (riv.), Burma, 68/B3
Irtysh (riv.), U.S.S.R., 58/G4
Irving, Tex., 19/J6
Ischia (isl.), Italy, 54/D4
Ise, Japan, 67/H6
Isère (riv.), France, 44/F5
Iserlohn, W. Ger., 47/B3
Iseyin, Nigeria, 83/E7
Isfahan, Iran, 74/F3
Ishim, U.S.S.R., 58/H4
Ishpeming, Mich., 20/M3
Iskenderun, Turkey, 74/C2
Islamabad (cap.), Pak., 75/K3
Islay (isl.), Scot., 40/C3
Isle Royale Nat'l Pk., Mich., 18/L2-3
Ismailia, Egypt, 81/K3
Isparta, Turkey, 74/B2
Israel, 76
Issoudun, France, 44/D4
Issyk-Kul' (lake), U.S.S.R., 58/H5
Istanbul, Turkey, 74/A1
Itabuna, Braz., 33/N6
Itaipu (dam), S. Amer., 34/J9
Italy, 54
Ithaca, N.Y., 20/O4
Itháki (isl.), Greece, 57/E6
Ivanovo, U.S.S.R., 60/E3
Ivory Coast, 83/C-D7
Ivory Coast (reg.), Afr., 83/C8
Ivugivik, Que., 25/J3
Iwo (isl.), Japan, 67/M4
Iwo, Nigeria, 83/E7
Iyo (sea), Japan, 66/E7
Izhevsk, U.S.S.R., 60/H3
Izmir, Turkey, 74/A2

J

Jabalpur, India, 72/D4
Jackson, Ala., 21/L7
Jackson, Mich., 20/M4
Jackson, Minn., 18/K4
Jackson (cap.), Miss., 19/L6
Jackson, Ohio, 20/N5
Jackson, Tenn., 19/L6
Jackson, Wyo., 16/E4
Jacksonville, Fla., 21/N7
Jacksonville, Ill., 18/L5
Jacksonville, Tex., 19/K6
Jacksonville Bch., Fla., 21/N7

Jaén, Spain, 53/E4
Jaffna, Sri Lanka, 73/E7
Jaipur, India, 72/D3
Jakarta (cap.), Indon., 70/D7
Jalalabad, Afghan., 75/K3
Jamaica, 28/C3
Jamama, Somalia, 85/H3
James (bay), Can., 25/H5
James (riv.), U.S., 15/G2
James (riv.), Va., 20/O5
James Ross (str.), N.W.T., 24/G1
Jamestown, N.Y., 20/O4
Jamestown, N. Dak., 18/J3
Jamestown (res.), N. Dak., 18/J3
Jammu, Kashmir, 75/K3
Jamma, Eth., 81/G6
Jamnagar, India, 72/B4
Jamshedpur, India, 72/F4
Janesville, Wis., 18/L4
Jan Mayen (isl.), Nor., 37/D1
Japan, 67
Japan (sea), Asia, 63/S6
Jars (plain), Laos, 68/F1
Jarvis (isl.), Pacific, 89/K6
Jasper, Ala., 21/M6
Jasper, Alta., 24/E5
Jasper, Tex., 19/K7
Jasper Nat'l Pk., Alta., 24/E5
Java (isl.), Indon., 70/D7
Java (sea), Indon., 70/D6
Jayapura, Indon., 71/K6
Jefferson City (cap.), Mo., 18/K5
Jeffersonville, Ind., 20/M5
Jena, E. Ger., 47/D3
Jennings, La., 19/K7
Jens Munk (isl.), N.W.T., 24/H2
Jerez de la Frontera, Spain, 53/D4
Jericho, West Bank, 76/C4
Jersey (isl.), Chan. Is., 41/E6
Jerusalem (cap.), Isr., 76/C4
Jesselton, Malaysia, see Kota Kinabalu
Jessore, Bang., 72/F4
Jesup, Ga., 21/N7
Jhang Sadar, Pak., 75/K3
Jhansi, India, 72/D3
Jhelum (riv.), Asia, 72/C2
Jidda, Saudi Arabia, 74/C5
Jihlava, Czech., 49/C2
Jilin, China, 65/L3
Jinja, Uganda, 84/F3
João Pessoa, Braz., 33/O5
Jodhpur, India, 72/C3
Johannesburg, S. Africa, 87/H6
John Day (riv.), Oreg., 16/C3
Johnson City, Tenn., 21/N5
Johnston (atoll), Pacific, 88/K4
Johnstown, Pa., 20/O4
Joliet, Ill., 18/L4
Joncs (plain), Asia, 68/E5
Jonesboro, Ark., 19/L6
Jönköping, Sweden, 39/H8
Jonquière, Que., 25/K6
Joplin, Mo., 19/K5
Jordan, 76/D4
Jordan (riv.), Asia, 76/D3
Juan de Fuca (str.), N. Amer., 24/D6
Juan Fernández (isls.), Chile, 34/D10
Juazeiro do Norte, Braz., 33/N5
Juba, Sudan, 81/F7
Juchitán, Mex., 26/F5
Judaea (reg.), Asia, 76/B-C 4-5
Juiz de Fora, Braz., 33/M8
Jujuy, Arg., 34/G8
Julesburg, Colo., 18/H4
Julian Alps (mts.), Europe, 54/D1
Julianehab, Greenl., 96/D9
Jullundur, India, 72/D2
Jumna (riv.), India, 72/E3
Junagadh, India, 72/B4
Junction, Tex., 19/H7
Junction City, Kans., 18/J5
Juneau (cap.), Alaska, 22/F4
Jungfrau (mt.), Switz., 50/D2
Junggar Pendi (reg.), China, 65/C2
Jura (mts.), Europe, 44/F-G4
Jutland (pen.), Den., 39/F9
Juventud (isl.), Cuba, 28/A2

K

K2 (mt.), Pak., 72/D1
Kaaawa, Hawaii, 23/C3
Kabarega Nat'l Pk., Uganda, 84/F3
Kabinda, Zaire, 84/D5
Kabul (cap.), Afghan., 75/J3
Kabwe, Zambia, 84/E6
Kadesh Barnea (ruins), Egypt, 77/A6
Kadugli, Sudan, 81/E5
Kaduna, Nigeria, 83/F6
Kaédi, Maur., 82/B5
Kaesŏng, N. Korea, 66/C4
Kagoshima, Japan, 66/E8
Kahala, Hawaii, 23/C5
Kahoolawe (isl.), Hawaii, 23/E3
Kahramanmaraş (Maraş), Turkey, 74/C2
Kahuku (pt.), Hawaii, 23/C3
Kahului, Hawaii, 23/E3

Kaieteur (fall), Guyana, 32/J3
Kaifeng, China, 65/H5
Kailua, Hawaii, 23/C4
Kailua (bay), Hawaii, 23/C4
Kairouan, Tun., 82/F1
Kaiserslautern, W. Ger., 47/B4
Kakamega, Kenya, 84/F3
Kakinada, India, 72/E5
Ka Lae (cape), Hawaii, 23/F5
Kalahari (des.), Afr., 86/C4
Kalahari Gemsbok Nat'l Pk., S. Africa, 86/B5
Kalamazoo, Mich., 20/M4
Kalātdlit-Nunât (Greenland), 96/B-C8
Kalaupapa, Hawaii, 23/E2
Kalemie, Zaire, 84/E5
Kalgoorlie, Austr., 91/C6
Kalimantan (reg.), Indon., 70-71/E6
Kalinin, U.S.S.R., 60/E3
Kaliningrad, U.S.S.R., 60/B4
Kalispell, Mont., 16/E2
Kalmar, Sweden, 39/K8
Kaluga, U.S.S.R., 60/E4
Kamakura, Japan, 67/O3
Kamchatka (pen.), U.S.S.R., 59/Q4
Kamina, Zaire, 84/D5
Kampong Cham, Camb., 68/E4
Kampong Chhnang, Camb., 68/D4
Kampong Saom, Camb., 68/D5
Kampot, Camb., 68/E5
Kampuchea, see Cambodia
Kanab, Utah, 17/E5
Kananga, Zaire, 84/D5
Kanazawa, Japan, 67/H5
Kanchenjunga (mt.), Asia, 72/F3
Kandahar (Qandahar), Afghan., 75/J3
Kandy, Sri Lanka, 73/E7
Kane (basin), N. Amer., 96/B10
Kane, Pa., 20/O4
Kanem (reg.), Chad, 80/C5
Kaneohe, Hawaii, 23/C4
Kaneohe (bay), Hawaii, 23/C4
Kangaroo (isl.), Austr., 91/F7
Kanin (pen.), U.S.S.R., 60/G1
Kankakee, Ill., 18/L4
Kankan, Guinea, 83/C6
Kannapolis, N.C., 21/N6
Kano, Nigeria, 82/F6
Kanpur, India, 72/E3
Kansas (riv.), Kans., 18/J5
Kansas (state), U.S., 15/G3
Kansas City, Kans., 18/K5
Kansas City, Mo., 18/K5
Kanye, Bots., 86/C5
Kaohsiung, China, 65/J7
Kaolack, Sen., 82/A6
Kapaa, Hawaii, 23/B1
Kara (sea), U.S.S.R., 58/G2
Karaganda, U.S.S.R., 58/H5
Karakoram (mts.), Asia, 72/D1
Karakorum (ruins), Mong., 65/F2
Kara-Kum (des.), U.S.S.R., 58/F5
Karamea (bight), N.Z., 94/C4
Karbalā', Iraq, 74/D3
Kariba (lake), Afr., 86/D3
Karl-Marx-Stadt, E. Ger., 47/E3
Karlovy Vary, Czech., 48/B1
Karlskrona, Sweden, 39/J8
Karlsruhe, W. Ger., 47/C4
Karlstad, Sweden, 39/H7
Karonga, Malawi, 84/F5
Kárpathos (isl.), Greece, 57/H8
Kars, Turkey, 74/D1
Kasai (riv.), Afr., 84/C4
Kashi (Kashgar), China, 65/A4
Kashmir (Jammu & Kashmir) (state), India, 72/D2
Kassala, Sudan, 81/G4
Kassel, W. Ger., 47/C3
Kasserine, Tun., 82/F1
Kastamonu, Turkey, 74/B1
Kastoría, Greece, 56/E5
Kasungu, Malawi, 84/F6
Katahdin (mt.), Maine, 20/R3
Katherina, Jebel (mt.), Egypt, 81/F2
Kathmandu (cap.), Nepal, 72/E3
Kati, Mali, 82/C6
Katmai Nat'l Pk., Alaska, 22/D4
Katowice, Pol., 51/D3
Kattegat (str.), Europe, 39/G8
Kauai (isl.), Hawaii, 23/B1
Kaukauna, Wis., 18/M3
Kaukauveld (mts.), Afr., 86/C3
Kaunas, U.S.S.R., 60/B4
Kavála, Greece, 56/G5
Kawasaki, Japan, 67/O2
Kaxgar (Kashi), China, 65/A4
Kaya, Upp. Volta, 82/D6
Kayenta, Ariz., 17/F5
Kayes, Mali, 82/B6
Kayseri, Turkey, 74/C2
Kazakh S.S.R., U.S.S.R., 58/G5
Kazan', U.S.S.R., 60/G3
Kazbek (mt.), U.S.S.R., 60/F6
Keahole (pt.), Hawaii, 23/E4
Kealakekua, Hawaii, 23/E4

Kearney, Nebr., 18/J4
Kecskemét, Hung., 49/E3
Keelung, China, 65/K6
Keene, N.H., 20/P4
Keetmanshoop, Namibia, 86/B5
Kefar Sava, Isr., 76/B3
Kékes (mt.), Hung., 49/E3
Kelang, Malaysia, 69/D7
Kellogg, Idaho, 16/D2
Kélo, Chad, 80/C6
Kelowna, Br. Col., 24/E6
Kelso, Wash., 16/C3
Kemerovo, U.S.S.R., 58/J4
Kemi, Fin., 38/O3
Kemmerer, Wyo., 16/E4
Kenai (pen.), Alaska, 22/D3
Kenai Fjords Nat'l Pk., Alaska, 22/E4
Kenedy, Tex., 19/J7
Kenema, S. Leone, 83/B7
Kenitra, Mor., 82/C2
Kenmare, N. Dak., 18/H2
Kenmare, Ire., 41/B5
Kennebec (riv.), Maine, 20/R3
Kennett, Mo., 19/L5
Kennewick, Wash., 16/C3
Kenogami (riv.), Ont., 24/H6
Kenora, Ont., 24/G5
Kenosha, Wis., 20/M4
Kentucky (lake), U.S., 15/J3
Kentucky (state), U.S., 15/J3
Kenya, 85/G3
Kenya (mt.), Kenya, 85/G4
Keokuk, Iowa, 18/L4
Kerguélen (isls.), 9/M8
Kérkira (isl.), Greece, 56/D6
Kermadec (isls.), N.Z., 88/J9
Kerman, Iran, 75/G3
Kermanshah, Iran, 74/E3
Kermit, Tex., 19/H7
Kerrville, Tex., 19/J7
Kerulen (riv.), Asia, 65/H2
Keta, Ghana, 83/E7
Ketchikan, Alaska, 22/F4
Kewanee, Ill., 18/L4
Keweenaw (pt.), Mich., 18/M3
Key West, Fla., 21/N8
Khabarovsk, U.S.S.R., 59/O5
Khamkeut, Laos, 68/E3
Khanía, Greece, 57/G8
Khanpur, Pak., 75/K4
Kharagpur, India, 72/F4
Khârga (oasis), Egypt, 81/F2
Khar'kov, U.S.S.R., 60/E5
Khartoum (cap.), Sudan, 81/F4
Khartoum North, Sudan, 81/F4
Khashm el Girba, Sudan, 81/G5
Khemis Miliana, Alg., 82/E1
Khemmarat, Thai., 68/E3
Khenifra, Mor., 82/C2
Kherson, U.S.S.R., 60/D5
Khíos (isl.), Greece, 57/G6
Khorramabad, Iran, 74/E3
Khorramshahr, Iran, 74/E3
Khotan, China, see Hotan
Khouribga, Mor., 82/C2
Khulna, Bang., 72/F4
Khyber (pass), Pak., 75/K3
Kidepo Nat'l Pk., Uganda, 84/F3
Kiel, W. Ger., 46/D1
Kiel (canal), W. Ger., 46/C1
Kielce, Pol., 51/E3
Kiev, U.S.S.R., 60/D4
Kiffa, Maur., 82/B5
Kigali (cap.), Rwanda, 84/F4
Kigoma-Ujiji, Tanz., 85/E4
Kikwit, Zaire, 84/C5
Kilauea, Hawaii, 23/B1
Kilauea (crater), Hawaii, 23/F4
Kildare, Ire., 41/C4
Kilgore, Tex., 19/K6
Kilimanjaro (mt.), Tanz., 84/G4
Kilkenny, Ire., 41/C4
Killarney, Ire., 41/B4
Killeen, Tex., 19/J7
Kimberley (plat.), Austr., 91/D3
Kimberley, S. Africa, 86/C5
Kinabalu (mt.), Malaysia, 71/F4
Kindersley, Sask., 24/F5
Kindia, Guinea, 83/B6
King (isl.), Austr., 95/H1
King City, Calif., 17/C5
King Cove, Alaska, 22/C5
Kingman, Ariz., 17/E6
Kings Canyon Nat'l Pk., Calif., 17/D5
Kingsford, Mich., 18/L3
Kingsport, Tenn., 21/N5
Kingston (cap.), Jam., 28/C3
Kingston, N.Y., 20/P4
Kingston (cap.), Norfolk I., 88/G8
Kingston, Ont., 25/J7
Kingston, Pa., 20/O4
Kingstown (cap.), St. Vinc. & Grens., 29/G4
Kingsville, Tex., 19/J8
King William (isl.), N.W.T., 24/G2
Kinross, Scot., 40/E2
Kinsale, Ire., 41/B5
Kinshasa (cap.), Zaire, 84/C4
Kinston, N.C., 21/O6
Kioga (lake), Uganda, 84/F3
Kirgiz S.S.R., U.S.S.R., 58/H5
Kiribati, 88/J6
Kirin, China, see Jilin
Kirkcaldy, Scot., 40/E2
Kirkcudbright, Scot., 40/E3

Kirkenes, Nor., 38/Q2
Kirksville, Mo., 18/K4
Kirkuk, Iraq, 74/D2
Kirkwall, Scot., 40/E1
Kirov, U.S.S.R., 60/G3
Kirovabad, U.S.S.R., 60/G6
Kirovograd, U.S.S.R., 60/D5
Kiruna, Sweden, 38/L3
Kisangani, Zaire, 84/E3
Kishinev, U.S.S.R., 60/C5
Kiska (isl.), Alaska, 22/E5
Kissidougou, Guinea, 83/B7
Kistna (riv.), India, 72/D5
Kisumu, Kenya, 84/F3
Kita, Mali, 82/C6
Kita Iwo (isl.), Japan, 88/D3
Kitakyushu, Japan, 66/E6
Kitale, Kenya, 85/G3
Kitchener, Ont., 15/N4
Kitimat, Br. Col., 24/D5
Kitwe, Zambia, 84/E6
Kitzbühel, Austria, 48/B3
Kiungchow (str.), China, see Qiongzhou
Kivu (lake), Afr., 84/E4
Kizel, U.S.S.R., 60/J3
Kizilirmak (riv.), Turkey, 74/B1
Kjölen (mts.), Europe, 39/K3
Kladno, Czech., 48/C1
Klagenfurt, Austria, 48/C3
Klaipeda, U.S.S.R., 60/B3
Klamath Falls, Oreg., 16/C4
Klerksdorp, S. Africa, 86/D5
Kleve, W. Ger., 47/B3
Kluane (lake), Yukon, 24/C3
Knoxville, Iowa, 18/K4
Knoxville, Tenn., 21/N5
Kobdo, Mong., see Hovd
Kobe, Japan, 67/H7
Kobenhavn, Den., see Copenhagen
Koblenz, W. Ger., 47/B3
Kobuk Valley Nat'l Pk., Alaska, 22/D2
Kodiak, Alaska, 22/D4
Kodiak (isl.), Alaska, 22/D4
Kodok, Sudan, 81/F6
Koforidua, Ghana, 83/D7
Koko (head), Hawaii, 23/D5
Kokomo, Ind., 20/M4
Koko Nor (lake), China, see Qinghai Hu
Koksoak (riv.), Que., 25/K4
Kola (pen.), U.S.S.R., 60/E1
Kolar Gold Fields, India, 72/D6
Kolding, Den., 39/F9
Kolguyev (isl.), U.S.S.R., 60/G1
Kolhapur, India, 72/C5
Köln (Cologne), W. Ger., 47/B3
Kolobrzeg, Pol., 51/B1
Kolwezi, Zaire, 84/E6
Kolyma (range), U.S.S.R., 59/Q3
Komárno, Czech., 49/D3
Kompong Thom, Camb., 68/E4
Komsomol'sk, U.S.S.R., 59/O4
Kongsberg, Nor., 39/F7
Königsberg (Kaliningrad), U.S.S.R., 60/B4
Königssee (lake), W. Ger., 47/C5
Konin, Pol., 51/D2
Köniz, Switz., 50/C2
Konstanz, W. Ger., 47/C5
Kontum (plat.), Viet., 68/E4
Konya, Turkey, 74/B2
Kootenay (lake), Br. Col., 24/E5
Koper, Yugo., 56/A3
Korachev, Camb., 68/E4
Korçë, Alb., 56/E5
Korčula (isl.), Yugo., 56/C4
Korea, 66
Korhogo, Iv. Coast, 83/C7
Koror, Belau, 88/D5
Korsakov, U.S.S.R., 59/P5
Kortrijk, Belg., 43/C7
Koryak (range), U.S.S.R., 59/R3
Kos (isl.), Greece, 57/H7
Kosciusko, Austr., 95/H2
Kosciusko, Miss., 19/L6
Košice, Czech., 49/F2
Kosti, Sudan, 81/F5
Kostroma, U.S.S.R., 60/F3
Koszalin, Pol., 51/C1
Kota Baharu, Malaysia, 68/D6
Kota Kinabalu, Malaysia, 71/F4
Kotka, Fin., 39/P6
Kotor, Yugo., 56/D4
Kotzebue, Alaska, 22/C2
Koudougou, Upp. Volta, 82/D6
Koulikoro, Mali, 82/C6
Koumra, Chad, 80/C6
Kouroussa, Guinea, 83/C6
Koutiala, Mali, 82/C6
Kowloon, Hong Kong, 65/H7
Koyuk, Alaska, 22/C2
Koyukuk (riv.), Alaska, 22/D2
Kozhikode, India, 72/D6
Kpalimé, Togo, 83/E7
Kra (isth.), Thai., 68/C5
Kragujevac, Yugo., 56/E3
Krakatau (isl.), Indon., 70/C7
Kraków, Pol., see Cracow
Krasnodar, U.S.S.R., 60/E6
Krasnovodsk, U.S.S.R., 58/F5
Krasnoyarsk, U.S.S.R., 58/K4
Krefeld, W. Ger., 47/B3

Kremenchug, U.S.S.R., 60/D5
Krishna (Kistna) (riv.), India, 72/D5
Kristiansand, Nor., 39/F8
Kristiansund, Nor., 39/E5
Kristinehamn, Sweden, 39/H7
Kristinestad, Fin., 39/N5
Krk (isl.), Yugo., 56/B3
Kroonstad, S. Africa, 86/D5
Kru Coast (reg.), Afr., 83/B8
Kruger Nat'l Pk., S. Africa, 86/E4
Krugersdorp, S. Africa, 86/H6
Krung Thep (Bangkok) (cap.), Thai., 68/D4
Ksar el Kebir, Mor., 82/C2
Kuala Lumpur (cap.), Malaysia, 68/D7
Kuching, Malaysia, 70/E5
Kufra (oasis), Libya, 80/D3
Kuldja, China, see Yining
Kuma (riv.), U.S.S.R., 60/G5
Kumamoto, Japan, 66/E7
Kumanovo, Yugo., 56/E4
Kumasi, Ghana, 83/D7
Kumbo, Cameroon, 84/A3
Kunlun (mts.), Asia, 65/A-D4
Kunming, China, 65/F6
Kuopio, Fin., 39/Q5
Kupang, Indon., 71/G8
Kura (riv.), U.S.S.R., 60/G6
Kürdzhali, Bulg., 56/G5
Kure, Japan, 67/F6
Kurgan, U.S.S.R., 58/G4
Kuril (isls.), U.S.S.R., 59/P5
Kursk, U.S.S.R., 60/E4
Kuskokwim (bay), Alaska, 22/C4
Kuskokwim (mts.), Alaska, 22/D3
Kutaisi, U.S.S.R., 60/F6
Kutch, Rann of (salt marsh), India, 72/B-C4
Kutum, Sudan, 80/D5
Kuusamo, Fin., 38/Q4
Kuwait, 74/E4
Kuybyshev, U.S.S.R., 60/H4
Kwajalein (atoll), Marshall Is., 88/G5
Kwangchow, China, see Canton
Kwangju, S. Korea, 66/C6
Kwangtung (prov.), China, see Guangdong
Kweiyang, China, see Guiyang
Kwigillingok, Alaska, 22/C4
Kyaukpyu, Burma, 68/B3
Kyoto, Japan, 67/J7
Kyushu (isl.), Japan, 66/E7
Kyustendil, Bulg., 56/F4
Kyzyl, U.S.S.R., 58/K4
Kyzyl-Kum (des.), U.S.S.R., 58/G5

L

Laayoune, W. Sahara, 82/B3
Labé, Guinea, 83/B6
Labrador (dist.), Newf., 25/K-L5
Labuan (isl.), Malaysia, 70/E4
Laccadive (isls.), India, 63/K8
La Ceiba, Hond., 27/C2
La Chaux-de-Fonds, Switz., 50/B1
Lackawanna, N.Y., 20/O4
Lac La Biche, Alta., 24/E4
Laconia, N.H., 20/R4
La Coruña, Spain, 52/B1
La Crosse, Wis., 18/L4
Ladakh (reg.), India, 72/D2
Ladoga (lake), U.S.S.R., 60/D2
Ladysmith, S. Africa, 86/D5
Ladysmith, Wis., 19/L3
Lae, Papua N.G., 88/E6
La Fayette, Ga., 21/M6
Lafayette, Ind., 20/M4
Lafayette, La., 19/L7
La Follette, Tenn., 21/M5
Laghouat, Alg., 82/E2
Lagos (cap.), Nigeria, 83/E7
La Grande, Oreg., 16/D3
La Grange, Ga., 21/M6
La Grange, Tex., 19/J7
La Guaira, Ven., 32/G1
Lahaina, Hawaii, 23/E3
Lahore, Pak., 75/K3
Lahti, Fin., 39/O6
Laï, Chad, 80/C6
Laie, Hawaii, 23/C3
La Junta, Colo., 18/G5
Lake Charles, La., 19/K7
Lake City, Fla., 21/N7
Lake Clark Nat'l Pk., Alaska, 22/C3
Lake Havasu City, Ariz., 17/E6
Lakeland, Fla., 21/N7
Lake Louise, Alta., 24/E5
Lake of the Woods, N. Amer., 24/G6
Lake Providence, La., 19/K6
Lakeview, Oreg., 16/C4
Lake Wales, Fla., 21/N8
Lakewood, Colo., 18/G5
Lakewood, Ohio, 20/N4
Lake Worth, Fla., 21/O8
La Línea, Spain, 53/D4

Lalitpur, Nepal, 72/E3
Lamar, Colo., 18/H5
Lamar, Mo., 18/K5
Lambaréné, Gabon, 84/B4
Lambeth, Eng., see detailed map p. 41
La Mesa, Calif., 17/D6
Lamesa, Tex., 19/H6
Lamia, Greece, 57/F6
Lamoni, Iowa, 18/K4
La Moure, N. Dak., 18/J3
Lampasas, Tex., 19/J7
Lanai (isl.), Hawaii, 23/D3
Lanai City, Hawaii, 23/E3
Lanark, Scot., 40/E3
Lancaster, Eng., 40/E3
Lancaster, Ohio, 20/N5
Lancaster, Pa., 20/O4
Lancaster, S.C., 21/N6
Lanchow, China, see Lanzhou
Lander, Wyo., 16/F4
Land's End (prom.), Eng., 41/D5
Landshut, W. Ger., 47/E4
Landskrona, Sweden, 39/H9
L'Anse, Mich., 18/L3
Lansing (cap.), Mich., 20/M4
Lanzhou, China, 65/F4
Laon, France, 44/E3
Laos, 68/D-E 3-4
La Palma (isl.), Spain, see Canary Is. map p. 52
La Paz (cap.), Bol., 32/G7
La Paz, Mex., 26/B3
Lapeer, Mich., 20/N4
La Pérouse (str.), Asia, 59/P5
Lapland (reg.), Europe, 38/K-R1
La Plata, Arg., 34/J11
La Porte, Ind., 20/M4
Lappeenranta, Fin., 39/P6
Laptev (sea), U.S.S.R., 59/N2
L'Aquila, Italy, 54/D3
Larache, Mor., 82/C1
Laramie, (riv.), U.S., 18/G4
Laramie, Wyo., 18/G4
Laredo, Tex., 19/J8
La Rioja, Arg., 34/G9
Lárisa, Greece, 56/F6
Larnaca, Cyprus, 74/B3
Larned, Kans., 18/J5
La Rochelle, France, 44/C4
La Romana, Dom. Rep., 28/E3
La Ronge, Sask., 24/F4
La Salle, Ill., 18/L4
Las Animas, Colo., 18/H5
La Sarre, Que., 25/J6
Las Cruces, N. Mex., 17/G6
Las Palmas, Spain, see Canary Is. map p. 52
La Spezia, Italy, 54/B2
Lassen (peak), Calif., 16/C4
Lassen Volcanic Nat'l Pk., Calif., 16/C4
Las Tablas, Pan., 27/F4
Lastoursville, Gabon, 84/B4
Las Vegas, Nev., 17/E5
Las Vegas, N. Mex., 19/G6
Latakia, Syria, 74/C2
Latina, Italy, 54/D4
Latvian S.S.R., U.S.S.R., 60/B3
Lau Group (isls.), Fiji, 88/J7
Launceston, Austr., 95/K3
Laurel, Miss., 19/L7
Laurens, S.C., 21/N6
Laurinburg, N.C., 21/O6
Lausanne, Switz., 50/B2
La Vega, Dom. Rep., 28/D3
Lavongai (isl.), Papua N.G., 88/F6
Lawrence, Kans., 18/K5
Lawrenceburg, Tenn., 21/M5
Lawton, Okla., 19/J6
Lead, S. Dak., 18/G3
Leadville, Colo., 18/F5
Leavenworth, Kans., 18/K5
Lebanon, 74/C3
Lebanon, Ky., 21/M5
Lebanon, Mo., 18/K5
Lebanon, Oreg., 16/C3
Lebanon, Pa., 20/O4
Lebanon, Tenn., 21/M5
Le Bourget, France, 44/B1
Lecce, Italy, 54/G4
Leech (lake), Minn., 18/K3
Leeds, Eng., 41/F4
Leesburg, Fla., 21/N7
Leesville, La., 19/K7
Leeuwarden, Neth., 42/H2
Leeward (isls.), W. Indies, 29/F3
Legazpi, Phil., 71/G3
Leghorn, Italy, 54/B3
Le Havre, France, 44/D3
Leicester, Eng., 41/F4
Leiden, Neth., 42/F4
Leipzig, E. Ger., 47/E3
Leiria, Port., 52/B3
Leizhou (pen.), China, 65/G7
Leland, Miss., 19/L6
Le Mans, France, 44/D3
Le Mars, Iowa, 18/J4
Lempa (riv.), El Sal., 27/B2
Lena (riv.), U.S.S.R., 59/N3
Leninabad, U.S.S.R., 58/G5
Leningrad, U.S.S.R., 60/C3
Leninsk, U.S.S.R., 58/G5
Leninsk-Kuznetskiy, U.S.S.R., 58/J4

Lens, France, 44/E2
Leoben, Austria, 49/C3
León, Mex., 26/E4
León, Nic., 27/C2
León, Spain, 53/D1
Léopoldville (Kinshasa) (cap.), Zaire, 84/C4
Le Port, Réunion, see Mascarene Is. map p. 87
Lérida, Spain, 53/G2
Lerwick, Scot., 40/G1
Les Cayes, Haiti, 28/C3
Lesotho, 86/D5
Lesser Antilles (isls.), W. Indies, 28-29/E-G 3-4
Lesser Slave (lake), Alta., 24/E4
Lésvos (isl.), Greece, 56/G6
Lethbridge, Alta., 24/E6
Levelland, Tex., 19/H6
Levkula, Fiji, 88/H7
Lewis (isl.), Scot., 40/C1
Lewiston, Idaho, 16/D3
Lewiston, Maine, 20/R3
Lewistown, Mont., 16/F3
Lewistown, Pa., 20/O4
Lexington, Ky., 20/M5
Lexington, Miss., 19/L6
Lexington, Nebr., 18/H4
Lexington, Va., 20/O5
Leyte (isl.), Phil., 71/H3
Lhasa, China, 65/D3
Liaodong (pen.), China, 65/K3
Liberal, Kans., 19/H5
Liberia, 83/C7
Liberia, C. Rica, 27/C3
Libreville (cap.), Gabon, 84/A3
Libya, 80/B-D2
Libyan (des.), Afr., 80/D2
Lichinga, Moz., 86/F2
Lido di Ostia, Italy, see detailed map p. 55
Lido di Venezia, Italy, 54/D2
Liechtenstein, 50/E1
Liège, Belg., 43/H7
Liffey (riv.), Ire., 41/C4
Ligurian (sea), Italy, 54/B3
Lihue, Hawaii, 23/B2
Lille, France, 44/E2
Lillehammer, Nor., 39/F6
Lilloodet, Br. Col., 24/D5
Lilongwe (cap.), Malawi, 86/E2
Lima, Ohio, 20/M4
Lima (cap.), Peru, 32/E6
Limassol, Cyprus, 74/B3
Limerick, Ire., 41/B4
Limoges, France, 44/D5
Limón, C. Rica, 27/D3
Limousin (reg.), France, 44/D5
Linares, Chile, 34/F11
Linares, Mex., 26/E3
Lincoln, Arg., 34/H10
Lincoln, Eng., 41/F4
Lincoln, Ill., 18/L4
Lincoln (cap.), Nebr., 18/J4
Lindesnes (cape), Nor., 39/E8
Lindi, Tanz., 85/G5
Line (isls.), Pacific, 89/K-L 5-6
Lingayen, Phil., 71/F2
Linköping, Sweden, 39/K7
Linton, Ind., 20/M5
Linz, Austria, 48/C2
Lions (gulf), France, 44/F6
Lipari (isls.), Italy, 54/E5
Lippe (riv.), W. Ger., 47/B3
Lisbon (cap.), Port., 52/B3
Lismore, Austr., 93/G1
Litchfield, Ill., 18/L5
Litchfield, Minn., 18/K3
Lithgow, Austr., 92/F3
Lithuanian S.S.R., U.S.S.R., 60/B3
Little America, Antarc., 35/B7
Little Cayman (isl.), Cayman Is., 28/B3
Little Colorado (riv.), U.S., 17/F6
Little Falls, Minn., 18/K3
Littlefield, Tex., 19/H6
Little Rock (cap.), Ark., 19/K6
Live Oak, Fla., 21/N7
Livingston, Mont., 16/F3
Livingstone (falls), Zaire, 84/B5
Livingstone, Zambia, 84/E7
Livorno (Leghorn), Italy, 54/C3
Ljubljana, Yugo., 56/B3
Llandudno, Wales, 41/E4
Llano, Tex., 19/J7
Llano Estacado (plain), U.S., 19/H6
Llanos del Orinoco (plains), S. Amer., 32/F-G 2-3
Lloydminster, Can., 24/E5
Llullaillaco (vol.), Chile, 34/F8
Loa (riv.), Chile, 32/F8
Lobatse, Bots., 86/D5
Lobito, Angola, 84/B6
Lockhart, Tex., 19/J7
Lock Haven, Pa., 20/O4
Lockport, N.Y., 20/O4
Loc Ninh, Viet., 68/E5
Lod (Lydda), Isr., 76/B4
Lodi, Calif., 16/C5
Łódź, Pol., 51/D3
Lofoten (isls.), Nor., 38/H2

Logan, Utah, 16/E4
Logan (mt.), Yukon, 24/B3
Logansport, Ind., 20/M4
Logroño, Spain, 53/E1
Loir (riv.), France, 44/D4
Loire (riv.), France, 44/C4
Loja, Ecua., 32/E4
Lombardy (reg.), Italy, 54/B2
Lombok (isl.), Indon., 71/F7
Lomé (cap.), Togo, 83/E7
Lomond (lake), Scot., 40/D2
Lompoc, Calif., 17/C6
London, Ont., 25/H7
London, Eng. (cap.), U.K., 41/F5
Londonderry, N. Ire., 40/C3
Long (isl.), Bah., 28/C2
Long (isl.), N.Y., 20/R4
Long Beach, Calif., 17/D6
Longford, Ire., 41/C4
Long Island (sound), U.S., 20/P4
Longmont, Colo., 18/G4
Longview, Tex., 19/K6
Longview, Wash., 16/C3
Long Xuyen, Viet., 68/E5
Lopatka (cape), U.S.S.R., 59/Q4
Lop Nur (Lop Nor) (dry lake), China, 65/D3
Lorain, Ohio, 20/N4
Lord Howe (isl.), Austr., see detailed map p. 93
Lordsburg, N. Mex., 17/F6
Lörrach, W. Ger., 47/B5
Los Alamos, N. Mex., 17/G6
Los Angeles, Calif., 17/D6
Los Angeles, Chile, 34/F11
Los Banos, Calif., 17/C5
Los Mochis, Mex., 26/C4
Los Mosquitos (gulf), Pan., 27/C6
Lot (riv.), France, 44/D5
Lötschberg (tunnel), Switz., 50/C2
Louang Namtha, Laos, 68/D2
Louangphrabang, Laos, 68/D3
Loubomo, Congo, 84/B4
Louisiade (arch.), Papua N.G., 88/F7
Louisiana (state), U.S., 15/H4
Louis Trichardt, S. Africa, 86/D4
Louisville, Ky., 20/M5
Lourdes, France, 44/C6
Lourenço Marques (Maputo) (cap.), Moz., 86/E5
Louvain, Belg., 43/F7
Loveland, Colo., 18/G4
Lovelock, Nev., 16/D4
Lovington, N. Mex., 19/H6
Lovisa, Fin., 39/P6
Lowell, Mass., 20/R4
Lower California (pen.), Mex., 13/G6-7
Lower Tunguska (riv.), U.S.S.R., 58/K4
Loyalty (isls.), New Cal., 89/H4
Loyang, China, see Luoyang
Luanda (cap.), Angola, 84/B5
Luanshya, Zambia, 86/E6
Lubango, Angola, 84/B6
Lubbock, Tex., 19/H6
Lübeck, W. Ger., 47/D2
Lublin, Pol., 51/F3
Lubumbashi, Zaire, 84/E6
Lucca, Italy, 54/C3
Lucerne, Switz., 50/D1
Lucerne (lake), Switz., 50/D2
Lucknow, India, 72/E3
Lüda, China, 65/K4
Ludhiana, India, 72/D2
Ludington, Mich., 20/M4
Ludwigsburg, W. Ger., 47/C4
Ludwigshafen, W. Ger., 47/C4
Lufkin, Tex., 19/K7
Lugano, Switz., 50/D2
Lugansk, U.S.S.R., see Voroshilovgrad
Lugo, Spain, 52/C1
Luichow (pen.), China, see Leizhou
Lukapa, Angola, 84/D5
Lulea, Sweden, 39/N4
Luling, Tex., 19/J7
Lumberton, N.C., 21/O6
Lund, Sweden, 39/H9
Lundy (isl.), Eng., 41/D5
Lünen, W. Ger., 47/B3
Lunenburg, N.S., 25/K7
Luoyang, China, 65/H5
Lusaka (cap.), Zambia, 84/E7
Lusatia (reg.), E. Ger., 47/F3
Lüshun, China, 65/K4
Lusk, Wyo., 18/G4
Luton, Eng., 41/F5
Luxembourg, 43/H-J9
Luxembourg (cap.), Lux., 43/J9
Luxor, Egypt, 81/F2
Luzon (isl.), Phil., 71/G2
L'vov, U.S.S.R., 60/B5
Lyallpur (Faisalabad), Pak., 75/K3
Lydda, Isr., 76/B4
Lynchburg, Va., 20/O5
Lynn, Mass., 20/R4
Lyon, France, 44/F5

M

Ma'an, Jordan, 76/D7
Maas (riv.), Neth., 42/G5
Maastricht, Neth., 43/H7
Macapá, Braz., 33/K3
Macau, 63/P7
Macclesfield, Eng., 41/E4
Macedonia (rep.), Yugo., 56/E5
Maceió, Braz., 33/N5
Macerata, Italy, 54/D3
Machala, Ecua., 32/D4
Machias, Maine, 20/S3
Machilipatnam, India, 72/E5
Machupicchu, Peru, 32/F6
Mackay, Austr., 91/H4
Mackenzie (riv.), N.W.T., 24/C2
Macomb, Ill., 18/L4
Mâcon, France, 44/F4
Macon, Ga., 21/N6
Macon, Mo., 18/K5
Ma'daba, Jordan, 76/D4
Madagascar, 87/H3-4
Madang, Papua N.G., 88/E6
Madeira (riv.), Braz., 32/H5
Madeira (isl.), Port., see detailed map p. 52
Madera, Calif., 17/D5
Madison, S. Dak., 18/J4
Madison (cap.), Wis., 18/L4
Madisonville, Ky., 21/L5
Madras, India, 72/E6
Madre Occidental, Sierra (mts.), Mex., 26/C1-3
Madre Oriental, Sierra (mts.), Mex., 26/E2-3
Madrid (cap.), Spain, 53/E2
Madura (isl.), Indon., 70/E7
Madurai, India, 72/D7
Mafeking (Mafikeng), S. Africa, 86/C5
Magadan, U.S.S.R., 59/P4
Magdalen (isls.), Que., 25/K6
Magdalena (riv.), Col., 32/F2
Magdeburg, E. Ger., 47/D2
Magellan (str.), S. Amer., 34/G14
Maggiore (lake), Europe, 50/D3
Magnitogorsk, U.S.S.R., 58/G4
Magnolia, Ark., 19/K6
Maguse River, N.W.T., 24/G3
Mahalapye, Bots., 86/D4
Mahanadi (riv.), India, 72/E4
Mahdia, Tun., 82/G1
Mahón, Spain, 53/J3
Maidstone, Eng., 41/G5
Maiduguri, Nigeria, 80/G6
Main (riv.), W. Ger., 47/C4
Maine (state), U.S., 15/N1
Mainz, W. Ger., 47/C4
Maipo (vol.), S. Amer., 34/G10
Maitland, Austr., 92/F3
Majorca (isl.), Spain, 53/H3
Majunga, Madag., 87/H3
Majuro (atoll), Marshall Is., 88/H5
Makale, Eth., 81/G5
Makapuu (pt.), Hawaii, 23/D4
Makassar (str.), Indon., 71/F6
Makawao, Hawaii, 23/E3
Makeni, S. Leone, 83/B7
Makeyevka, U.S.S.R., 60/E5
Makgadikgadi (salt pan), Bots., 86/D3
Makhachkala, U.S.S.R., 60/G6
Makhtesh Ramon (depr.), Isr., 77/B6
Makó, Hung., 49/F3
Makoua, Congo, 84/C3
Makurdi, Nigeria, 83/F7
Malabar (coast), India, 72/C6
Malabo (cap.), Equat. Guin., 84/A3
Malacca (str.), Asia, 68/D7
Malad City, Idaho, 16/E4
Málaga, Spain, 53/D4
Malagasy Rep., see Madagascar
Malaita (isl.), Sol. Is., 88/G6
Malakal, Sudan, 81/F6
Malang, Indon., 70/E7
Malange, Angola, 84/C5
Malatya, Turkey, 74/C2
Malawi, 85/F6
Malay (pen.), Asia, 68/C-D 5-7
Malaya (reg.), Malaysia, 68/D6
Malaysia, 70/C-E4
Maldives, 73/C8
Maldonado, Urug., 34/K11
Male (cap.), Maldives, 73/C8
Malebo (Stanley Pool) (lake), Afr., 84/C4
Malheur (lake), Oreg., 16/D4
Mali, 80/C-D 5-6
Malindi, Kenya, 85/H4
Malmédy, Belg., 43/J8
Malmö, Sweden, 39/H9
Malone, N.Y., 20/P3
Malta, 55/E7
Malvern, Ark., 19/K6
Mammoth Cave Nat'l Pk., Ky., 21/M5
Mamoutzou (cap.), Mayotte, see Dzaoudzi
Man, Isle of (isl.), 40/D3
Man, Iv. Coast, 83/C7
Manado, Indon., 71/G5

Managua (cap.), Nic., 27/C2
Manama (cap.), Bahrain, 74/E4
Manatí, P. Rico, see detailed map p. 29
Manaus, Braz., 32/H4
Mancha, La (reg.), Spain, 53/E3
Manchester, Eng., 41/E4
Manchester, N.H., 20/R4
Manchuria (reg.), China, 63/R5
Mandalay, Burma, 68/C2
Mandan, N. Dak., 18/H3
Mandeb, Bab el (str.), 74/D7
Mangareva (isl.), Fr. Poly., 89/N8
Manhattan, Kans., 18/J5
Manicouagan (riv.), Que., 25/K5
Manihiki (atoll), Cook Is., 89/K7
Manila (cap.), Phil., 71/F3
Manistee, Mich., 20/M3
Manistique, Mich., 20/M3
Manitoba (prov.), Can., 24/G5
Manitoba (lake), Man., 24/G5
Manitoulin (isl.), Ont., 25/H6
Manitou Springs, Colo., 18/G5
Manitowoc, Wis., 18/M4
Manizales, Col., 32/E2
Mankato, Minn., 18/K4
Mannar (gulf), Asia, 72/D7
Mannheim, W. Ger., 47/C4
Mansa, Zambia, 84/E6
Mansfield, Eng., 41/F4
Mansfield, La., 19/K6
Mansfield, Ohio, 20/N4
Mantiqueira (mts.), Braz., 33/M8
Mantua, Italy, 54/C2
Manus (isl.), Papua N.G., 88/E6
Manzanillo, Mex., 26/D4
Manzini, Swaziland, 86/E5
Mao, Chad, 80/C5
Maple Creek, Sask., 24/F6
Maputo (cap.), Moz., 86/E5
Maquela do Zombo, Angola, 84/C5
Maquoketa, Iowa, 18/L4
Mar (mts.), Braz., 34/L9
Maracaibo, Ven., 32/F1
Maracay, Ven., 32/G1
Maradi, Niger, 82/F6
Marajó (isl.), Braz., 33/K4
Marañón (riv.), Peru, 32/E5
Maraş, Turkey, 74/C2
Marathon, Ont., 24/H6
March (riv.), Austria, 48/D2
Mar del Plata, Arg., 34/J11
Marfa, Tex., 19/G7
Margarita (isl.), Ven., 32/H1
Marianao, Cuba, 28/A2
Marianas, Northern (isls.), 88/E4
Marianna, Ark., 19/L6
Marianna, Fla., 21/M7
Maria van Diemen (cape), N.Z., 94/D1
Maribor, Yugo., 56/B2
Maricourt, Que., 25/J3
Marie Byrd Land, Antarc., 35/B8-9
Marie-Galante (isl.), Guad., 29/G4
Mariehamn, Fin., 39/M7
Mariental, Namibia, 86/B4
Marietta, Ga., 21/M6
Marietta, Ohio, 20/N5
Marinette, Wis., 18/L3
Marion, Ill., 18/L5
Marion, Ind., 20/M4
Marion, Kans., 18/J5
Marion, Ohio, 20/N4
Marion, S.C., 21/O6
Maritime Alps (mts.), Europe, 44/G5
Marken (isls.), Neth., 42/G4
Marlin, Tex., 19/J7
Marmara (sea), Turkey, 74/A1
Marne (riv.), France, 44/E3
Maroni (riv.), Fr. Guiana, 32/J2
Maroua, Cameroon, 84/B1
Marovoay, Madag., 87/H3
Marquesas (isls.), Fr. Poly., 89/N6
Marquette, Mich., 20/M3
Marrakech, Mor., 82/C2
Marsabit, Kenya, 85/G3
Marsa el Brega, Libya, 80/D1
Marseille, France, 44/F6
Marshall, Lib., 83/B7
Marshall, Minn., 18/K3
Marshall, Mo., 18/K5
Marshall, Tex., 19/K6
Marshall Is., 88/G4
Marshalltown, Iowa, 18/K4
Marshfield, Wis., 18/L3
Martha's Vineyard (isl.), Mass., 15/M2
Martinique, 29/G4
Martinsburg, W. Va., 20/O5
Martinsville, Va., 21/N5
Mary, U.S.S.R., 58/G6
Maryland (state), U.S., 15/L3
Marysville, Calif., 16/C5
Marysville, Kans., 18/J5
Maryville, Mo., 18/K4
Maryville, N. Dak., 18/K3
Maryville, Tenn., 21/M6
Masaya, Nic., 27/C3
Masbate (isl.), Phil., 71/G3
Mascara, Alg., 82/D1
Mascarene (isls.), Afr., see map p. 87

Maseru (cap.), Lesotho, **86/D5**
Mashonaland (reg.), Zim., **86/E3**
Masindi, Uganda, **84/F3**
Masira (isl.), Oman, **75/G5**
Mason City, Iowa, **18/K4**
Massa, Italy, **54/C2**
Massachusetts (state), U.S., **15/M2**
Massawa, Eth., **81/G4**
Massena, N.Y., **20/P3**
Massillon, Ohio, **20/N4**
Masterton, N.Z., **94/E4**
Matadi, Zaire, **84/B5**
Matagalpa, Nic., **27/C2**
Matamoros, Mex., **26/F3**
Matabeleland (reg.), Zim., **86/D3**
Matanzas, Cuba, **28/B2**
Matapan (cape), Greece, **57/F7**
Matara, Sri Lanka, **73/E7**
Matarani, Peru, **32/F7**
Mata Utu (cap.), Wallis & Futuna, **88/J7**
Mato Grosso (plat.), Braz., **32/K7**
Matrah, Oman, **75/G5**
Matsu (isl.), China, *see Mazu*
Matsumoto, Japan, **67/H5**
Mattawa, Ont., **25/J6**
Matterhorn (mt.), Switz., **50/C3**
Mattoon, Ill., **18/L5**
Maturín, Ven., **32/H2**
Maui (isl.), Hawaii, **23/E4**
Mauna Kea (mt.), Hawaii, **23/F4**
Mauna Loa (mt.), Hawaii, **23/F4**
Maunawili, Hawaii, **23/C4**
Mauritania, **82/B5**
Mauritius, *see map p. 87*
May (cape), N.J., **20/P5**
Mayaguana (isl.), Bah., **28/D2**
Mayagüez, P. Rico, *see detailed map p. 29*
Mayfield, Ky., **19/L5**
Mayo, Yukon, **24/C3**
Mayotte (isl.), Comoros, **87/G2**
Maysville, Ky., **20/M5**
Mazagan (El Jadida), Mor., **82/C2**
Mazar-e Sharif, Afghan., **75/J2**
Mazaruni (riv.), Guyana, **32/H2**
Mazatlán, Mex., **26/C3**
Mazu (Matsu) (isl.), China, **65/K6**
Mbabane (cap.), Swaz., **86/E5**
Mbale, Uganda, **84/F3**
Mbandaka, Zaire, **84/C5**
Mbanza Congo, Angola, **84/B5**
Mbarara, Uganda, **84/F4**
Mbeya, Tanz., **84/F5**
Mbinda, Congo, **84/B4**
M'Bour, Sen., **82/A4**
M'Bout, Maur., **82/B5**
Mbuji-Mayi, Zaire, **84/D5**
McAlester, Okla., **19/K6**
McAllen, Tex., **19/J8**
McCamey, Tex., **19/H7**
McComb, Miss., **21/L7**
McConaughy (lake), Nebr., **18/H4**
McDonald (isls.), Austr., **9/N8**
McKeesport, Pa., **20/N4**
McKinley (mt.), Alaska, **22/E3**
M'Clintock (chan.), N.W.T., **24/F1**
M'Clure (isl.), N.W.T., **24/E1**
M'Clure (str.), N.W.T., **24/E1**
McMinnville, Oreg., **16/C3**
McMinnville, Tenn., **21/M6**
McPherson, Kans., **18/J5**
Mead (lake), U.S., **17/E5**
Meade, Kans., **18/H5**
Meadville, Pa., **20/O4**
Mecca, Saudi Arabia, **74/C5**
Mecklenburg (reg.), E. Ger., **47/E2**
Medan, Indon., **70/B5**
Médéa, Alg., **82/E1**
Medellín, Col., **32/E2**
Medford, Oreg., **16/C4**
Medicine Bow (range), Wyo., **16/G4**
Medicine Hat, Alta., **24/E5**
Medicine Lodge, Kans., **18/J5**
Medina, Saudi Arabia, **74/C5**
Mediterranean (sea), **8-9/K4**
Médoc (reg.), France, **44/C5**
Médenine, Tun., **82/F2**
Meeker, Colo., **16/F4**
Meerut, India, **72/D3**
Megiddo, Isr., **76/C2**
Meiningen, E. Ger., **47/D3**
Meissen, E. Ger., **47/E3**
Meknès, Mor., **82/C2**
Mekong (riv.), Asia, **68/E4**
Melaka, Malaysia, **68/D7**
Melanesia (reg.), Pacific, **88/E-H 5-8**
Melbourne, Austr., **92/C5**
Melbourne, Fla., **21/N7**
Melfort, Sask., **24/F5**
Melilla, Spain, **82/D1**
Melrose, Scot., **40/E3**
Melville (isl.), Austr., **91/D2**
Melville (lake), Newf., **25/L6**
Melville (isl.), N.W.T., **25/M3**
Melville (pen.), N.W.T., **24/H2**
Melville, Sask., **24/F5**
Memphis (ruins), Egypt, **81/F2**
Memphis, Tenn., **19/L6**
Menard, Tex., **19/J7**
Mendocino (cape), Calif., **16/B4**
Mendoza, Arg., **34/G10**

Menominee, Mich., **20/L3**
Menomonie, Wis., **18/L3**
Menongue, Angola, **84/C6**
Menton, France, **44/G6**
Menzel Bourguiba, Tun., **82/F1**
Merced, Calif., **16/C5**
Mercedes, Tex., **19/J8**
Mercedes, Urug., **34/J10**
Mérida, Mex., **26/G4**
Mérida, Spain, **53/C3**
Mérida, Ven., **32/F2**
Meridian, Miss., **21/L6**
Meroe (ruins), Sudan, **81/F4**
Merowe, Sudan, **81/F4**
Merrill, Wis., **18/L3**
Mersa Matrûh, Egypt, **81/E1**
Mersey (riv.), Eng., **41/E4**
Merthyr Tydfil, Wales, **41/E5**
Mesa, Ariz., **17/F6**
Mesa Verde Nat'l Pk., Colo., **17/F5**
Meshed, Iran, **74/H2**
Mesolóngion, Greece, **57/E6**
Mesopotamia (reg.), Iraq, **74/D-E3**
Messina, Italy, **54/E5**
Metairie, La., **15/H4**
Metlakatla, Alaska, **22/F4**
Metz, France, **44/G3**
Meuse (riv.), Europe, **44/F3**
Mexia, Tex., **19/J7**
Mexicali, Mex., **26/A1**
Mexico, **26**
Mexico, Mo., **18/L5**
Mexico (gulf), N. Amer., **13/K7**
Mexico (city) (cap.), Mex., **26/E4**
Miami, Fla., **21/N8**
Miami, Okla., **19/K5**
Miami Beach, Fla., **21/O8**
Michigan (lake), U.S., **15/J3**
Michigan (state), U.S., **15/J2**
Micronesia (reg.), Pacific, **88/E-H 4-6**
Middlebury, Vt., **20/P3**
Middlesboro, Ky., **21/M5**
Middletown, Ohio, **20/M5**
Midland, Mich., **20/M4**
Midland, Tex., **19/H6**
Midway (isls.), Pacific, **89/J3**
Mikkeli, Fin., **39/P6**
Míkonos (isl.), Greece, **57/G7**
Mikumi Nat'l Pk., Tanz., **85/G5**
Milan, Italy, **54/B2**
Mildura, Austr., **92/A4**
Miles City, Mont., **18/F3**
Milford, Del., **20/P5**
Milledgeville, Ga., **21/N6**
Mille Lacs (lake), Minn., **18/K3**
Millen, Ga., **21/N6**
Miller, S. Dak., **18/J3**
Millinocket, Maine, **20/R3**
Millville, N.J., **20/P5**
Milwaukee, Wis., **18/M4**
Milwaukie, Oreg., **16/C3**
Minas, Urug., **34/K10**
Minas Gerais (state), Braz., **32/L-M7**
Mindanao (isl.), Phil., **71/H4**
Mindelo, Cape Verde, **82/A7**
Minden, La., **19/K6**
Minden, Nebr., **18/J4**
Mindoro (isl.), Phil., **71/G3**
Mineola, Tex., **19/K6**
Mineral del Monte, Mex., **26/E4**
Mineral Wells, Tex., **19/J6**
Mingan, Que., **25/K5**
Minho (riv.), Port., **52/B2**
Minneapolis, Minn., **18/K3**
Minnesota (riv.), Minn., **15/H2**
Minnesota (state), U.S., **15/H1**
Miño (riv.), Spain, **52/B1**
Minorca (isl.), Spain, **53/J2**
Minot, N. Dak., **18/H2**
Minsk, U.S.S.R., **60/C4**
Minya Konka (mt.), China, *see Gongga Shan*
Mirim (lagoon), S. Amer., **34/K10**
Mirtóön (sea), Greece, **57/F7**
Mishawaka, Ind., **20/M4**
Miskolc, Hung., **49/F2**
Missinaibi (riv.), Ont., **24/H6**
Mission, Tex., **19/J8**
Mississippi (delta), U.S., **15/J5**
Mississippi (riv.), U.S., **15/H4**
Mississippi (state), U.S., **15/H4**
Missoula, Mont., **16/E3**
Missouri (riv.), U.S., **15/G2**
Missouri (state), U.S., **15/H3**
Mistassini (lake), Que., **25/J5**
Misti, El (mt.), Peru, **32/F7**
Misurata, Libya, **80/C1**
Mitchell (mt.), N.C., **21/N6**
Mitchell, S. Dak., **18/J4**
Mitilíni, Greece, **57/H6**
Mitla (ruin), Mex., **26/F5**
Mitsamíouli, Comoros, **87/G2**
Mittenwald, W. Ger., **47/D5**
Miyazaki, Japan, **66/E8**
Moab, Utah, **17/F5**
Moberly, Mo., **18/K5**
Mobile, Ala., **21/M7**
Mobile (bay), N. Amer., **15/J4-5**
Mobutu Sese Seko (lake), Afr., **84/F3**
Moçâmbique, Moz., **86/G3**

Moçâmedes, Angola, **84/B7**
Modena, Italy, **54/C2**
Modesto, Calif., **16/C5**
Mogadishu (Muqdisho) (cap.), Somalia, **85/J3**
Mogador (Essaouira), Mor., **82/B2**
Mogilev, U.S.S.R., **60/C4**
Mohács, Hung., **49/E3**
Mohaleshoek, Les., **86/D6**
Mohammedia, Mor., **80/C2**
Mohéli (isl.), Comoros, **87/G2**
Mojave (des.), Calif., **16/D6**
Mokapu, Hawaii, **23/C4**
Moknine, Tun., **82/G1**
Mokp'o, S. Korea, **66/C6**
Moldau (Vltava) (riv.), Czech., **48/C2**
Moldavian S.S.R., U.S.S.R., **60/C5**
Molepolole, Bots., **86/C4**
Moline, Ill., **18/L4**
Mollendo, Peru, **32/F7**
Molokai (isl.), Hawaii, **23/D2**
Moluccas (isls.), Indon., **71/H5-7**
Mombasa, Kenya, **85/G4**
Mona (passage), W. Indies, **28/E3**
Monaco, **44/G6**
Monaghan, Ire., **41/C3**
Monahans, Tex., **19/H7**
Monastir, Tun., **82/G1**
Mönchengladbach, W. Ger., **47/B3**
Monclova, Mex., **26/E2**
Moncton, N. Br., **25/K6**
Monett, Mo., **19/K5**
Mongalla, Sudan, **81/F6**
Mongolia, **65/B-J2**
Monmouth, Ill., **18/L4**
Monmouth, Wales, **41/E5**
Monroe, La., **19/L6**
Monroe, N.C., **21/N6**
Monrovia (cap.), Lib., **83/B7**
Mons, Belg., **43/D8**
Montana (state), U.S., **14/E1**
Montaña, La (reg.), Peru, **32/F5-6**
Mont Cenis (tunnel), Europe, **44/G5**
Monte Carlo, Monaco, **44/G6**
Montecristi, Dom. Rep., **28/D3**
Montecristo (isl.), Italy, **54/C3**
Montego Bay, Jam., **28/B3**
Montenegro (rep.), Yugo., **56/D4**
Monterey, Calif., **17/C5**
Monterey (bay), Calif., **16/C5**
Monterrey, Mex., **26/E2**
Montevideo, Minn., **18/J3**
Montevideo (cap.), Urug., **34/J11**
Montgomery (cap.), Ala., **21/M6**
Monticello, Ark., **19/L6**
Mont-Joli, Que., **25/K6**
Mont-Laurier, Que., **25/J6**
Montpelier, Idaho, **16/F4**
Montpelier (cap.), Vt., **20/P3**
Montpellier, France, **44/E6**
Montréal, Que., **25/J6**
Montreux, Switz., **50/C2**
Montrose, Colo., **17/F5**
Mont-St-Michel, France, **44/C3**
Montserrat, **29/G3**
Moorabbin, Austr., **92/J5**
Moorea (isl.), Fr. Poly., **89/S13**
Moorehead, Minn., **18/J3**
Moosehead (lake), Maine, **20/R3**
Moose Jaw, Sask., **24/F5**
Moosomin, Sask., **24/F5**
Moosonee, Ont., **25/H5**
Mopti, Mali, **82/D6**
Moradabad, India, **72/D3**
Moratuwa, Sri Lanka, **74/D7**
Morava (riv.), Czech., **48/D2**
Morava (riv.), Yugo., **56/E3**
Moray (firth), Scot., **40/E2**
Morehead City, N.C., **21/O6**
Morelia, Mex., **26/E4**
Morena, Sierra (mts.), Spain, **53/E3**
Morenci, Ariz., **17/F6**
Morgan City, La., **19/L7**
Morgantown, W. Va., **20/N5**
Moro (gulf), Phil., **71/G4**
Morocco, **82/C2**
Morogoro, Tanz., **85/G5**
Moroni (cap.), Comoros, **87/G2**
Morrilton, Ark., **19/K6**
Morris, Minn., **18/K3**
Moscow, Idaho, **16/D3**
Moscow (cap.), U.S.S.R., **60/E3**
Mosel (riv.), Europe, **47/B3**
Moselle (riv.), France, **44/G3**
Moses Lake, Wash., **16/D3**
Moshi, Tanz., **85/G4**
Mosi-Oa-Tunya (falls), Afr., **84/E7**
Moskva, U.S.S.R., *see Moscow*
Moss, Nor., **39/G7**
Mossaka, Congo, **84/C4**
Mossel Bay, S. Africa, **86/C6**
Mossendjo, Congo, **84/B4**
Mostaganem, Alg., **82/D1**
Mosul, Iraq, **74/D2**
Moulmein, Burma, **68/C3**
Moultrie, Ga., **21/N7**
Moundou, Chad, **80/C6**
Moundsville, W. Va., **20/N5**
Mountainair, N. Mex., **17/G6**
Mountain Home, Ark., **19/K5**
Mountain Home, Idaho, **16/E4**

Mountainview, Hawaii, **23/F4**
Mountain Village, Alaska, **22/C3**
Mountain Zebra Nat'l Pk., S. Africa, **86/C6**
Mount Airy, N.C., **21/N5**
Mount Carmel, Ill., **18/L5**
Mount Isa, Austr., **91/F4**
Mount Pleasant, Mich., **20/M4**
Mount Pleasant, Tex., **19/K6**
Mount Rainier Nat'l Pk., Wash., **16/C3**
Mount Shasta, Calif., **16/C4**
Mount Sterling, Ky., **20/N5**
Mount Vernon, Ill., **18/L5**
Mount Vernon, Ohio, **20/N4**
Mount Vernon, Wash., **16/C2**
Mozambique, **86/E-F 2-4**
Mozambique (chan.), Afr., **86/F-G3**
Mtwara-Mikindani, Tanz., **85/H6**
Muang Khammoun, Laos, **68/E3**
Muang Xaignabouri, Laos, **68/D3**
Mufulira, Zambia, **84/E6**
Muğla, Turkey, **74/A2**
Mühlhausen (Thomas-Müntzer-Stadt), E. Ger., **47/D3**
Mukalla, P.D.R. Yemen, **74/E7**
Mukden, China, *see Shenyang*
Mulhacén (mt.), Spain, **53/E4**
Mülheim, W. Ger., **47/B3**
Mulhouse, France, **44/G4**
Mull (isl.), Scot., **40/D2**
Mullingar, Ire., **41/C4**
Multan, Pak., **75/K3**
München, W. Ger., *see Munich*
Muncie, Ind., **20/M4**
Münden, W. Ger., **47/C3**
Munich, W. Ger., **47/D4**
Munising, Mich., **20/M3**
Münster, W. Ger., **47/B3**
Muonio (riv.), Europe, **39/M1**
Muqdisho (cap.), Somalia, **85/J3**
Mur (Mura) (riv.), Europe, **48/B2**
Murchison (falls), Uganda, **84/F3**
Murcia, Spain, **53/F4**
Mureş (riv.), Rom., **56/E2**
Murfreesboro, Tenn., **21/M6**
Murmansk, U.S.S.R., **60/D1**
Murray (riv.), Austr., **91/G6**
Murray, Ky., **21/L5**
Murray, Utah, **16/F4**
Murrumbidgee (riv.), Austr., **92/C4**
Murwillumbah, Austr., **92/G1**
Murzuk, Libya, **80/B2**
Muş, Turkey, **74/D2**
Musala (mt.), Bulg., **56/F4**
Musandam, Ras (cape), Oman, **75/G4**
Muscat (cap.), Oman, **75/G5**
Muscat and Oman, *see Oman*
Muscatine, Iowa, **18/L4**
Musgrave (ranges), Austr., **91/E5**
Mushandike Nat'l Pk., Zim., **86/D4**
Muskegon, Mich., **20/M4**
Muskegon Hts., Mich., **20/M4**
Muskogee, Okla., **19/K6**
Musoma, Tanz., **84/F4**
Musselshell (riv.), Mont., **16/F3**
Muzaffarabad, Pak., **72/C2**
Muzaffarpur, India, **72/E3**
Muztag (mt.), China, **65/B4**
Muztagata (mt.), China, **65/A4**
Mwanza, Tanz., **84/F4**
Mweru (lake), Afr., **79/E5**
Myitkyina, Burma, **68/C1**
Myrtle Beach, S.C., **21/O6**
Mysore, India, **72/D6**
My Tho, Viet., **68/E5**

N

Naas, Ire., **41/C4**
Nablus (Nabulus), West Bank, **76/C3**
Nacogdoches, Tex., **19/K7**
Nadi, Fiji, **89/P10**
Naganol Japan, **67/J5**
Nagaoka, Japan, **67/J5**
Nagasaki, Japan, **66/D7**
Nagishot, Sudan, **81/F7**
Nagoya, Japan, **67/H6**
Nagpur, India, **72/D4**
Nagykanizsa, Hung., **49/D3**
Naha, Japan, **67/N6**
Nahariyya, Isr., **76/C1**
Nahuel Huapi (lake), Arg., **34/F12**
Nairn, Scot., **40/E2**
Nairobi (cap.), Kenya, **85/G4**
Naivasha, Kenya, **85/G4**
Najin, N. Korea, **66/E2**
Nakhichevan', U.S.S.R., **60/F7**
Nakhon Ratchasima, Thai., **68/D4**
Nakhon Si Thammarat, Thai., **68/D5**
Nakina, Ont., **24/H5**
Nakon Sawan, Thai., **68/D4**
Nakskov, Den., **39/G9**
Nakuru, Kenya, **85/G4**
Namangan, U.S.S.R., **58/H5**
Nam Dinh, Viet., **68/E2**
Namib (des.), Namibia, **86/A3-4**

Namibia, **86/B4**
Nampa, Idaho, **16/D4**
Nampula, Moz., **86/F3**
Namsos, Nor., **39/G4**
Namur, Belg., **43/F7**
Nanaimo, Br. Col., **24/D6**
Nanakuli, Hawaii, **23/B4**
Nanchang, China, **65/H6**
Nancy, France, **44/G3**
Nanda Devi (mt.), India, **72/D2**
Nanga Parbat (mt.), Pak., **72/D1**
Nanjing (Nanking), China, **65/J5**
Nanning, China, **65/G7**
Nan Shan (mts.), China, *see Qilian Shan*
Nanterre, France, **44/A1**
Nantes, France, **44/C4**
Nantucket (isl.), Mass., **20/R4**
Nanyuki, Kenya, **85/G3**
Napa, Calif., **16/C5**
Napier, N.Z., **94/F3**
Naples, Fla., **21/N8**
Naples, Italy, **54/E4**
Napoleon, N. Dak., **18/J3**
Nara, Japan, **67/J8**
Narayanganj, Bang., **72/G4**
Narbonne, France, **44/E6**
Narmada (riv.), India, **72/D4**
Nasca, Peru, **32/F6**
Nashua, N.H., **20/R4**
Nashville (cap.), Tenn., **21/M5**
Nasirabad, Bang., **72/G4**
Nassau (cap.), Bah., **28/C1**
Nàssjö, Sweden, **39/J8**
Natal, Braz., **33/O5**
Natal (prov.), S. Africa, **86/E5**
Natashquan (riv.), Can., **25/K5**
Natchez, Miss., **21/L7**
Natchitoches, La., **19/K7**
National City, Calif., **16/D6**
Natitingou, Benin, **83/E6**
Nauru, **88/G6**
Navarin (cape), U.S.S.R., **59/T3**
Navojoa, Mex., **26/C2**
Nawabganj, Bang., **72/G4**
Náxos (isl.), Greece, **57/G7**
Nazaré, Braz., **33/N6**
Nazareth, Isr., **76/C2**
Nazret, Eth., **81/G6**
Ndalatando, Angola, **84/B5**
N'Djamena (cap.), Chad, **80/C5**
Ndola, Zambia, **84/E6**
Neagh (lake), N. Ire., **40/C3**
Near (isls.), Alaska, **22/D4**
Nebo (mt.), Jordan, **76/D4**
Nebraska (state), U.S., **15/G2**
Nebraska City, Nebr., **18/J4**
Neckar (riv.), W. Ger., **47/C4**
Needles, Calif., **16/E6**
Neenah, Wis., **18/L3**
Nefud (des.), Saudi Arabia, **74/C-D4**
Negev (reg.), Isr., **76/B6**
Negombo, Sri Lanka, **73/D7**
Negro (riv.), S. Amer., **32/H4**
Negros (isl.), Phil., **71/G4**
Neiva, Col., **32/F3**
Nejd (reg.), Saudi Arabia, **74/C-E 4-5**
Neligh, Nebr., **18/J4**
Nelson, Br. Col., **24/E6**
Nelson (riv.), Man., **24/G5**
Nelson, N.Z., **94/D4**
Nenagh, Ire., **41/B4**
Nenana, Alaska, **22/E3**
Neosho, Mo., **19/K5**
Nepal, **72/E3**
Nephi, Utah, **16/F5**
Ness (lake), Scot., **40/D2**
Netanya, Isr., **76/B3**
Netherlands, **42**
Netherlands Antilles, **28/E4, F3**
Nettilling (lake), N.W.T., **25/J2**
Neubrandenburg, E. Ger., **47/E2**
Neuchâtel, Switz., **50/B2**
Neuilly, France, **44/B1**
Neumünster, W. Ger., **47/C1**
Neuquén, Arg., **34/G11**
Neuse (riv.), N.C., **21/O6**
Neusiedler (lake), Europe, **48/D3**
Neuss, W. Ger., **47/B3**
Neustadt an der Weinstrasse, W. Ger., **47/B4**
Neu-Ulm, W. Ger., **47/D4**
Nevada, Mo., **18/K5**
Nevada (state), U.S., **14/C3**
Nevada, Sierra (mts.), Spain, **53/E4**
Nevada, Sierra (mts.), U.S., **16/C-D5**
Nevers, France, **44/E4**
Nevis (isl.), St. Chris.-Nevis, **29/F3**
New Albany, Ind., **20/M5**
New Amsterdam, Guyana, **32/J2**
Newark, Eng., **41/F4**
Newark, N.J., **20/O4**
Newark, N.Y., **20/O4**
Newark, Ohio, **20/N4**
New Bedford, Mass., **20/R4**
New Bern, N.C., **21/O6**
Newberry, S.C., **21/N6**
New Braunfels, Tex., **19/J7**
New Britain (isl.), Papua N.G., **89/B2**

New Brunswick (prov.), Can., **25/K6**
Newburgh, N.Y., **20/P4**
New Caledonia, **89/G4**
Newcastle, Austr., **92/F3**
Newcastle, Eng., **41/E4**
Newcastle, N. Br., **25/K7**
Newcastle, N. Ire., **40/D3**
New Castle, Pa., **20/N4**
Newcastle upon Tyne, Eng., **41/E3**
New Delhi (cap.), India, **72/D3**
Newfoundland (prov.), Can., **25/K-L 5-6**
Newfoundland (isl.), Newf., **25/L6**
New Georgia (isl.), Sol. Is., **89/F6**
New Guinea (isl.), Pacific, **88/D-E6**
New Hampshire (state), U.S., **15/M2**
New Haven, Conn., **20/P4**
New Hebrides (isls.), Pacific, *see Vanuatu*
New Iberia, La., **19/L7**
New Ireland (isl.), Papua N.G., **89/B1**
New Jersey (state), U.S., **15/M2**
New London, Conn., **15/M2**
New Madrid, Mo., **19/L5**
New Mexico (state), U.S., **14/E4**
Newnan, Ga., **21/M6**
New Orleans, La., **19/L7**
New Plymouth, N.Z., **94/D3**
Newport, Ark., **19/L6**
Newport, Ky., **21/M5**
Newport, Oreg., **16/B3**
Newport, Vt., **20/P3**
Newport, Wales, **41/E5**
Newport News, Va., **20/P5**
New Providence (isl.), Bah., **28/C1**
Newry, N. Ire., **40/C3**
New Siberian (isls.), U.S.S.R., **59/P2**
New Smyrna Beach, Fla., **21/N7**
New South Wales (state), Austr., **92**
Newton, Iowa, **18/K4**
Newton, Kans., **18/J5**
New Ulm, Minn., **18/K4**
New Westminster, Br. Col., **24/D6**
New York, N.Y., **20/P4**
New York (state), U.S., **15/L2**
New Zealand, **94**
Neyshabur, Iran, **74/H2**
Ngami (lake), Bots., **86/C4**
N'Gaoundéré, Cameroon, **84/B2**
Ngorongoro (crater), Tanz., **84/F4**
N'Guigmi, Niger, **82/B4**
Ngunza, Angola, **84/B6**
Nha Trang, Viet., **68/F4**
Niafunké, Mali, **82/D5**
Niagara Falls, N.Y., **20/O4**
Niagara Falls, Ont., **25/J7**
Niamey (cap.), Niger, **82/E6**
Nias (isl.), Indon., **71/B5**
Nicaragua, **27/C2**
Nice, France, **44/G6**
Nicobar (isls.), India, **72/G7**
Nicosia (cap.), Cyprus, **74/B2**
Nicoya (gulf), C. Rica, **27/C3**
Nieuw-Nickerie, Sur., **32/J2**
Niğde, Turkey, **74/B2**
Niger, **82/F-G5**
Niger (riv.), Afr., **83/F7**
Nigeria, **83/F6**
Niğrlta, Greece, **57/F5**
Niigata, Japan, **67/J5**
Niihau (isl.), Hawaii, **23/A2**
Nijmegen, Neth., **42/H5**
Nikolayev, U.S.S.R., **60/D5**
Nile (riv.), Afr., **79/F2**
Niles, Mich., **20/M4**
Nîmes, France, **44/F6**
Ningbo (Ningpo), China, **65/K6**
Ningsia, China, *see Yinchuan*
Niobrara (riv.), U.S., **15/F2**
Nioro, Mali, **82/B5**
Nioro-du-Rip, Sen., **83/A6**
Niort, France, **44/C4**
Nipigon, Ont., **24/H7**
Nipigon (lake), Ont., **24/H7**
Niš, Yugo., **56/E4**
Nishinomiya, Japan, **67/H8**
Niterói, Braz., **34/M8**
Niuafo'ou (isl.), Tonga, **88/J7**
Niue, **88/K7**
Nizhniy Tagil, U.S.S.R., **58/G4**
Nkayi, Congo, **84/B4**
Nkhotakota, Malawi, **84/F6**
Nkongsamba, Cameroon, **84/B3**
Noatak, Alaska, **22/C2**
Nogales, Ariz., **17/F7**
Nome, Alaska, **22/C3**
Nondalton, Alaska, **22/D3**
Noorvik, Alaska, **22/C2**
Noranda, Que., **25/J7**
Nordhausen, E. Ger., **47/D3**
Nordkapp (cape), Nor., **39/P1**
Nordkinn (cape), Nor., **39/Q1**
Nord-Ostsee (canal), W. Ger., **47/C1**
Norfolk, Nebr., **18/J4**
Norfolk, Va., **20/P5**
Norfolk I. (terr.), Austr., **88/G8**
Noril'sk, U.S.S.R., **58/J3**

Norman, Okla., **19**/J6
Norman Wells, N.W.T., **24**/D2
Norrköping, Sweden, **39**/K7
Norrtälje, Sweden, **39**/L7
North (slope), Alaska, **22**/C-D1
North (sea), Europe, **37**/E3
North (isl.), N.Z., **94**/F1
North (Nordkapp) (cape), Nor., **39**/P1
North (chan.), U.K., **41**/D3
North Adams, Mass., **20**/P4
Northampton, Eng., **41**/F4
North Battleford, Sask., **24**/F5
North Bay, Ont., **25**/J7
North Bend, Oreg., **16**/B4
North Carolina (state), U.S., **15**/L3
North Cascades Nat'l Pk., Wash., **14**/B1
North Dakota (state), U.S., **15**/G1
Northern Dvina (riv.), U.S.S.R., **60**/F2
Northern Ireland, **40**/C3
Northern Territory, Austr., **91**/E-F 3-4
Northfield, Minn., **18**/K3
North Frisian (isls.), Europe, **46**/C1
North Korea, **66**/D3-4
North Little Rock, Ark., **19**/L6
North Magnetic Pole, N.W.T., **96**/B1
North Miami, Fla., **21**/O8
North Platte, Nebr., **18**/H4
North Platte (riv.), U.S., **14**/F2
North Pole, **96**
North Saskatchewan (riv.) Can., **24**/F5
North Vancouver, Br. Col., **24**/D6
North West (cape), Austr., **91**/A4
Northwest Territories, Can., **24-25**/C-K 2-3
Norton (sound), Alaska, **22**/C3
Norway, **39**
Norway House, Man., **24**/G5
Norwegian (sea), Europe, **37**/D-E2
Norwich, Eng., **41**/G4
Nosy Be (isl.), Madag., **87**/H2
Nosy Boraha (isl.), Madag., **87**/J3
Nottingham, Eng., **41**/F4
Nouadhibou, Maur., **82**/A4
Nouakchott (cap.), Maur., **82**/A5
Nouméa (cap.), New Cal., **89**/H5
Nova Lisboa, Angola, *see Huambo*
Novara, Italy, **54**/B2
Nova Scotia (prov.), Can., **25**/K7
Novaya Zemlya (isls.), U.S.S.R., **60**/H1
Novgorod, U.S.S.R., **60**/D3
Novo Redondo, Angola, *see Ngunza*
Novorossiysk, U.S.S.R., **60**/E6
Novosibirsk, U.S.S.R., **58**/J4
Nowra, Austr., **92**/F4
Nsawam, Ghana, **83**/D7
Nubia (lake), Sudan, **81**/F3
Nueces (riv.), Tex., **15**/G5
Nueltin (lake), N.W.T., **24**/G3
Nueva San Salvador, El Sal., **27**/B2
Nuevo Laredo, Mex., **26**/E2
Nûk (cap.), Greenl., **96**/C8
Nuku'alofa (cap.), Tonga, **88**/J8
Nunivak (isl.), Alaska, **22**/C4
Nuremberg (Nürnberg), W. Ger., **47**/D4
Nutak, Newf., **25**/K4
Nyala, Sudan, **81**/E5
Nyasa (lake), Afr., **84**/F6
Nyasaland, *see Malawi*
Nyborg, Den., **39**/G9
Nykobing, Den., **39**/H9
Nyköping, Sweden, **39**/K7
N'Zérékoré, Guinea, **83**/C7

O

Oahe (lake), U.S., **18**/H3
Oahu (isl.), Hawaii, **23**/B3
Oakland, Calif., **16**/C5
Oak Ridge, Tenn., **21**/M5
Oamaru, N.Z., **94**/C6
Oaxaca, Mex., **26**/F5
Ob' (riv.), U.S.S.R., **58**/G3
Oba, Ont., **24**/H6
Oban, Scot., **40**/D2
Oberammergau, W. Ger., **47**/D5
Oberhausen, W. Ger. **47**/B3
Oberlin, Kans., **18**/H5
Óbidos, Braz., **32**/J4
Obuasi, Ghana, **83**/D7
Ocala, Fla., **21**/N7
Ocean (Banaba) (isl.), Kiribati, **88**/G6
Oceanside, Calif., **16**/C6
Oconto, Wis., **18**/L3
Ocumare, Ven., **32**/G1
Odense, Den., **39**/G9
Odenwald (for.), W. Ger., **47**/C4
Oder (riv.), Europe, **47**/L5
Odessa, Tex., **19**/H7
Odessa, U.S.S.R., **60**/D5

Odongk, Camb., **68**/E5
Oelwein, Iowa, **18**/L4
Offenbach am Main, W. Ger., **47**/C3
Offenburg, W. Ger., **47**/B4
Ogaden (reg.), Eth., **81**/H6
Ogallala, Nebr., **18**/H4
Ogbomosho, Nigeria, **83**/E7
Ogden, Utah, **16**/E4
Ogdensburg, N.Y., **20**/P3
O'Higgins (lake), Chile, **34**/F13
Ohio (riv.), U.S., **15**/K3
Ohio (state), U.S., **15**/K2
Ohrid (lake), Europe, **56**/E5
Oil City, Pa., **20**/O4
Oildale, Calif., **16**/D6
Oise (riv.), France, **44**/E3
Oita, Japan, **67**/E7
Ojos del Salado (mt.), S. Amer., **34**/G9
Okanagan (lake), Br. Col., **24**/D6
Okayama, Japan, **67**/F6
Okeechobee (lake), Fla., **21**/N8
Okhotsk (sea), U.S.S.R., **59**/P4
Okinawa (state), U.S., **15**/K3
Oklahoma (state), U.S., **15**/G3
Oklahoma City (cap.), Okla., **19**/J6
Okmulgee, Okla., **19**/J6
Okovanggo (riv.), Afr., **86**/C3
Öland (isl.), Sweden, **39**/K8
Olbia, Italy, **54**/B4
Oldenburg, W. Ger., **47**/C2
Old Town, Maine, **20**/R3
Olduvai (gorge), Tanz., **85**/G4
Olean, N.Y., **20**/O4
Olenek (riv.), U.S.S.R., **59**/M3
Olinda, Braz., **33**/N5
Olives (mt.), Isr., *see detailed map p. 76*
Olney, Ill., **18**/L5
Olomouc, Czech., **48**/D2
Olsztyn, Pol., **51**/E2
Olt (riv.), Rom., **56**/F3
Olten, Switz., **50**/C1
Olympia (cap.), Wash., **16**/C3
Olympic (mts.), Wash., **16**/C3
Olympic Nat'l Pk., Wash., **16**/B3
Olympus (mt.), Greece, **57**/F5
Omagh, N. Ire., **40**/C3
Omaha (beach), France, **44**/C3
Omaha, Nebr., **18**/J4
Oman, **75**/G4-6
Oman (gulf), Asia, **75**/G5
Omdurman, Sudan, **81**/F4
Omsk, U.S.S.R., **58**/H4
Omuta, Japan, **66**/E7
Ondangua, Namibia, **86**/B3
Onega (lake), U.S.S.R., **60**/E2
Oneida, N.Y., **20**/P4
Oneonta, N.Y., **20**/P4
Onitsha, Nigeria, **83**/F7
Onon, Mong., **65**/H2
Onslow, Austr., **91**/B4
Ontario (prov.), Can., **24**/G-H5
Ontario (lake), N. Amer., **15**/L2
Ontario, Oreg., **16**/D3
Ontonagon, Mich., **20**/L3
Ontong Java (atoll), Sol. Is., **88**/G6
Ootacamund, India, **72**/D6
Opava, Czech., **48**/E2
Opelika, Ala., **21**/M6
Opelousas, La., **19**/L7
Opole, Pol., **51**/C3
Oporto (Porto), Port., **52**/B2
Opp, Ala., **21**/M6
Oradea, Rom., **56**/E2
Oran, Alg., **82**/D1
Orange (riv.), Afr., **86**/B5
Orange, Austr., **92**/E3
Orange, France, **44**/F5
Orange, Tex., **19**/K7
Orangeburg, S.C., **21**/N6
Orange Free State (prov.), S. Africa, **86**/D5
Orange Walk, Belize, **27**/B1
Oranjemund, Namibia, **86**/B5
Oranjestad, Neth. Ant., **28**/D4
Orava (riv.), Czech., **48**/E2
Ord (riv.), Austr., **91**/D3
Ord, Nebr., **18**/J4
Ordos (reg.), China, **65**/G4
Ordzhonikidze, U.S.S.R., **60**/F6
Örebro, Sweden, **39**/J7
Oregon (state), U.S., **14**/B2
Oregon City, Oreg., **16**/C3
Orel, U.S.S.R., **60**/D4
Orenburg, U.S.S.R., **60**/J4
Orense, Spain, **52**/C1
Orinoco (riv.), S. Amer., **32**/G2
Oristano (gulf), Italy, **54**/B5
Orizaba, Mex., **26**/F4
Orkney (isls.), Scot., **40**/E1
Orland, Calif., **16**/C5
Orlando, Fla., **21**/N7
Orléans, France, **44**/D3
Orléansville, Alg., *see El Asnam*
Orly, France, **44**/B2
Ormond Beach, Fla., **21**/N7
Orne (riv.), France, **44**/C3
Orofino, Idaho, **16**/E3
Orontes (riv.), Syria, **74**/C2
Oroville, Calif., **16**/C5
Oroville, Wash., **16**/D2
Orsk, U.S.S.R., **60**/J4

Oruro, Bol., **32**/G7
Osaka, Japan, **67**/G6
Osawatomie, Kans., **18**/K5
Osceola, Ark., **19**/L6
Osh, U.S.S.R., **58**/H5
Oshkosh, Wis., **18**/L3
Oshogbo, Nigeria, **83**/F7
Oskaloosa, Iowa, **18**/K4
Oskarshamn, Sweden, **39**/K8
Oslo (cap.), Nor., **39**/G6
Osnabrück, W. Ger., **47**/C2
Osorno, Chile, **34**/F12
Ostend, Belg., **42**/B6
Ostrava, Czech., **48**/E2
Oswego, N.Y., **20**/O4
Oświecim, Pol., **51**/D3
Otago (pen.), N.Z., **94**/C6
Otaru, Japan, **67**/K2
Otavalo, Ecua., **32**/E3
Otranto (str.), Europe, **56-57**/D6
Otsu, Japan, **67**/J7
Ottawa (cap.), Can., **25**/J7
Ottawa (riv.), Can., **25**/J7
Ottawa, Ill., **18**/L4
Ottawa, Kans., **18**/K5
Ottumwa, Iowa, **18**/K4
Ötztal Alps (mts.), Europe, **54**/C1
Ouachita (mts.), U.S., **15**/H4
Ouagadougou (cap.), Upp. Volta, **82**/D6
Ouahigouya, Upp. Volta, **82**/D6
Ouargla, Alg., **82**/F2
Oudtshoorn, S. Africa, **86**/C6
Oued Zem, Mor., **82**/C2
Ouesso, Congo, **84**/C3
Ouezzane, Mor., **82**/C2
Ouidah, Benin, **83**/E7
Oujda, Mor., **82**/D2
Oulu, Fin., **39**/O4
Our (riv.), Europe, **43**/J9
Ouray, Colo., **17**/G5
Ouro Preto, Braz., **33**/M8
Ouse (riv.), Eng., *see Great Ouse*
Outer Hebrides (isls.), Scot., **40**/C2
Ovalle, Chile, **34**/F10
Ovamboland (reg.), Namibia, **86**/B3
Oviedo, Spain, **53**/C1
Owando, Congo, **84**/C4
Owatonna, Minn., **18**/K3
Owendo, Gabon, **84**/A3
Owensboro, Ky., **21**/M5
Owen Sound, Ont., **25**/H6
Owosso, Mich., **20**/M4
Owyhee (lake), Oreg., **16**/D4
Owyhee (riv.), U.S., **16**/D4
Oxford, Eng., **41**/F5
Oxford, Miss., **21**/L6
Oxnard, Calif., **16**/D6
Oyapock (riv.), S. Amer., **32**/K3
Oyd, Nigeria, **83**/E7
Oyem, Gabon, **84**/B3
Ozark (mts.), U.S., **15**/H3
Ozark (plateau), U.S., **15**/H3
Ozarks, Lake of the, Mo., **18**/K5

P

Paarl, S. Africa, **86**/B6
Pabna, Bang., **72**/F4
Pachua, Mex., **26**/E4
Pacific Grove, Calif., **17**/C5
Pacific Islands, Territory of the, **88**/D-G5
Pacific Ocean, **88-89**
Pacific Palisades, Hawaii, **23**/C4
Padang, Indon., **71**/C6
Paderborn, W. Ger., **47**/C3
Padlei, N.W.T., **24**/G3
Padloping Islands, N.W.T., **25**/K2
Padre (isls.), Tex., **19**/J8
Padua, Italy, **54**/C2
Paducah, Ky., **21**/L5
Pago Pago (cap.), Amer. Samoa, **88**/J7
Pahala, Hawaii, **23**/F4
Pahang (riv.), Malaysia, **69**/D7
Pahlavi, Iran, *see Enzeli*
Painesville, Ohio, **20**/N4
Painted (des.), Ariz., **17**/D5
Paintsville, Ky., **20**/N5
Paisley, Scot., **40**/D3
Pakistan, **75**/J4
Pakxé, Laos, **68**/E4
Palatka, Fla., **21**/N7
Palau (isls.), Pacific, *see Belau*
Palawan (isl.), Phil., **71**/F4
Palembang, Indon., **71**/D6
Palencia, Spain, **53**/D2
Palenque, Mex., **26**/G5
Palermo, Italy, **54**/D5
Palestine, Tex., **19**/K7
Palk (str.), Asia, **72**/D7
Palma, Spain, **53**/H3
Palmas (gulf), Italy, **54**/B5
Palmas (gulf), Lib., **82**/C8
Palm Beach, Fla., **21**/O8
Palmerston North, N.Z., **94**/E4
Palm Springs, Calif., **16**/D6
Palmyra (ruins), Syria, **74**/C2
Palo Alto, Calif., **16**/C5
Palos (cape), Spain, **53**/F4
Pamir (plat.), Asia, **75**/K2

Pamlico (sound), N.C., **21**/O6
Pampa, Tex., **19**/H6
Pampas (plain), Arg., **34**/H10-11
Pamplona, Spain, **53**/F1
Pana, Ill., **18**/L5
Panama, **27**/D-E3
Panamá (cap.), Pan., **27**/E3
Panama (gulf), Pan., **27**/E4
Panama City, Fla., **21**/M7
Panama City (Panamá) (cap.), Pan., **27**/E3
Panay (isl.), Phil., **71**/G3
Panda-Likasi, Zaire, **84**/E6
Pangani, Tanz., **85**/G5
Pangnirtung, N.W.T., **25**/K3
Panguitch, Utah, **17**/E5
Pánuco, Mex., **26**/F4
Paoy Pet, Camb., **68**/D4
Papeete (cap.), Fr. Poly., **89**/S10
Papua New Guinea, **88**/E6
Paragould, Ark., **19**/L5
Paraguaná (pen.), Ven., **32**/F1
Paraguarí, Par., **34**/J9
Paraguay, **32**, **34**/J8-9
Paraguay (riv.), S. Amer., **31**/J8
Paraíba, Braz., **33**/O5
Paramaribo (cap.), Sur., **32**/K2
Paraná, Arg., **34**/J10
Paraná (state), Braz., **34**/K8
Paraná (riv.), S. Amer., **34**/J9
Paranaíba, Braz., **33**/K7
Pardubice, Czech., **48**/C1
Paria (gulf), **29**/G5
Parima (mts.), S. Amer., **32**/H3
Paris (cap.), France, **44**/E3
Paris, Ill., **18**/L5
Paris, Ky., **21**/M5
Paris, Tenn., **21**/L5
Paris, Tex., **19**/K6
Parker, Ariz., **17**/E6
Parker (dam), U.S., **17**/E6
Parkersburg, W. Va., **20**/N5
Parkes, Austr., **92**/E3
Parkston, S. Dak., **18**/J4
Parma, Italy, **54**/C2
Parma, Ohio, **20**/N4
Parnaíba, Braz., **33**/M4
Parnassus (mt.), Greece, **57**/F6
Pärnu, U.S.S.R., **60**/B3
Paro, Bhutan, **72**/F3
Paropamisus (mts.), Afghan., **75**/H3
Páros (isl.), Greece, **57**/G7
Parowan, Utah, **17**/E5
Parramatta, Austr., **92**/F3
Parry (chan.), N.W.T., **24**/E-H1
Parry (isls.), N.W.T., **25**/M3
Parry Sound, Ont., **25**/J7
Parsons, Kans., **18**/K5
Pasadena, Calif., **16**/D6
Pasadena, Tex., **19**/K7
Pascagoula, Miss., **21**/L7
Pasco, Wash., **16**/D3
Paso de los Toros, Urug., **34**/J10
Paso Robles, Calif., **16**/C6
Passau, W. Ger., **47**/E4
Passo Fundo, Braz., **34**/K9
Pasto, Col., **32**/E3
Patagonia (reg.), Arg., **34**/F-G 12-14
Patchogue, N.Y., **20**/P4
Paterson, N.J., **20**/P4
Pathfinder (res.), Wyo., **16**/G4
Patiala, India, **72**/D2
Pátmos (isl.), Greece, **57**/H7
Patna, India, **72**/F3
Patos (lagoon), Braz., **34**/K10
Pátrai, Greece, **57**/E6
Pau, France, **44**/C6
Paulatuk, N.W.T., **24**/D2
Pauls Valley, Okla., **19**/J6
Pavia, Italy, **54**/B2
Pavlodar, U.S.S.R., **58**/H4
Pawhuska, Okla., **19**/J5
Paysandú, Urug., **34**/J10
Pazardzhik, Bulg., **56**/F4
Peace River, Alta., **24**/E4
Pearl (hbr.), Hawaii, **23**/C4
Pearl City, Hawaii, **23**/C4
Pearsall, Tex., **19**/H7
Peary (chan.), N.W.T., **25**/M3
Peary Land (reg.), Greenl., **96**/A8
Péc, Yugo., **56**/E4
Pechora (riv.), U.S.S.R., **60**/H1
Pecos, Tex., **19**/H7
Pecos (riv.), U.S., **14**/F4
Pécs, Hung., **48**/E3
Peebles, Scot., **40**/E3
Pee Dee (riv.), S.C., **15**/L4
Peel (riv.), Can., **24**/C2
Peel, Isle of Man, **41**/D3
Pegasus (bay), N.Z., **94**/D5
Pegu, Burma, **68**/C3
Peipus (lake), U.S.S.R., **60**/C3
Pekin, Ill., **18**/L4
Peking (Beijing) (cap.), China, **65**/J3
Pelée (vol.), Mart., **29**/G4
Pelican, Alaska, **22**/F4
Pelly (riv.), Yukon, **24**/C3
Pelly Bay, N.W.T., **24**/G2
Pelotas, Braz., **34**/K10
Pemba, Moz., **86**/G2
Pemba (isl.), Tanz., **85**/G5
Pembroke, Ont., **25**/J7

Pembroke, Wales, **41**/D5
Pendembu, S. Leone, **83**/B7
Pendleton, Oreg., **16**/D3
Pend Oreille (lake), Idaho, **16**/D2
Penghu (isls.), China, **65**/J7
Penibética (riv.), Spain, **53**/E4
Pennine Alps (mts.), Europe, **54**/A2
Pennsylvania (state), U.S., **15**/L2
Penonomé, Pan., **27**/D3
Penrhyn (Tongareva) (atoll), Cook Is., **89**/L6
Penrith, Austr., **92**/F3
Pensacola, Fla., **21**/M7
Pentland (firth), Scot., **40**/E1
Penza, U.S.S.R., **60**/G4
Penzance, Eng., **41**/D5
Peoria, Ill., **18**/L4
Perche (reg.), France, **44**/D3
Pereira, Col., **32**/E3
Pergamino, Arg., **34**/M11
Péribonca (riv.), Que., **25**/J6
Périgueux, France, **44**/D5
Perim (isl.), P.D.R. Yemen, **74**/D7
Perlas (arch.), Pan., **27**/E3
Perm', U.S.S.R., **60**/J3
Pernambuco (Recife), Braz., **33**/O5
Perpignan, France, **44**/E6
Perry, Fla., **21**/N7
Perry, Okla., **19**/J5
Perryton, Tex., **19**/H5
Perryville, Mo., **18**/L5
Persia, *see Iran*
Persian (gulf), Asia, **74**/E-F4
Perth, Austr., **91**/B6
Perth, Scot., **40**/E2
Peru, **32**/D5
Peru, Ind., **20**/M4
Perugia, Italy, **54**/D3
Pesaro, Italy, **54**/D3
Pescadores (Penghu) (isls.), China, **65**/J7
Pescara, Italy, **54**/E3
Peshawar, Pak., **75**/K3
Petah Tiqwa, Isr., **76**/B3
Petaluma, Calif., **16**/C5
Petén-Itzá (lake), Guat., **27**/B1
Peterborough, Eng., **41**/F4
Peterborough, Ont., **25**/J7
Peterhead, Scot., **40**/E2
Petersburg, Alaska, **22**/F4
Petersburg, Va., **20**/O5
Petoskey, Mich., **20**/M3
Petra (ruins), Jordan, **76**/D6
Petrified Forest Nat'l Pk., Ariz., **17**/F6
Petrolina, Braz., **33**/M5
Petropavlovsk, U.S.S.R., **58**/K4
Petrópolis, Braz., **34**/M8
Petrozavodsk, U.S.S.R., **60**/D2
Pforzheim, W. Ger., **47**/C4
Phan Rang, Viet., **68**/F5
Phenix City, Ala., **21**/M6
Phet Buri, Thai., **68**/C4
Phichit, Thai., **68**/D3
Philadelphia, Miss., **21**/L6
Philadelphia, Pa., **20**/P4
Philippeville, Alg., *see Skikda*
Philippines, **71**/H3
Phnom Penh (cap.), Camb., **68**/E5
Phoenix (cap.), Ariz., **17**/E6
Phoenix (isls.), Kiribati, **88**/J6
Phuket, Thai., **68**/C6
Phu Tho, Viet., **68**/E2
Piacenza, Italy, **54**/B2
Piatra Neamţ, Rom., **56**/G2
Piave (riv.), Italy, **54**/D2
Pibor Post, Sudan, **81**/F6
Picayune, Miss., **21**/L7
Picton, N.Z., **94**/D4
Piedmont (reg.), Italy, **54**/A-B2
Piedras Negras, Mex., **26**/E2
Pierre (cap.), S. Dak., **18**/H3
Pietermaritzburg, S. Africa, **86**/E5
Pietersburg, S. Africa, **86**/D4
Pikes (peak), Colo., **18**/G5
Pikeville, Ky., **21**/N5
Pilcomayo (riv.), S. Amer., **32**/H8
Pinang, Malaysia, *see George Town*
Pinar del Río, Cuba, **28**/A2
Pincher Creek, Alta., **24**/E6
Pindus (mts.), Greece, **57**/E6
Pine Bluff, Ark., **19**/K6
Pine Ridge, S. Dak., **18**/H4
Pines (Juventud) (isl.), Cuba, **28**/A2
Pines, Isle of, New Cal., **89**/H5
Pineville, La., **19**/K7
Pingtung, China, **65**/K7
Pingxiang (Pingsiang), China, **65**/G7
Pinsk, U.S.S.R., **60**/C4
Pioche, Nev., **17**/E5
Piombino, Italy, **54**/C3
Pipestone, Minn., **18**/J3
Piqua, Ohio, **20**/M4
Piraiévs, Greece, **57**/F7
Pírgos, Greece, **57**/E7
Pirmasens, W. Ger., **47**/B4
Pisa, Italy, **54**/C3
Pisco, Peru, **32**/E6

Pistoia, Italy, **54**/C2
Pitcairn (isl.), Pacific, **89**/O8
Piteşti, Rom., **56**/G3
Pittsburg, Kans., **18**/K5
Pittsburgh, Pa., **20**/O4
Pittsfield, Mass., **20**/P4
Piura, Peru, **32**/D5
Plainview, Tex., **19**/H6
Plant City, Fla., **21**/N7
Plaquemine, La., **19**/L7
Plasencia, Spain, **53**/C2
Plata, Río de la (est.), S. Amer., **34**/J11
Platte (riv.), Nebr., **15**/G2
Platteville, Wis., **18**/L4
Plattsburgh, N.Y., **20**/P4
Plattsmouth, Nebr., **18**/J4
Plauen, E. Ger., **47**/E3
Pleiku, Viet., **68**/E4
Plenty (bay), N.Z., **94**/F2
Pletipi (lake), Que., **25**/K5
Pleven, Bulg., **56**/G4
Plock, Pol., **51**/D2
Ploieşti, Rom., **56**/H3
Plovdiv, Bulg., **56**/G4
Plymouth, Eng., **41**/E5
Plymouth (cap.), Montserrat, **29**/F3
Plzeň, Czech., **48**/B2
Po (riv.), Italy, **54**/C2
Pobeda (peak), Asia, **58**/J5
Pocatello, Idaho, **16**/E4
Podol'sk, U.S.S.R., **60**/E3
Pointe-à-Pitre, Guad., **29**/G3
Pointe-Noire, Congo, **84**/B5
Point Hope, Alaska, **22**/C2
Point Lay, Alaska, **22**/C2
Poitiers, France, **44**/D4
Pokhara, Nepal, **72**/E3
Pola (Pula), Yugo., **56**/A3
Poland, **51**
Poltava, U.S.S.R., **60**/D5
Polynesia (reg.), Pacific, **88-89**/J-K 4-8
Pomerania (reg.), Europe, **47**/E2
Pompeii (ruins), Italy, **54**/F4
Ponape (isl.), Fed. States of Micronesia, **88**/F5
Ponca City, Okla., **19**/J5
Ponce, P. Rico, *see detailed map p. 29*
Pondicherry (terr.), India, **72**/E6
Ponta Grossa, Braz., **34**/K9
Pontchartrain (lake), La., **15**/J4
Pontecorvo, Italy, **54**/D4
Pontiac, Ill., **18**/L4
Pontiac, Mich., **20**/N4
Pontianak, Indon., **70**/D5
Pontic (mts.), Turkey, **74**/C1
Pontine (isls.), Italy, **54**/D4
Pontoise, France, **44**/E3
Poona, India, **72**/C5
Poopó (lake), Bol., **32**/G7
Popayán, Col., **32**/E3
Poplar, Mont., **18**/G2
Poplar Bluff, Mo., **19**/L5
Porbandar, India, **72**/B4
Porcupine (riv.), N. Amer., **13**/D3
Pordenone, Italy, **54**/D2
Pori, Fin., **39**/M6
Porrentruy, Switz., **50**/B1
Porsanger (fjord), Nor., **39**/O1
Porsgrunn, Nor., **39**/F7
Portage, Wis., **18**/L4
Portage la Prairie, Man., **24**/G5
Portales, N. Mex., **19**/H6
Port Angeles, Wash., **16**/C2
Port Antonio, Jam., **28**/C3
Port Arthur, China, *see Lüshun*
Port Arthur, Tex., **19**/K7
Port Augusta, Austr., **91**/F6
Port-au-Prince (cap.), Haiti, **28**/D3
Port Blair, India, **72**/G6
Port-Bouet, Iv. Coast, **83**/D7
Port-Cartier-Ouest, Que., **25**/K6
Port Elizabeth, S. Africa, **86**/D6
Porterville, Calif., **17**/D5
Port Fairy, Austr., **92**/B6
Port-Francqui (Ilebo), Zaire, **84**/D4
Port-Gentil, Gabon, **84**/A4
Port Harcourt, Nigeria, **83**/F8
Port Hedland, Austr., **90**/B3
Port Huron, Mich., **20**/N4
Port Kembla, Austr., **92**/E4
Port Kindu, Zaire, **84**/E4
Portland, Bill of (pen.), Eng., **41**/E5
Portland, Maine, **20**/R4
Portland, Oreg., **16**/C3
Portlaoighise, Ire., **41**/C4
Port Lavaca, Tex., **19**/J7
Port Lincoln, Austr., **91**/E6
Port Louis (cap.), Mauritius, *see Mascarene Is. map p. 87*
Port-Lyautey (Kenitra), Mor., **82**/C2
Port Macquarie, Austr., **92**/G2
Port Maria, Jam., **28**/C3
Port Melbourne, Austr., **92**/H5
Port-Menier, Que., **25**/K6
Port Moresby (cap.), Papua N.G., **88**/E6
Port Nelson, Man., **24**/G4
Port Nolloth, S. Africa, **86**/B5

Port-Nouveau-Québec, Que., 25/K4
Porto, Port., 52/B2
Porto Alegre, Braz., 34/K10
Portofino, Italy, 54/B2
Port of Spain (cap.), Trin. & Tob., 29/K4
Portola, Calif., 16/C5
Porto-Novo (cap.), Benin, 83/E7
Portoviejo, Ecua., 32/D4
Port Pirie, Austr., 91/F6
Port Radium, N.W.T., 24/E3
Port Said, Egypt, 81/F1
Port St. Joe, Fla., 21/M7
Port Shepstone, S. Africa, 86/E6
Portsmouth, Eng., 41/F5
Portsmouth, N.H., 20/R4
Portsmouth, Ohio, 21/N5
Portsmouth, Va., 21/05
Port Sudan, Sudan, 81/G4
Port Swettenham, Malaysia, 69/D7
Port Talbot, Wales, 41/E5
Port Townsend, Wash., 16/C2
Portugal, 52
Portuguese Guinea, see Guinea-Bissau
Port-Vendres, France, 44/E6
Port Weld, Malaysia, 69/D6
Posadas, Arg., 34/J9
Poschiavo, Switz., 50/F2
Poste-de-la-Baleine, Que., 25/J5
Potchefstroom, S. Africa, 86/D5
Potenza, Italy, 54/E4
Potosí, Bol., 32/G7
Potsdam, E. Ger., 47/F2
Potsdam, N.Y., 20/P4
Pottsville, Pa., 20/04
Poughkeepsie, N.Y., 20/P4
Pouthisat, Camb., 68/D4
Povungnituk, Que., 25/J3
Powder (riv.), U.S., 18/G3
Powell (lake), U.S., 17/F5
Poyang Hu (lake), China, 65/J6
Poznań, Pol., 51/C2
Prague (Praha) (cap.), Czech., 48/C2
Prairie du Chien, Wis., 18/L4
Pratt, Kans., 19/J5
Prescott, Ariz., 17/E6
Prescott, Ark., 19/K6
Presidente Prudente, Braz., 33/K8
Presidio, Tex., 19/G7
Prespa (lake), Europe, 56/E5
Presque Isle, Maine, 20/R3
Preston, Austr., 93/J5
Preston, Eng., 40/E4
Preston, Idaho, 16/E4
Prestwick, Scot., 40/D3
Pretoria (cap.), S. Africa, 86/D5
Préveza, Greece, 57/E6
Prey Veng, Camb., 68/E5
Pribilof (isls.), Alaska, 22/C4
Příbram, Czech., 48/B2
Price, Utah, 16/F5
Prilep, Yugo., 56/E5
Prince Albert (pen.), N.W.T., 24/E1
Prince Albert (sound), N.W.T., 24/E1
Prince Albert, Sask., 24/F5
Prince Albert Nat'l Pk., Sask., 24/F5
Prince Charles (isl.), N.W.T., 24/J2
Prince Edward (isls.), S. Africa, 9/L8
Prince Edward Island (prov.), Can., 25/K6
Prince George, Br. Col., 24/D5
Prince of Wales (cape), Alaska, 22/C2
Prince of Wales (isl.), N.W.T., 24/G1
Prince of Wales (str.), N.W.T., 25/E1
Prince Patrick (isl.), N.W.T., 25/M3
Prince Rupert, Br. Col., 24/C5
Princeton, Ind., 20/M5
Princeton, Ky., 21/M5
Princeton, W. Va., 21/N5
Príncipe (isl.), São T. & Pr., 83/F8
Prineville, Oreg., 16/C3
Priština, Yugo., 56/E4
Prizren, Yugo., 56/E4
Progreso, Mex., 26/H4
Prokop'yevsk, U.S.S.R., 58/J4
Prome, Burma, 68/B3
Proserpine, Austr., 91/H4
Prostějov, Czech., 48/D2
Providence (cap.), R.I., 20/R4
Providencia (isl.), Col., 28/B4
Provo, Utah, 16/F4
Prudhoe Bay, Alaska, 22/E1
Pruszków, Pol., 51/E2
Prut (riv.), Europe, 56/J2
Przemyśl, Pol., 51/F4
Pskov, U.S.S.R., 60/C3
Puebla, Mex., 26/E4
Pueblo, Colo., 18/G5
Puente-Genil, Spain, 53/D4
Puerto Aisén, Chile, 34/F13
Puerto Ángel, Mex., 26/F5
Puerto Ayacucho, Ven., 32/G2

Puerto Barrios, Guat., 27/B2
Puerto Cabello, Ven., 32/G1
Puerto Colombia, Col., 32/E1
Puerto Cortés, Hond., 27/C2
Puerto de Hierro, Ven., 32/H1
Puerto Deseado, Arg., 34/G13
Puertollano, Spain, 53/D3
Puerto La Cruz, Ven., 32/H1
Puerto Montt, Chile, 34/F12
Puerto Peñasco, Mex., 26/B1
Puerto Plata, Dom. Rep., 28/D3
Puerto Princesa, Phil., 71/F4
Puerto Real, Spain, 53/D4
Puerto Rico, 29/E3
Puerto Suárez, Bol., 32/J7
Puget (sound), Wash., 16/C3
Pukapuka (atoll), Cook Is., 89/K7
Pula, Yugo., 56/A3
Pulaski, Va., 21/N5
Pulicat (lake), India, 72/E6
Pullman, Wash., 16/D3
Punakha, Bhutan, 72/F3
Pune, India, 72/C5
Punjab (state), India, 72/D2
Punjab (prov.), Pak., 72/C2
Puno, Peru, 32/F7
Punta Arenas, Chile, 34/F14
Punta Gorda, Fla., 21/N8
Puntarenas, C. Rica, 27/C3
Puri, India, 72/F5
Purulia, India, 72/F4
Purus (riv.), S. Amer., 32/H5
Pusan, S. Korea, 66/D6
Pushkin, U.S.S.R., 60/C3
Puttalam, Sri Lanka, 73/D7
Putumayo (riv.), S. Amer., 32/F4
Puunene, Hawaii, 23/E3
Puyallup, Wash., 16/C3
Puy-de-Dôme (mt.), France, 44/E5
Pyapon, Burma, 68/B3
P'yŏngyang (cap.), N. Korea, 66/B4
Pyramid (lake), Nev., 16/D4
Pyramids, Giza (ruins), Egypt, 81/J3
Pyrenees (mts.), Europe, 36/D4
Pyuthan, Nepal, 72/E3

Q

Qandahar, Afghan., 75/J3
Qatar, 74/F4
Qattâra (depr.), Egypt, 81/E2
Qazvin, Iran, 75/E2
Qena, Egypt, 81/F2
Qeshm (isl.), Iran, 74/G4
Qilian Shan (mts.), China, 65/E4
Qingdao, China, 65/K4
Qiqihar, China, 65/K2
Qiryat Gat, Isr., 76/B4
Qiryat Motzkin, Isr., 76/C2
Qiryat Shemona, Isr., 76/C1
Qiryat Yam, Isr., 76/C2
Qishn, P.D.R. Yemen, 74/F6
Quanah, Tex., 19/H6
Quang Ngai, Viet., 68/F4
Quang Tri, Viet., 68/F3
Quartzsite, Ariz., 17/E6
Québec (prov.), Can., 25/J5
Québec (cap.), Que., 25/J5
Queen Charlotte (isls.), Br. Col., 24/C5
Queen Elizabeth (isls.), N.W.T., 25/M-N3
Queen Maud (gulf), N.W.T., 24/F2
Queensland (state), Austr., 91/G4
Queenstown, Austr., 95/B4
Queenstown (Cóbh), Ire., 41/B5
Quelimane, Moz., 86/F3
Quemoy (isl.), China, see Jinmen
Que Que, Zim., see Kwekwe
Querétaro, Mex., 26/E4
Quesnel, Br. Col., 24/D5
Quetta, Pak., 75/J3
Quezaltenango, Guat., 27/A2
Quibdó, Col., 32/E2
Quiberon, France, 44/B4
Quillacollo, Bol., 32/G7
Quilon, India, 73/D7
Quimper, France, 44/A4
Quincy, Fla., 21/M7
Quincy, Ill., 18/L5
Quinhagak, Alaska, 22/C4
Qui Nhon, Viet., 68/F4
Quito (cap.), Ecua., 32/E3
Qum (Qom), Iran, 74/F3
Qumran, Khirbet, West Bank, 76/C4

R

Raahe, Fin., 39/04
Rabat (cap.), Mor., 82/C2
Rabaul, Papua N.G., 89/B2
Rabba, Jordan, 76/C5
Race (cape), Newf., 25/L6
Rach Gia, Viet., 68/E5

Racibórz, Pol., 51/C3
Racine, Wis., 18/L4
Radium Hill, Austr., 91/G6
Radom, Pol., 51/E3
Radville, Sask., 24/F5
Rae (isth.), N.W.T., 24/H4
Rae-Edzo, N.W.T., 24/E3
Rafah, Gaza Strip, 76/A5
Ragusa, Italy, 54/E6
Ragusa (Dubrovnik), Yugo., 56/C4
Raiatea (isl.), Fr. Poly., 89/L7
Rainier (mt.), Wash., 16/C3
Rainy (lake), N. Amer., 18/02
Rainy (riv.), N. Amer., 18/02
Rainy River, Ont., 24/G6
Raivavae (isl.), Fr. Poly., 89/M8
Rajahmundry, India, 72/E5
Rajkot, India, 72/C3
Rajpur, India, 72/F2
Rajshahi, Bang., 72/F4
Raleigh (cap.), N.C., 21/06
Ramâllah, West Bank, 76/C4
Ramat Gan, Isr., 76/B3
Rambouillet, France, 44/D3
Ramla, Isr., 76/B4
Ramsey, Isle of Man, 40/D3
Ramsgate, Eng., 41/G5
Rancagua, Chile, 34/F10
Ranchi, India, 72/F4
Randers, Den., 39/G8
Randfontein, S. Africa, 86/G6
Randwick, Austr., 92/J3
Ranger, Tex., 19/J6
Rangoon (cap.), Burma, 68/C3
Rantoul, Ill., 18/L4
Rapa (isl.), Fr. Poly., 89/M8
Rapallo, Italy, 54/B2
Rapa Nui (Easter) (isl.), Chile, 8/D7
Rapid City, S. Dak., 18/H3
Raroia (atoll), Fr. Poly., 89/M7
Rarotonga (isl.), Cook Is., 89/K8
Ras al Khaimah, U.A.E., 74/G4
Ras Asèr (cape), Somalia, 85/K1
Ras Dashan (mt.), Eth., 81/G5
Rasht, Iran, 74/E2
Ras Tanura, Saudi Arabia, 74/F4
Rat (isls.), Alaska, 22/E5
Raton, N. Mex., 19/G5
Ravenna, Italy, 54/D2
Ravensburg, W. Ger., 47/C5
Ravi (riv.), Asia, 72/C2
Rawalpindi, Pak., 72/C2
Rawlins, Wyo., 16/G4
Raymond, Alta., 24/E6
Raymond, Wash., 16/C3
Raymondville, Tex., 19/J8
Ré (isl.), France, 44/C4
Reading, Eng., 41/F5
Reading, Pa., 20/P4
Real (mts.), S. Amer., 32/G7
Recife, Braz., 33/05
Recklinghausen, W. Ger., 46/B3
Reconquista, Arg., 34/H9
Red (sea), 81/G3
Red (riv.), Asia, 68/E2
Red (lake), Minn., 18/K3
Red (riv.), U.S., 19/K6
Red Bluff, Calif., 16/C4
Red Deer, Alta., 24/E5
Redding, Calif., 16/C4
Red Lake (riv.), Minn., 18/K3
Red Lake, Ont., 24/G5
Red Lodge, Mont., 16/F3
Red Oak, Iowa, 18/K4
Red River of the North (riv.), U.S., 18/J3
Red Volta (riv.), Afr., 82/D6
Red Wing, Minn., 18/K3
Redwood Falls, Minn., 18/J3
Redwood Nat'l Pk., Calif., 16/B4
Ree (lake), Ire., 41/B4
Reed City, Mich., 20/M4
Refugio, Tex., 19/J7
Regensburg, W. Ger., 47/E4
Reggio, Italy, 54/C2
Reggio di Calabria, Italy, 54/E5
Regina (cap.), Sask., 24/F5
Rehovot, Isr., 76/B4
Reidsville, N.C., 21/05
Reigate, Eng., 41/F5
Reims, France, 44/E3
Reindeer (lake), Can., 24/F4
Reindeer Station, N.W.T., 24/C2
Reinosa, Mex., 26/E2
Remscheid, W. Ger., 47/B3
Renfrew, Ont., 25/J6
Renfrew, Scot., 40/A1
Rennes, France, 44/C3
Reno, Nev., 16/D5
Renton, Wash., 16/C3
Republican (riv.), U.S., 18/J5
Repulse Bay, N.W.T., 24/H2
Resistencia, Arg., 34/H9
Reşiţa, Rom., 56/E3
Resolute Bay, N.W.T., 25/M3
Resolution (isl.), N.W.T., 25/K3
Retalhuleu, Guat., 27/A2
Réunion, see Mascarene Is. map p. 87
Reutlingen, W. Ger., 47/C4
Revelstoke, Br. Col., 24/E5
Revillagigedo (isls.), Mex., 26/B4
Rewa, India, 72/E4
Rexburg, Idaho, 16/E4

Reykjavík (cap.), Icel., 38/W2
Rhaetian Alps (mts.), Europe, 50/E2
Rheydt, W. Ger., 47/B3
Rhine (riv.), Europe, 37/E4
Rhinelander, Wis., 18/L3
Rhino Camp, Uganda, 84/F3
Rhode Island (state), U.S., 15/M2
Rhodes (Ródhos), Greece, 57/H7
Rhodesia, see Zimbabwe
Rhodes Inyanga Nat'l Pk., Zim., 86/E3
Rhodope (mts.), Europe, 56/G5
Rhön (mts.), Ger., 47/D3
Rhondda, Wales, 41/E5
Rhône (riv.), Europe, 37/E5
Rhum (isl.), Scot., 40/C2
Riau (arch.), Indon., 70/C5
Ribeirão Preto, Braz., 33/L8
Riberalta, Bol., 32/G6
Rice Lake, Wis., 18/L3
Richfield, Utah, 16/E5
Richland, Wash., 16/D3
Richmond, Austr., 93/J5
Richmond, Calif., 16/C5
Richmond, Ind., 20/M5
Richmond, Ky., 21/M5
Richmond (cap.), Va., 20/05
Riding Mtn. Nat'l Pk., Man., 24/F5
Ried, Austria, 48/B2
Riehen, Switz., 50/C1
Rieti, Italy, 54/D3
Rifle, Colo., 16/G5
Riga, U.S.S.R., 60/B3
Rigestan (reg.), Afghan., 75/H3
Rigi (mt.), Switz., 50/D1
Rigolet, Newf., 25/L5
Riihimäki, Fin., 39/06
Rijeka, Yugo., 56/B3
Rimini, Italy, 54/D2
Rimouski, Que., 25/K6
Riobamba, Ecua., 32/E4
Río Caribe, Ven., 32/H1
Rio de Janeiro, Braz., 34/M8
Rio Grande, Braz., 34/K10
Rio Grande (riv.), N. Amer., 13/H7
Riohacha, Col., 32/F1
Río Muni (reg.), Equat. Guin., 84/B3
Rio Tinto, Braz., 33/05
Rishon Le Ziyyon, Isr., 76/B4
Rivas, Nic., 27/C3
Rivera, Urug., 34/J10
Riverside, Calif., 17/D6
Riverton, Man., 24/G5
Riverton, Wyo., 16/F4
Riviera (reg.), Europe, 45/G6
Rivière-du-Loup, Que., 25/K6
Riyadh (cap.), Saudi Arabia, 74/F5
Road Town (cap.), V.I. (Br.), see detailed map p. 29
Roanoke, Ala., 21/M6
Roanoke, Va., 20/N5
Roanoke Rapids, N.C., 21/05
Robertsport, Lib., 83/B7
Roberval, Que., 25/J5
Robson (mt.), Br. Col., 24/D5
Robstown, Tex., 19/J8
Rocha, Urug., 34/K10
Rochefort, France, 44/C4
Rocher River, N.W.T., 24/E4
Rochester, Eng., 41/G5
Rochester, Minn., 18/K4
Rochester, N.Y., 20/04
Rockall (isl.), Scot., 37/C3
Rockdale, Austr., 93/J5
Rockford, Ill., 18/L4
Rockhampton, Austr., 93/J4
Rock Hill, S.C., 21/N6
Rockingham, Austr., 91/B6
Rock Island, Ill., 18/L4
Rockland, Maine, 20/R3
Rock Rapids, Iowa, 18/K4
Rocksprings, Tex., 19/H7
Rock Springs, Wyo., 16/F4
Rocky (mts.), N. Amer., 13/F-H 4-6
Rocky Mount, N.C., 21/05
Rocky Mountain Nat'l Pk., Colo., 18/G4
Rocky Mountain House, Alta., 24/E5
Rodez, France, 44/E5
Ródhos, Greece, 57/J7
Rodrigues (isl.), Mauritius, 63/K11
Roeselare, Belg., 43/C7
Roes Welcome (sound), N.W.T., 24/H3
Rogers, Ark., 19/K5
Rolla, Mo., 19/L5
Rolla, N. Dak., 18/J2
Roma, Austr., 91/H5
Romania, 56/G3
Romanshorn, Switz., 50/E1
Rome, Ga., 21/M6
Rome (cap.), Italy, 54/D4
Rome, N.Y., 20/P4
Ronda, Spain, 53/D4
Rondônia (terr.), Braz., 32/H6
Ronne, Den., 39/J9
Roodeport, S. Africa, 86/H6
Roosevelt (isl.), Antarc., 35/A7
Roosevelt (riv.), Braz., 32/H5

Roosevelt, Utah, 16/F4
Rorschach, Switz., 50/E1
Rosa (mt.), Europe, 54/A1
Rosario, Arg., 34/H10
Rosario, Mex., 26/D3
Roscommon, Ire., 41/B4
Roseau (cap.), Dominica, 29/G4
Roseau, Minn., 18/J2
Roseburg, Oreg., 16/B4
Rosenberg, Tex., 19/K7
Rosetown, Sask., 24/F5
Rosetta, Egypt, 81/J2
Roseville, Calif., 16/C5
Rosignol, Guyana, 32/J2
Ross (sea), Antarc., 35/B7
Rossland, Br. Col., 24/E6
Rosso, Maur., 82/A5
Rosthern, Sask., 24/F5
Rostock, E. Ger., 46/E1
Rostov, U.S.S.R., 60/D4
Roswell, N. Mex., 19/G6
Rothesay, Scot., 40/D3
Roti (isl.), Indon., 71/G8
Rotorua, N.Z., 94/F3
Rotterdam, Neth., 42/E5
Rottweil, W. Ger., 47/C4
Rotuma (isl.), Fiji, 88/H7
Roubaix, France, 44/E2
Rouen, France, 44/D3
Roundup, Mont., 16/F3
Rouyn, Que., 25/J6
Rovaniemi, Fin., 38/03
Rovereto, Italy, 54/C2
Rovigo, Italy, 54/C2
Rovno, U.S.S.R., 60/C4
Rovuma (riv.), Afr., 85/G6
Royale, Isle (isl.), Mich., 18/L2
Royal Natal Nat'l Pk., S. Africa, 86/F5
Ruaha Nat'l Pk., Tanz., 85/F5
Ruapehu (mt.), N.Z., 94/E3
Rub' al Kahli (des.), Asia, 74/E-F5
Ruda Śląska, Pol., 51/A4
Rudolf (lake), Afr., 85/G3
Rudolstadt, E. Ger., 47/D3
Rufiji (riv.), Tanz., 85/G5
Rufisque, Sen., 82/A6
Rugby, Eng., 41/F4
Rügen (isl.), E. Ger., 47/E1
Ruhr (riv.), W. Ger., 47/B3
Rukwa (lake), Tanz., 85/F5
Rum (cay), Bah., 28/C2
Rum (isl.), Scot., 40/C2
Rum Jungle, Austr., 91/E2
Rumford, Maine, 20/R3
Rupert House, Que., 25/J5
Rupununi (riv.), Guyana, 32/J3
Ruse, Bulg., 56/H4
Russell, Kans., 18/J5
Russellville, Ark., 19/K6
Russellville, Ky., 21/M5
Russian Mission, Alaska, 22/C3
Russian S.F.S.R., U.S.S.R., 58/D-S 3-4
Ruston, La., 19/K6
Rutland, Vt., 20/P4
Ruwenzori (mts.), Afr., 84/E3
Rwanda, 84/E4
Ryazan', U.S.S.R., 60/D3
Rybinsk, U.S.S.R., 60/E3
Ryde, Austr., 92/J3
Ryukyu (isls.), Japan, 67/K7
Rzeszów, Pol., 51/E3

S

Saale (riv.), E. Ger., 47/D3
Saar (riv.), Europe, 47/B4
Saarbrücken, W. Ger., 47/B4
Saaremaa (isl.), U.S.S.R., 60/A3
Saba (isl.), Neth. Ant., 29/F3
Sabadell, Spain, 53/H2
Sabah (state), Malaysia, 71/F4
Sabinas, Mex., 26/E2
Sabine (riv.), U.S., 15/H4
Sable (cape), Fla., 15/N6
Sable (cape), N.S., 25/K7
Sable (isl.), N.S., 25/L7
Sabrathah, Libya, 80/B1
Sabzevar, Iran, 74/G2
Sachs Harbour, N.W.T., 24/D1
Sacramento (cap.), Calif., 16/C5
Sacramento (riv.), Calif., 14/B3
Sacramento (mts.), N. Mex., 19/G6
Safford, Ariz., 17/F6
Safi, Mor., 82/C2
Saga, Japan, 67/E7
Sagaing, Burma, 68/B2
Sagar, India, 72/D4
Saginaw, Mich., 20/N4
Saginaw (bay), Mich., 15/N2
Saglouc, Que., 25/J3
Saguache, Colo., 18/G5
Sagua la Grande, Cuba, 28/B2
Saguenay (riv.), Que., 13/L5
Sagunto, Spain, 53/F3
Sahara (des.), Afr., 79/A-E2
Saharanpur, India, 72/D2
Sahuaripa, Mex., 26/C2
Saïda, Alg., 82/E2
Saigon (Ho Chi Minh City), Viet., 68/E5

St. Albans, Eng., 41/F5
St. Albans, Vt., 20/P3
St. Albans, W. Va., 20/N5
St. Andrews, Scot., 40/E2
St. Anthony, Idaho, 16/E4
St. Augustine, Fla., 21/N7
St. Austell, Eng., 41/D5
St-Barthélémy (isl.), Guad., 29/F3
St. Christopher (isl.), St. Chris.-Nevis, 29/F3
St. Christopher-Nevis, 29/F3
St. Clair (lake), Mich., 15/C5
St-Cloud, France, 44/A2
St. Cloud, Minn., 18/K3
St. Croix (isl.), V.I. (U.S.), see detailed map p. 29
St-Denis, France, 44/B1
St-Denis (cap.), Réunion, see Mascarene Is. map p. 87
St. Elias (mts.), N. Amer., 22/E3
St-Étienne, France, 44/F5
St. Eustatius (isl.), Neth. Ant., 29/F3
St-Florent (gulf), France, 44/B6
St. Francis, Kans., 18/H5
St. George, Utah, 17/E5
St. George's (chan.), Europe, 41/D4
St. George's (cap.), Grenada, 29/G4
St-Germain, France, 44/D3
St. Gotthard (tunnel), Switz., 50/D2
St. Helena (isl.), 79/B6
St. Helens, Eng., 41/E4
St. Helens, Oreg., 16/C3
St. Helens (mt.), Wash., 16/C3
St. Helier (cap.), Jersey, Chan. Is., 41/E6
St-Jean (lake), Que., 25/J6
St. John, N. Br., 25/K7
St. John (riv.), N. Amer., 15/N1
St. John (isl.), V.I. (U.S.), see detailed map p. 29
St. Johns (cap.), Ant. & Bar., 29/G3
St. John's (cap.), Newf., 25/L6
St. Johnsbury, Vt., 20/P3
St. Joseph, Mo., 18/K5
St. Kilda, Austr., 92/H5
St. Kitts (St. Christopher) (isl.), St. Chris.-Nevis, 29/F3
St. Lawrence (isl.), Alaska, 22/B3
St. Lawrence (gulf), Can., 25/K6
St. Lawrence (riv.), N. Amer., 13/L5
St-Lô, France, 44/C3
St. Louis, Mo., 18/L5
St-Louis, Sen., 82/A5
St. Louis Park, Minn., 18/K3
St. Lucia, 29/G4
St-Malo, France, 44/B3
St. Martin (isl.), Guad. & Neth. Ant., 29/F3
St. Marys, Pa., 20/04
St. Matthew (isl.), Alaska, 22/B3
Ste-Mère-Eglise, France, 44/C3
St-Mihiel, France, 44/F3
St-Nazaire, France, 44/B4
St. Paul (isl.), Alaska, 22/C4
St. Paul (cap.), Minn., 18/K3
St. Paul, Nebr., 18/J4
St. Peter, Minn., 18/K3
St. Peter Port (cap.), Guernsey, Chan. Is., 41/E6
St. Petersburg, Fla., 21/N8
St. Pierre & Miquelon, 25/L6
St-Quentin, France, 44/E3
St. Stephen, N. Br., 25/K6
St. Thomas (isl.), V.I. (U.S.), see detailed map p. 29
St-Tropez, France, 44/G6
St. Vincent & The Grenadines, 29/G4
Saipan (isl.), N. Marianas, 88/E4
Sakakawea (lake), N. Dak., 18/H3
Sakarya (riv.), Turkey, 74/B1
Sakhalin (isl.), U.S.S.R., 59/P4
Sakishima (isls.), Japan, 67/K7
Salado del Norte (riv.), Arg., 34/G11, H9
Salamanca, Mex., 26/E4
Salamanca, Spain, 53/D2
Sala y Gómez (isl.), Chile, 8/D7
Salé, Mor., 82/C2
Salekhard, U.S.S.R., 58/G3
Salem, India, 72/D6
Salem, Mo., 19/L5
Salem (cap.), Oreg., 16/C3
Salerno, Italy, 54/E4
Salina, Kans., 18/J5
Salina Cruz, Mex., 26/F5
Salinas, Calif., 17/C5
Salinas, Ecua., 32/D4
Salisaw, Okla., 19/K6
Salisbury, Eng., 41/F5
Salisbury, Md., 20/P5
Salisbury, N.C., 21/N6
Salisbury, N.W.T., 25/K2
Salisbury (cap.), Zim., 86/E3
Salmon, Idaho, 16/E3
Salmon (riv.), Idaho, 14/C1
Salmon River (mts.), Idaho, 16/E3
Salonga Nat'l Pk., Zaire, 84/D4

Salonika (Thessaloníki), Greece, 57/F5
Salt (riv.), Ariz., 14/D4
Salta, Arg., 34/G8
Saltillo, Mex., 26/E3
Salt Lake City (cap.), Utah, 16/F4
Salto, Urug., 34/J10
Salûm, Egypt, 81/E1
Salvador, Braz., 33/N6
Salween (riv.), Asia, 68/C3
Salzach (riv.), Europe, 48/B2
Salzburg, Austria, 48/B3
Salzgitter, W. Ger., 47/D3
Samaná (bay), Dom. Rep., 28/E3
Samar (isl.), Phil., 71/H3
Samaria (reg.), Jordan, 76/C3
Samarinda, Indon., 71/F6
Samarkand, U.S.S.R., 58/G5
Sambhar (lake), India, 72/C3
Samawa, Iraq, 75/D3
Sámos (isl.), Greece, 57/H7
Samothráki (isl.), Greece, 57/G5
Samsun, Turkey, 74/C1
Samut Prakan, Thai., 68/D4
Samut Sakhon, Thai., 68/D4
San, Mali, 82/D6
San (riv.), Pol., 51/F3
San'a (cap.), Yemen Arab Rep., 74/D6
San Andrés (isl.), Col., 32/D1
San Andrés Tuxtla, Mex., 26/F4
San Angelo, Tex., 19/H7
San Antonio, Tex., 19/J7
San Antonio (riv.), Tex., 15/J5
San Benito, Tex., 19/J8
San Bernardino, Calif., 17/D6
San Bernardino (mts.), Calif., 17/E6
San Blas (cape), Fla., 21/M7
San Blas (gulf), Pan., 27/E3
San Carlos, Nic., 27/C3
San Carlos, Ven., 32/G2
San Carlos de Bariloche, Arg., 34/F12
Sánchez, Dom. Rep., 28/E3
San Clemente (isl.), Calif., 17/D6
San Cristóbal (isl.), Solomon Is., 88/G7
San Cristóbal, Ven., 32/F2
Sancti-Spíritus, Cuba, 28/B2
Sandakan, Malaysia, 71/F4
Sanderson, Tex., 19/H7
Sandersville, Ga., 21/N6
Sandgate, Austr., 91/J5
San Diego, Calif., 17/D6
Sand Hills (mts.), Nebr., 18/H4
Sandoway, Burma, 68/B3
Sandusky, Ohio, 20/N4
San Fernando, Chile, 34/F10
Sanford, Fla., 21/N7
Sanford, Maine, 20/R4
Sanford, N.C., 21/O6
San Francisco, Calif., 16/C5
San Francisco de Macorís, Dom. Rep., 28/E3
San Francisco del Oro, Mex., 26/C2
San Gabriel, Mex., 26/F4
San Germán, P. Rico, see detailed map p. 29
Sangre de Cristo (mts.), U.S., 19/G6
San Joaquin (riv.), Calif., 14/B3
San Jose, Calif., 16/C5
San José (cap.), C. Rica, 27/D3
San José, Guat., 27/B2
San José, Urug., 34/J10
San José de Chiquitos, Bol., 32/H7
San Juan, Arg., 34/G10
San Juan (riv.), Cent. Amer., 27/C3
San Juan (cap.), P. Rico, see detailed map p. 29
San Juan (riv.), U.S., 14/E3
San Juan del Norte, Nic., 27/D3
Sankt Gallen, Switz., 50/E1
Sankt Pölten, Austria, 48/C2
San Lorenzo de El Escorial, Spain, 53/E2
San Lucas (cape), Mex., 26/B3
San Luis, Arg., 34/G10
San Luis Obispo, Calif., 17/C6
San Luis Potosí, Mex., 26/E3
San Marcos, Tex., 19/J7
San Marino, 53/E3
San Matéo, Calif., 16/C5
San Miguel, El Sal., 27/C2
San Miguel de Tucumán, Arg., 34/H9
San Nicolas (isl.), Calif., 17/C6
San Pedro, Par., 34/J8
San Pedro Sula, Hond., 27/B2
San Rafael, Arg., 34/G10
San Rafael, Calif., 16/C5
San Remo, Italy, 54/A3
San Salvador (isl.), Bah., 28/C1
San Salvador (cap.), El Sal., 27/B2
San Sebastián, Spain, 53/E1
Santa Ana, Calif., 17/D6
Sta. Ana, El Sal., 27/B2
Sta. Barbara, Calif., 17/D6
Sta. Barbara (chan.), Calif., 17/C6

Sta. Barbara (isls.), Calif., 17/C6
Sta. Bárbara, Hond., 27/C2
Sta. Bárbara, Mex., 26/D2
Sta. Catalina (isl.), Calif., 17/D6
Sta. Catarina (isl.), Braz., 34/L9
Sta. Clara, Cuba, 28/B2
Sta. Cruz, Bol., 32/H7
Sta. Cruz (isl.), Calif., 17/D6
Sta. Cruz (isls.), Sol. Is., 71/G6
Sta. Cruz, Calif., 16/C5
Sta. Cruz de Tenerife, Spain, see Canary Is. map p. 52
Sta. Elena, Ecua., 32/B4
Santa Fe (cap.), N. Mex., 17/G6
Sta. Isabel (isl.), Sol. Is., 71/F6
Sta. Maria, Braz., 34/K9
Sta. Maria, Calif., 17/D6
Sta. Maria, Italy, 54/E4
Sta. María (riv.), Mex., 26/C1
Sta. Marta, Col., 32/F1
Santana do Livramento, Braz., 34/K10
Santander, Col., 32/E3
Santander, Spain, 53/D1
Sta. Paula, Calif., 17/D6
Santarém, Braz., 32/J4
Santarém, Port., 52/B3
Sta. Rosa, Arg., 34/H11
Sta. Rosa, Calif., 16/C5
Sta. Rosa (isl.), Calif., 17/D6
Sta. Rosa (mts.), Nev., 16/D4
Sta. Rosa de Copán, Hond., 27/B2
Sta. Rosalía, Mex., 26/B2
Santee (riv.), S.C., 15/L4
Santiago (cap.), Chile, 34/F10
Santiago, Dom. Rep., 28/D3
Santiago, Pan., 27/D3
Santiago, Spain, 53/B1
Santiago (mts.), Tex., 19/H7
Santiago de Cuba, Cuba, 28/C2
Santiago del Estero, Arg., 34/H9
Säntis (mt.), Switz., 50/E1
Santo Amaro, Braz., 33/N6
Sto. Ângelo, Braz., 34/K9
Sto. Antão (isl.), Cape Verde, 83/A7
Sto. Antônio, São T. & Pr., 83/F8
Santo Domingo (cap.), Dom. Rep., 28/E3
Santos, Braz., 34/L8
San Vito, Italy, 54/D2
São Bernardo do Campo, Braz., 34/L8
São Francisco (riv.), Braz., 33/N5
São João da Boa Vista, Braz., 33/L8
São José do Rio Prêto, Braz., 33/K8
São Leopoldo, Braz., 34/K9
São Luís, Braz., 33/M4
Saône (riv.), France, 44/F4
São Paulo, Braz., 34/L8
São Roque (cape), Braz., 33/O5
São Sebastião (pt.), Moz., 86/F4
São Tiago (isl.), Cape Verde, 83/B8
São Tomé (cap.), São T. & Pr., 83/F8
São Tomé e Príncipe, 83/F8
São Vicente (isl.), Cape Verde, 83/A7
São Vincent (cape), Port., 52/B4
Sapporo, Japan, 67/K2
Sapulpa, Okla., 19/K6
Saragossa, Spain, 53/F2
Sarajevo, Yugo., 56/D4
Saranac Lake, N.Y., 20/P3
Saransk, U.S.S.R., 60/G4
Sarasota, Fla., 21/N8
Saratoga Springs, N.Y., 20/P4
Saratov, U.S.S.R., 60/G4
Sarawak (state), Malaysia, 70/E5
Sardinia (isl.), Italy, 54/B4
Sargodha, Pak., 75/K3
Sarh, Chad, 80/C2
Sark (isl.), Chan. Is., 41/E6
Sarnath, India, 72/E3
Sarnia, Ont., 25/K7
Sarthe (riv.), France, 44/D4
Sasebo, Japan, 66/D7
Saskatchewan (prov.), Can., 24/F5
Saskatchewan (riv.), Can., 24/F5
Saskatoon, Sask., 24/F5
Sassandra, Iv. Coast, 83/C8
Sassari, Italy, 54/B4
Satpura (range), India, 72/D4
Satu Mare, Rom., 56/F2
Saudi Arabia, 74/C-E 4-5
Sauer (riv.), Europe, 43/J9
Sauerland (reg.), W. Ger., 46/B3
Sauk Center, Minn., 18/K3
Sauk Rapids, Minn., 18/K3
Sault Ste. Marie, Mich., 20/M3
Sault Ste. Marie, Ont., 24/H6
Saumur, France, 44/D4
Saurimo, Angola, 84/D3
Sava (riv.), Yugo., 56/D3
Savai'i (isl.), W. Samoa, 89/L8
Savalou, Benin, 83/E7
Savannah, Ga., 21/N6
Savannah (riv.), U.S., 21/N6
Savannakhét, Laos, 68/E3

Savanna la Mar, Jam., 28/B3
Save (riv.), Moz., 86/E4
Shatt-al-'Arab (riv.), Asia, 74/E3
Savona, Italy, 54/B2
Savonlinna, Fin., 39/G6
Sawtooth (mts.), U.S., 16/E4
Sawu (sea), Indon., 71/G7
Saxony (reg.), E. Ger., 47/E3
Sayre, Pa., 20/P4
Scapa Flow (chan.), Scot., 40/E1
Scarborough, Eng., 41/F3
Scarborough, Trin. & Tob., 29/G5
Schaffhausen, Switz., 50/D1
Schefferville, Que., 25/K4
Scheldt (riv.), Belg., 43/C7
Schenectady, N.Y., 20/P4
Scheveningen, Neth., 42/E4
Schiedam, Neth., 42/E5
Schleswig, W. Ger., 47/C1
Schofield Barracks, Hawaii, 23/B4
Schwäbisch Gmünd, W. Ger., 47/C4
Schwarzwald (Black) (for.), W. Ger., 47/C4
Schweinfurt, W. Ger., 47/D3
Schwerin, E. Ger., 47/D2
Schwyz, Switz., 50/D1
Scilly (isls.), Eng., 41/C6
Scotia (sea), Antarc., 35/D11
Scotland, 40/D2
Scottsbluff, Nebr., 16/H4
Scranton, Pa., 20/P4
Scutari (lake), Europe, 56/D4
Sea (isls.), U.S., 21/N7
Searcy, Ark., 19/L6
Seattle, Wash., 16/C3
Sebha, Libya, 80/B2
Sebring, Fla., 21/N8
Secunderabad, India, 72/D5
Sedalia, Mo., 18/K5
Sedan, France, 44/F3
Sefrou, Mor., 82/D2
Ségou, Mali, 82/C6
Segovia, Spain, 53/D2
Segre (riv.), Spain, 53/G2
Seguin, Tex., 19/J7
Seine (riv.), France, 44/D3
Sekondi, Ghana, 83/D8
Seldovia, Alaska, 22/D4
Selebi-Pikwe, Bots., 86/D4
Selenga (riv.), Asia, 65/G1
Sélibaby, Maur., 82/B5
Selkirk, Man., 24/G5
Selkirk, Scot., 40/E3
Selma, Ala., 21/M6
Semarang, Indon., 70/E7
Seminole, Okla., 19/J6
Seminole, Tex., 19/H6
Semipalatinsk, U.S.S.R., 58/H4
Semnan, Iran, 74/F2
Sendai, Japan, 67/K4
Senegal, 82/B-C6
Senegal (riv.), Afr., 82/B5
Sennar, Sudan, 81/F5
Sens, France, 44/E3
Seoul (cap.), S. Korea, 66/C5
Sept-Îles, Que., 25/K5
Sequoia Nat'l Pk., Calif., 17/D5
Serbia (rep.), Yugo., 56/E4
Seremban, Malaysia, 69/D7
Serengeti Nat'l Pk., Tanz., 84/F4
Serowe, Bots., 86/D4
Serpents Mouth (str.), 29/G5
Serpukhov, U.S.S.R., 60/E4
Sérrai, Greece, 57/F5
Sète, France, 44/E6
Setúbal, Port., 52/B3
Sevastopol', U.S.S.R., 60/D6
Sevenoaks, Eng., 41/C6
Severn (riv.), Ont., 24/G5
Severn (riv.), U.K., 41/E5
Severnaya Zemlya (isls.), U.S.S.R., 58/K-M 1-2
Sevier (lake), Utah, 14/D3
Sevier (riv.), Utah, 14/D3
Seville, Spain, 53/D4
Seward, Alaska, 22/C2
Seward (pen.), Alaska, 22/C2
Seward, Nebr., 18/J5
Seychelles, see detailed map p. 87
Seydhisfjördhur, Icel., 38/X1
Seymour, Ind., 20/M5
Sfax, Tun., 82/G2
's Gravenhage (The Hague) (cap.), Neth., 42/E4
Shache, China, 65/A4
Shageluk, Alaska, 22/D3
Shahat, Libya, 80/D1
Shahjahanpur, India, 72/E3
Shaktoolik, Alaska, 22/C3
Shammar, Jebel (plat.), Saudi Arabia, 74/D4
Shamrock, Tex., 19/H6
Shan (plat.), Burma, 68/C2
Shandong (Shantung) (prov.), China, 65/K4
Shanghai, China, 65/K5
Shannon (riv.), Ire., 40/B4
Shantou, China, 65/J7
Shari (riv.), Afr., 80/C5
Sharjah, U.A.E., 74/G4
Sharon, Pa., 20/N4
Shasta (dam), Calif., 16/C4
Shasta (lake), Calif., 16/C4

Shasta (mt.), Calif., 16/C4
Shaunavon, Sask., 24/F5
Shawano, Wis., 18/L3
Shawinigan, Que., 25/J6
Shawnee, Okla., 19/J6
Sheboygan, Wis., 18/L4
Sheerness, Eng., 41/G5
Sheffield, Ala., 21/M6
Sheffield, Eng., 41/F4
Shelby, Mont., 16/F2
Shelby, N.C., 21/N6
Shelbyville, Ind., 20/M5
Shelbyville, Tenn., 21/M6
Sheldon, Iowa, 18/K4
Shellbrook, Sask., 24/F5
Shenandoah, Iowa, 18/K4
Shenandoah Nat'l Pk., Va., 20/O5
Shenyang, China, 65/K3
Sherbrooke, Que., 25/J7
Sheridan, Mont., 16/F3
Sheridan, Wyo., 16/G4
Sherman, Tex., 19/J6
Sherridon, Man., 24/G5
's Hertogenbosch, Neth., 42/G5
Shetland (isls.), Scot., 40/G1
Sheyenne (riv.), N. Dak., 15/G1
Shijiazhuang (Shihkiachwang), China, 65/J4
Shikoku (isl.), Japan, 67/F7
Shillong, India, 72/G3
Shimizu, Japan, 67/J6
Shimoga, India, 72/D6
Shimonoseki, Japan, 67/E6
Shindand, Afghan., 75/H3
Shinkolobwe, Zaire, 84/E6
Shinyanga, Tanz., 84/F5
Shipki (pass), Asia, 72/D2
Shiraz, Iran, 74/F4
Shire (riv.), Afr., 85/G7
Shishmaref, Alaska, 22/C2
Shizuoka, Japan, 67/H6
Shkodër, Alb., 56/D5
Sholapur, India, 72/D5
Shorewood, Wis., 18/M4
Shreveport, La., 19/K6
Shrewsbury, Eng., 41/E4
Shumen, Bulg., 56/H4
Shungnak, Alaska, 22/D2
Shuswap (lake), Br. Col., 24/D5
Sialkot, Pak., 75/K3
Siam, see Thailand
Şian, China, see Xi'an
Sichuan (prov.), China, 65/F5
Sicily (isl.), Italy, 54/D-E6
Sidi Barrani, Egypt, 81/E1
Sidi Bel Abbès, Alg., 82/E1
Sidney, Nebr., 16/H4
Sidney, Ohio, 20/M4
Sidra (gulf), Libya, 80/C1
Siegen, W. Ger., 47/C3
Siemreab, Camb., 68/D4
Siena, Italy, 54/C3
Sierra Leone, 82/E7
Sierra Nevada (mts.), Calif., 14/B-C3
Sighişoara, Rom., 56/G2
Siguiri, Guinea, 83/C6
Sikasso, Mali, 82/C6
Sikeston, Mo., 19/L5
Sikhote-Alin' (range), U.S.S.R., 59/P5
Si Kiang (riv.), China, see Xi Jiang
Sikkim (state), India, 72/F3
Silchar, India, see Izmir
Silesia (reg.), Pol., see Slask
Silistra, Bulg., 56/H3
Silkeborg, Den., 39/F8
Sillsbee, Tex., 19/K7
Silver Peak (range), Nev., 17/D5
Silver City, N. Mex., 17/F6
Silverton, Colo., 17/F5
Simferopol', U.S.S.R., 60/D6
Simonstown, S. Africa, 86/E7
Simplon (tunnel), Europe, 50/D2
Simpson (des.), Austr., 91/F5
Sinai (pen.), Egypt, 81/F2
Sind (reg.), Pak., 75/J4
Singapore, see detailed map p. 69
Singapore (cap.), Sing., 69/D7
Singaraja, Indon., 71/F7
Singida, Tanz., 84/F4
Sining, China, see Xining
Sinkiang (prov.), China, see Xinjiang Uygur Zizhiqu
Sinnamary, Fr. Guiana, 32/K2
Sinoia, Zim., 86/D3
Sinop, Turkey, 74/C1
Sinsiang, China, see Xinxiang
Sinton, Tex., 19/J7
Sintra, Port., 52/B3
Sinúiju, N. Korea, 66/B3
Sion, Switz., 50/C2
Sioux City, Iowa, 18/J4
Sioux Falls, S. Dak., 18/J4
Sioux Lookout, Ont., 24/G5
Siracusa (Syracuse), Italy, 54/E6
Siret (riv.), Rom., 56/H2
Síros (isl.), Greece, 57/G7
Sisophon, Camb., 68/D4
Sisseton, S. Dak., 18/J3
Sitka, Alaska, 22/F4

Sittang (riv.), Burma, 68/C3
Sittwe, Burma, 68/B2
Sivas, Turkey, 74/C2
Siwa (oasis), Egypt, 81/E2
Sixth Cataract (falls), Sudan, 81/F4
Skagen, Den., 39/G8
Skagerrak (str.), Europe, 39/E-G8
Skagway, Alaska, 22/F4
Skeena (riv.), Br. Col., 24/D5
Skeleton Coast (reg.), Afr., 86/A3
Skellefteå, Sweden, 39/M4
Skien, Nor., 39/F7
Skikda, Alg., 82/F1
Skopje, Yugo., 56/E5
Skowhegan, Maine, 20/R3
Skye (isl.), Scot., 40/C2
Slaton, Tex., 19/H6
Slave (riv.), Can., 24/E3
Slave Coast (reg.), Afr., 83/E7
Slavgorod, U.S.S.R., 58/H4
Sleetmute, Alaska, 22/D3
Sliema, Malta, 54/E7
Sligo, Ire., 40/B3
Slovak Socialist Rep., Czech., 49/E2
Slovenia (rep.), Yugo., 56/B2
Slupsk, Pol., 51/C1
Smallwood (res.), Newf., 25/K5
Smithers, Br. Col., 24/D5
Smoky (riv.), Can., 24/C4
Smolensk, U.S.S.R., 60/D4
Smyrna, Turkey, see Izmir
Snake (riv.), U.S., 14/D2
Sneeukop (mt.), S. Africa, 86/F6
Snowdon (mt.), Wales, 41/D4
Snow Lake, Man., 24/G5
Snowy (riv.), Austr., 92/E5
Snyder, Tex., 19/H6
Sochi, U.S.S.R., 60/E6
Society (isls.), Fr. Poly., 89/L7
Socorro, N. Mex., 17/G6
Socotra (isl.) P.D.R. Yemen, 74/F7
Söderhamn, Sweden, 39/K6
Södertälje, Sweden, 39/K7
Soest, W. Ger., 47/C3
Sofia (cap.), Bulg., 56/F4
Sogamoso, Col., 32/F2
Sognafjorden (fjord), Nor., 39/D6
Sohâg, Egypt, 81/F2
Soissons, France, 44/E3
Sokna, Libya, 80/C2
Sokodé, Togo, 83/E7
Sokoto, Nigeria, 83/F6
Sollefteå, Sweden, 39/K5
Sologne (reg.), France, 44/E4
Solomon (isls.), Pacific, 89/C-E 2-3
Solomon (sea), Pacific, 88/F6
Solomon Islands, 88/F6
Solothurn, Switz., 50/C1
Solway (firth), U.K., 40/D3
Somalia, 85/J3
Somerset, Ky., 21/M5
Somerset (isl.), N.W.T., 24/G1
Somme (riv.), France, 44/D2
Sonderborg, Den., 39/G9
Sondrio, Italy, 54/B1
Songea, Tanz., 85/G6
Songhua (riv.), China, 65/M2
Söngjin, N. Korea, 66/C2
Songkhla, Thai., 68/D6
Sonora, Calif., 16/C5
Sonora (state), Mex., 26/B1-2
Sonora, Texas, 19/H7
Sonsonate, El Sal., 27/B2
Soochow, China, see Suzhou
Sopot, Pol., 51/D1
Sopron, Hung., 49/D3
Soria, Spain, 53/E2
Sorocaba, Braz., 34/L8
Sorrento, Italy, 54/E4
Souris, Man., 24/F5
Souris, P.E.I., 25/K6
Souris (riv.), N. Amer., 15/F1
Sousse, Tun., 82/G1
South (isl.), N.Z., 94/B5
South Africa, 86/C-D 4-6
South America, 30-31
South Australia (state), Austr., 91/E5
South Bend, Ind., 20/M4
South Boston, Va., 21/O5
South Carolina (state), U.S., 15/K4
South China (sea), Asia, 70/E3
South Dakota (state), U.S., 15/G2
Southend-on-Sea, Eng., 41/G5
Southern Alps (mts.), N.Z., 94/C5
Southern Cross, Austr., 91/B6
South Georgia (isl.), Falk. Is., 34/J14
South Korea, 66/B-D 2-3
South Magnetic Pole, Antarc., 35/C5
South Orkney (isls.), Antarc., 35/C11
South Platte (riv.), U.S., 15/F2
South Pole, 35/A3
Southport, Eng., 41/D4
South Sandwich (isls.), Antarc., 35/C12

South Shetland (isls.), Antarc., 35/C10
South Suburban, India, 72/F2
South-West Africa, see Namibia
Sovetskaya Gavan', U.S.S.R., 59/P5
Soweto, S. Africa, 86/H6
Soyo, Angola, 84/B5
Spain, 53
Spandau, W. Ger., 47/E3
Spanish Fork, Utah, 16/E4
Spanish Sahara, see Western Sahara
Spanish Town, Jam., 28/C3
Sparks, Nev., 16/D5
Sparta, Greece, 57/C4
Sparta, Wis., 18/L3
Spartanburg, S.C., 21/N6
Spenard, Alaska, 22/C3
Spencer, Iowa, 18/K4
Spencer (gulf), Austr., 91/F6
Speyer, W. Ger., 47/C4
Spiez, Switz., 50/C2
Spirit River, Alta., 24/E4
Spitsbergen (isl.), Nor., 39/C2
Split, Yugo., 56/C4
Splügen (pass), Europe, 50/E2
Spokane, Wash., 16/D3
Spoleto, Italy, 54/D3
Spooner, Wis., 18/L3
Spree (riv.), Ger., 47/F3
Springdale, Ark., 19/K5
Springerville, Ariz., 17/F6
Springfield (cap.), Ill., 18/L5
Springfield, Mass., 20/P4
Springfield, Mo., 18/K5
Springfield, Ohio, 20/N5
Springfield, Oreg., 16/C3
Springfield, Tenn., 21/M5
Springs, S. Africa, 86/J6
Springville, Utah, 16/E4
Spur, Texas, 19/H6
Sri Lanka, 73/E7
Srinagar, India, 72/D2
Stafford, Eng., 41/E4
Staked (Llano Estacado) (plain), U.S., 19/H6
Stalingrad (Volgograd), U.S.S.R., 60/F5
Stamford, Eng., 41/F4
Stanley (cap.), Falk. Is., 34/J14
Stanley (falls), Zaire, 84/E3
Stanley Pool (lake), Afr., 84/C4
Stanleyville, see Kisangani, Zaire
Stanovoy (range), U.S.S.R., 59/N4
Stara Zagora, Bulg., 56/G4
Starkville, Miss., 19/L6
State College, Pa., 20/O4
Staten (Estados) (isl.), Arg., 34/H14
Statesboro, Ga., 21/N6
Statesville, N.C., 21/N6
Staunton, Va., 20/O5
Stavanger, Nor., 39/D7
Stavropol', U.S.S.R., 60/F5
Steamboat Springs, Colo., 16/G4
Steinkjer, Nor., 39/G4
Stellenbosch, S. Africa, 86/F6
Stendal, E. Ger., 47/D2
Stepanakert, U.S.S.R., 60/G7
Stephenville, Newf., 25/L6
Sterling, Colo., 18/H4
Sterling, Ill., 18/L4
Stettin (Szczecin), Pol., 51/B2
Stettler, Alta., 24/E5
Steubenville, Ohio, 20/N4
Stevens Village, Alaska, 22/E3
Stewart, Br. Col., 24/D4
Stewart (isl.), N.Z., 94/A7
Stewart (riv.), Yukon, 24/C3
Stewart River, Yukon, 24/C3
Steyr, Austria, 48/C2
Stikine (riv.), Br. Col., 24/C4
Stillwater, Okla., 19/J5
Stip, Yugo., 56/F5
Stirling, Scot., 40/D2
Stockholm (cap.), Sweden, 39/L7
Stockport, Eng., 41/F4
Stockton, Calif., 16/C5
Stoeng Treng, Camb., 68/E4
Stoke-on-Trent, Eng., 41/E4
Storm Lake, Iowa, 18/K4
Stornoway, Scot., 40/C1
Stralsund, E. Ger., 47/E1
Strasbourg, France, 44/G3
Stratford-on-Avon, Eng., 41/F4
Streator, Ill., 18/L4
Stromboli (isl.), Italy, 54/E6
Strumica, Yugo., 56/F5
Stuart (range), Austr., 91/E5
Sturgeon Bay, Wis., 20/M3
Sturgeon Falls, Ont., 25/H6
Sturgis, Mich., 20/M4
Sturt (des.), Austr., 91/G5
Stuttgart, Ark., 19/L6
Stuttgart, W. Ger., 47/C4
Suakin, Sudan, 81/G4
Subotica, Yugo., 56/D2
Sucre (cap.), Bol., 32/G7
Sudan, 81/E4
Sudan (reg.), Afr., 81/C-F5
Sudbury, Ont., 25/H6
Sudeten (mts.), Europe, 48/C1-3
Suez, Egypt, 81/F1
Suez (canal), Egypt, 81/F1

Suffolk, Va., **21/O5**
Sukhumi, U.S.S.R., **60/F6**
Sulaimaniya, Iraq, **74/D2**
Sulawesi (Celebes) (isl.), Indon., **71/G6**
Sulitjelma (mt.), Europe, **39/K3**
Sullivan, Mo., **18/L5**
Sulphur, La., **19/K7**
Sulphur, Okla., **19/J6**
Sulphur Springs, Tex., **19/K6**
Sulu (sea), Asia, **71/F4**
Sulu (arch.), Phil., **71/G4**
Sumatra (isl.), Indon., **70/B-C 5-6**
Sumba (isl.), Indon., **71/F7**
Sumbawa (isl.), Indon., **71/F7**
Sumbawanga, Tanz., **84/F5**
Summerville, Ga., **21/M6**
Sumter, S.C., **21/N6**
Sunbury, Pa., **20/O4**
Sunda (str.), Indon., **70/C7**
Sundarbans (swamp), Asia, **72/F4**
Sunderland, Eng., **41/F3**
Sundsvall, Sweden, **39/K5**
Sungari (riv.), China, see Songhua
Sunnyside, Wash., **16/D3**
Sunnyvale, Calif., **14/B3**
Sun Valley, Idaho, **16/E4**
Suo (sea), Japan, **66/F7**
Superior (lake), N. Amer., **15/J1**
Superior, Wis., **20/K3**
Sur, Leb., **74/C1**
Surabaya, Indon., **70/E7**
Surakarta, Indon., **70/E7**
Surat, India, **72/C4**
Suriname, **32/J3**
Susanville, Calif., **16/C4**
Susten (pass), Switz., **50/D2**
Sutherland, Austr., **93/J4**
Sutlej (riv.), Asia, **72/C3**
Suva (cap.), Fiji, **89/Q11**
Suwannee (riv.), U.S., **15/K5**
Suzhou, China, **65/K6**
Svalbard (isls.), Nor., **39/C2**
Svay Rieng, Camb., **68/E5**
Svendborg, Den., **39/G9**
Sverdlovsk, U.S.S.R., **58/F4**
Sverdrup (isls.), N.W.T., **25/M3**
Swabian Jura (mts.), W. Ger., **47/C4**
Swakopmund, Namibia, **86/A4**
Swan (isls.), Hond., **27/C1**
Swan River, Man., **24/G5**
Swansea, Wales, **41/D5**
Swatow, China, see Shantou
Swaziland, **86/E5**
Sweden, **39**
Sweetwater, Tex., **19/H6**
Swift Current, Sask., **25/F5**
Swindon, Eng., **41/E5**
Switzerland, **50**
Sydney, Austr., **92/F3**
Sydney, N.S., **25/L6**
Sylacauga, Ala., **21/M6**
Syracuse, Italy, **54/E6**
Syracuse, N.Y., **20/O4**
Syrdar'ya (riv.), U.S.S.R., **58/G5**
Syria, **74/C2**
Syrian (des.), Asia, **74/C-D3**
Syrte, Libya, **80/C1**
Szczecin, Pol., **51/B2**
Szechwan (prov.), China, see Sichuan
Szeged, Hung., **49/E3**

T

Table (bay), S. Africa, **86/E6**
Tabor (mt.), Isr., **76/C2**
Tabora, Tanz., **85/F5**
Tabou, Iv. Coast, **83/C8**
Tabriz, Iran, **74/E2**
Tacna, Peru, **32/F7**
Tacoma, Wash., **16/C3**
Tacuarembó, Urug., **34/J10**
Tadjoura, Djibouti, **81/H5**
Tadmor (Palmyra) (ruins), Syria, **74/C3**
Tadmur, Syria, **74/C3**
Tadoussac, Que., **25/J6**
Tadzhik S.S.R., U.S.S.R., **59/H6**
Taegu, S. Korea, **66/D6**
Taejŏn, S. Korea, **66/C5**
Taganrog, U.S.S.R., **60/E5**
Tagus (riv.), Europe, **52/B3**
Tahiti (isl.), Fr. Poly., **89/S13**
Tahlequah, Okla., **19/K6**
Tahoua, Niger, **82/F6**
Tahoe (lake), U.S., **16/C5**
Taichung, China, **65/J7**
Taif, Saudi Arabia, **74/D5**
Tainan, China, **65/J7**
Taipei (cap.), Taiwan (Rep. of China), **65/K7**
Taiwan (isl.), China, **65/K7**
Taiyuan, China, **65/H4**
Ta'izz, Yemen Arab Rep., **74/D7**
Tajo (Tagus) (riv.), Spain, **53/D3**
Taklamakan Shamo (des.), China, **65/A-C4**
Takoradi, Ghana, **83/D8**
Talara, Peru, **32/D4**
Talca, Chile, **34/F11**
Talcahuano, Chile, **34/F11**

Talladega, Ala., **21/M6**
Tallahassee (cap.), Fla., **21/M7**
Tallinn, U.S.S.R., **60/B3**
Tallulah, La., **19/L6**
Tamale, Ghana, **83/D7**
Tamanrasset, Alg., **82/F4**
Tambacaounda, Sen., **83/B6**
Tambov, U.S.S.R., **60/F4**
Tampa, Fla., **21/N8**
Tampa (bay), Fla., **15/K5**
Tampere, Fin., **39/N6**
Tampico, Mex., **26/F3**
Tamworth, Austr., **92/F2**
Tana (lake), Eth., **81/G5**
Tanacross, Alaska, **22/E3**
Tanana, Alaska, **22/D2**
Tanana (riv.), Alaska, **22/E3**
Tanarive, Madag., see Antananarivo
Tandil, Arg., **34/J11**
Tanezrouft (des.), Afr., **82/D-E4**
Tanga, Tanz., **85/G4**
Tanganyika, see Tanzania
Tanganyika (lake), Afr., **84/E5**
Tangier, Mor., **82/C1**
Tangshan, China, **65/J4**
Tanta, Egypt, **81/F1**
Tanzania, **85/F5**
Taormina, Italy, **54/E6**
Taos, N. Mex., **19/G5**
Tapachula, Mex., **26/F5**
Tapajós (riv.), Braz., **32/J5**
Tarascon, France, **44/F6**
Tarawa (atoll), Kiribati, **88/H5**
Tarboro, N.C., **21/O6**
Taree, Austr., **92/G2**
Tarfaya, Mor., **82/B3**
Tarhuna, Libya, **80/B1**
Tarija, Bol., **32/H8**
Tarim He (riv.), China, **65/C3**
Tarkio, Mo., **18/K4**
Tarnów, Pol., **51/E4**
Taroudant, Mor., **82/C2**
Tarpon Springs, Fla., **21/N7**
Tarragona, Spain, **53/G2**
Tarsus, Turkey, **74/B2**
Tartu, U.S.S.R., **60/C3**
Taschereau, Que., **25/J6**
Tashkent, U.S.S.R., **58/G5**
Tasman (sea), Pacific, **88/G9**
Tasmania (state), Austr., **95**
Tata, Hung., **49/E3**
Tatar (str.), U.S.S.R., **59/P4**
Tatnam (cape), Man., **24/G4**
Tatra, High (mts.), Europe, **48/E2**
Taubaté, Braz., **34/L8**
Taunton, Eng., **41/E5**
Taunus (mts.), W. Ger., **47/C3**
Taupo (lake), N.Z., **94/F3**
Taurus (mts.), Turkey, **74/B2**
Tavoy, Burma, **68/C4**
Taxco, Mex., **26/E4**
Tay (firth), Scot., **40/E2**
Taylor, Tex., **19/J7**
Taylorville, Ill., **18/L5**
Taymyr (pen.), U.S.S.R., **58/L2**
Tay Ninh, Viet., **68/E5**
Tbilisi, U.S.S.R., **60/F6**
Tchibanga, Gabon, **84/B4**
Tczew, Pol., **51/D1**
Tébessa, Alg., **82/F1**
Tees (riv.), Eng., **41/F3**
Tegucigalpa (cap.), Hond., **27/C2**
Tehachapi (mts.), Calif., **17/D6**
Tehran (cap.), Iran, **74/F2**
Tehuantepec, Mex., **26/F5**
Tejo (Tagus) (riv.), Port., **52/B3**
Tel Aviv-Jaffa, Isr., **76/B3**
Telluride, Colo., **17/F5**
Tema, Ghana, **83/E7**
Tempe, Ariz., **17/F6**
Temple, Tex., **19/J7**
Temuco, Chile, **34/F11**
Tenasserim, Burma, **68/C5**
Tenerife (isl.), see Canary Is. map p. 52
Tennessee (riv.), U.S., **15/J3**
Tennessee (state), U.S., **15/J3**
Ten Thousand (isls.), Fla., **21/N8**
Teófilo Otoni, Braz., **33/M7**
Tepic, Mex., **26/D4**
Teplice, Czech., **48/B1**
Teresina, Braz., **33/M4**
Termini Imerese, Italy, **54/D6**
Ternate, Indon., **71/H5**
Terni, Italy, **54/D3**
Terrace, Br. Col., **24/D5**
Terre Haute, Ind., **20/M5**
Teruel, Spain, **53/F2**
Teslin (lake), Yukon, **24/C3**
Tete, Moz., **86/E3**
Teutoburger Wald (for.), W. Ger., **47/C2**
Texarkana, Ark., **19/K6**
Texarkana, Tex., **19/K6**
Texas (state), U.S., **15/G4**
Texas City, Tex., **19/K7**
Texel (isl.), Neth., **42/F2**
Texoma (lake), U.S., **19/J6**
Thailand, **68**
Thai Nguyen, Viet., **68/E2**
Thames (riv.), Eng., **41/F5**

Thásos (isl.), Greece, **57/G5**
The Dalles, Oreg., **16/C3**
Theodore Roosevelt (lake), Ariz., **17/F6**
Theodore Roosevelt Nat'l Pk., N. Dak., **18/G3**
Thessalon, Ont., **24/H6**
Thessaloníki, Greece, **57/F5**
Thief River Falls, Minn., **18/J2**
Thiès, Sen., **83/A6**
Thika, Kenya, **85/G4**
Thimphu (cap.), Bhutan, **72/F3**
Third Cataract (rapids), Sudan, **81/F4**
Thisted, Den., **39/F8**
Thívai, Greece, **57/F6**
Thomas-Müntzer-Stadt, E. Ger., **47/D3**
Thomasville, Ga., **21/N7**
Thompson, Man., **24/G4**
Thon Buri, Thai., **68/D4**
Three Forks, Mont., **16/E3**
Thule A.F.B. (Dundas), Greenl., **96/M3**
Thun, Switz., **50/C2**
Thunder Bay, Ont., **24/H6**
Thüringer Wald (for.), E. Ger., **47/D3**
Thuringia (reg.), E. Ger., **47/D3**
Thursday Island, Austr., **91/G2**
Thurso, Scot., **40/E1**
Tianjin, China, **65/J4**
Tiber (riv.), Italy, **54/D3**
Tiberias, Isr., **76/C2**
Tibesti (mts.), Chad, **80/C3**
Tibet (reg.), China, see Xizang
Ticonderoga, N.Y., **20/P4**
Tidjikja, Maur., **82/B5**
Tien Shan (mts.), Asia, **65/A-B3**
Tientsin, China, see Tianjin
Tierra del Fuego (isl.), S. Amer., **34/G14**
Tiffin, Ohio, **20/N4**
Tifton, Ga., **21/N7**
Tigris (riv.), Asia, **74/E3**
Tihama (reg.), Asia, **74/C-D 5-7**
Tijuana, Mex., **26/A1**
Tilburg, Neth., **42/G5**
Tillamook, Oreg., **16/B3**
Timaru, N.Z., **94/C6**
Timbuktu, Mali, **82/D5**
Timiskaming (lake), Can., **25/J4**
Timişoara, Rom., **56/E3**
Timmins, Ont., **25/H6**
Timor (isl.), Indon., **71/H7**
Timor (sea), **71/D2**
Tinian (isl.), N. Marianas, **88/E4**
Tipperary, Ire., **40/B4**
Tiranë (Tirana) (cap.), Alb., **56/E5**
Tîrgovişte, Rom., **56/G3**
Tîrgu Neamţ, Rom., **56/G2**
Tirich Mir (mt.), Pak., **75/K2**
Tirol (prov.), Austria, **48/A3**
Tiruchirappalli, India, **72/D6**
Tisa (riv.), Europe, **49/F3**
Titicaca (lake), S. Amer., **32/F7**
Titograd, Yugo., **56/D4**
Titusville, Fla., **21/N7**
Tiverton, Eng., **41/E5**
Tizi Ouzou, Alg., **82/E1**
Tjirebon, Indon., **70/D7**
Tlaxcala, Mex., **26/F4**
Tlemcen, Alg., **82/D2**
Toamasina, Madag., **87/H3**
Tobago (isl.), Trin. & Tob., **29/G5**
Tobol'sk, U.S.S.R., **58/G4**
Tobruk, Libya, **81/D1**
Tocantins (riv.), Braz., **33/L4**
Toccoa, Ga., **21/N6**
Tocopilla, Chile, **32/F8**
Toggenburg (dist.), Switz., **50/E1**
Togo, **83/E7**
Tokaj, Hung., **49/F2**
Tokelau (isls.), **88/J6**
Tokushima, Japan, **67/G7**
Tokyo (cap.), Japan, **67/O2**
Toledo, Ohio, **20/N4**
Toledo, Spain, **53/D3**
Toledo Bend (res.), U.S., **15/H4**
Toliary, Madag., **87/G4**
Tolima (mt.), Col., **32/E3**
Tolosa, Spain, **53/F1**
Toluca, Mex., **26/E4**
Tombigbee (riv.), U.S., **15/J4**
Tombouctou, Mali, see Timbuktu
Tomsk, U.S.S.R., **58/J4**
Tonga, **88/J8**
Tongareva (atoll), Cook Is., **89/L6**
Tongatapu (isls.), Tonga, **88/J8**
Tongue (riv.), U.S., **18/G3**
Tonkin (gulf), Asia, **68/E3**
Tonle Sap (lake), Camb., **68/D4**
Tonopah, Nev., **16/D4**
Tooele, Utah, **16/E4**
Topeka (cap.), Kans., **18/K5**
Toppenish, Wash., **16/C3**
Torino (Turin), Italy, **54/A2**
Toronto (cap.), Ont., **25/H7**
Torquay, Eng., **41/E5**
Torrance, Calif., **14/C4**
Torre Annunziata, Italy, **54/E4**
Torreón, Mex., **26/D3**
Torres (str.), **91/G1**
Tórshavn, Faeroe Is., **37/D2**

Tortola (isl.), V.I. (Br.), see detailed map, p. 29
Tortuga (isl.), Haiti, **28/D2**
Toruń, Pol., **51/D2**
Touggourt, Alg., **82/F2**
Toul, France, **44/F3**
Toulon, France, **44/F6**
Toulouse, France, **44/D6**
Toungoo, Burma, **68/C3**
Tournai, Belg., **43/C7**
Tours, France, **44/D4**
Townsville, Austr., **91/H3**
Toyama, Japan, **67/H5**
Toyohashi, Japan, **67/H6**
Trabzon, Turkey, **74/C1**
Trafalgar (cape), Spain, **53/C4**
Trail, Br. Col., **24/E6**
Tranquebar, India, **72/E6**
Trans-Himalaya (mts.), China, see Gangdisê Shan
Transkei (aut. rep.), S. Africa, **86/D6**
Transvaal (prov.), S. Africa, **86/D4**
Transylvanian Alps (mts.), Rom., **56/G3**
Trapani, Italy, **54/D5**
Traverse City, Mich., **18/M3**
Travancore (reg.), India, **72/D7**
Treinta y Tres, Urug., **34/K10**
Trelleborg, Sweden, **39/H9**
Trent (riv.), Eng., **41/F4**
Trento, Italy, **54/C1**
Trenton, Mo., **18/K4**
Trenton (cap.), N.J., **20/P4**
Trier, W. Ger., **47/B4**
Trieste, Italy, **54/D1**
Tríkkala, Greece, **56/F6**
Trincomalee, Sri Lanka, **73/E7**
Trinidad, Bol., **32/H6**
Trinidad, Colo., **18/G5**
Trinidad (isl.), Trin. & Tob., **29/G5**
Trinidad, Urug., **34/J10**
Trinidad & Tobago, **29/G5**
Trinity (riv.), Calif., **16/C4**
Trinity (riv.), Tex., **14/G4**
Tripoli (Tarabulus), Leb., **74/C3**
Tripoli (cap.), Libya, **80/B1**
Tripolis, Greece, **57/F7**
Tripolitania (reg.), Libya, **80/B1**
Tristan da Cunha (isl.), St. Helena, **8/J6**
Trivandrum, India, **72/D7**
Trois-Rivières, Que., **25/J6**
Tromsø, Nor., **39/L2**
Trondheim, Nor., **39/F5**
Troy, Ala., **21/M7**
Troy, N.Y., **20/P4**
Troy, Ohio, **20/M4**
Troyes, France, **44/F3**
Trucial States, see United Arab Emirates
Trujillo, Hond., **27/C2**
Trujillo, Peru, **32/E5**
Trujillo, Ven., **32/F2**
Truk (isls.), Fed. States of Micronesia, **88/F5**
Trumann, Ark., **19/L6**
Truro, Eng., **41/D5**
Truro, N.S., **25/K7**
Truth or Consequences, N. Mex., **17/G6**
Tsingtao, China, see Qingdao
Tsitsihar, China, see Qiqihar
Tsumeb, Namibia, **86/B3**
Tuamotu (arch.), Fr. Poly., **89/M7**
Tubai (Austral) (isls.), Fr. Poly., **89/M8**
Tubmanburg, Lib., **83/B7**
Tucson, Ariz., **17/F6**
Tucumcari, N. Mex., **19/G6**
Tuktoyaktuk, N.W.T., **24/C1**
Tula, U.S.S.R., **60/E4**
Tulare (lake), Calif., **17/C6**
Tularosa, N. Mex., **19/G6**
Tulia, Tex., **19/H6**
Tullahoma, Tenn., **21/M6**
Tulsa, Okla., **19/K5**
Tunis (cap.), Tun., **82/G1**
Tunisia, **82/G1**
Tunja, Col., **32/F2**
Tununak, Alaska, **22/C3**
Tupelo, Miss., **19/L6**
Turin, Italy, **54/A2**
Turkana (lake), Afr., **85/G3**
Turkestan, U.S.S.R., **58/G5**
Turkey, **74/A-D2**
Turkmen S.S.R., U.S.S.R., **58/F6**
Turks (isls.), Turks & Caicos Is., **28/D2**
Turks & Caicos Is., **28/D2**
Turku, Fin., **39/N6**
Turlock, Calif., **16/C5**
Turneffe (isls.), Belize, **27/C1**
Turnhout, Belg., **43/F6**
Tuscaloosa, Ala., **19/M6**
Tuscany (reg.), Italy, **54/C3**
Tutuila (isl.), Amer. Samoa, **88/J7**
Tuvalu, **88/H6**
Tuxtla Gutiérrez, Mex., **26/G5**
Tweed (riv.), Eng., **41/E3**
Twin Falls, Idaho, **16/E4**
Two Harbors, Minn., **18/L3**
Tyler, Tex., **19/K6**
Tyne (riv.), Eng., **41/F3**

Tyre (Sur), Leb., **74/C1**
Tyrrhenian (sea), Italy, **54/C-E 4-5**
Tzepo, China, see Zibo

U

Ubangi (riv.), Afr., **84/C3**
Uberaba, Braz., **33/L7**
Ubon, Thai., **68/E4**
Ucayali (riv.), Peru, **32/E5**
Udine, Italy, **54/D1**
Udon Thani, Thai., **68/D3**
Ufa, U.S.S.R., **60/J4**
Uganda, **84/F3**
Uige, Angola, **84/C5**
Uitenhage, S. Africa, **86/C6**
Ujjain, India, **72/D4**
Ujung Pandang, Indon., **71/F6**
Ukiah, Calif., **16/C5**
Ukrainian S.S.R., U.S.S.R., **58/C5**
Ulaanbaatar (cap.), Mong., **65/G2**
Ulan-Ude, U.S.S.R., **58/L4**
Uliastay (Uliassutai), Mong., **65/E2**
Ulm, W. Ger., **47/C4**
Ul'yanovsk, U.S.S.R., **60/G4**
Ulysses, Kans., **19/H5**
Umeå, Sweden, **39/M5**
Umm al Qaiwain, U.A.E., **74/G4**
Umnak (isl.), Alaska, **22/C5**
Umpqua (riv.), Oreg., **16/C4**
Umtali, Zim., **86/E3**
Unalaska, Alaska, **22/C5**
Unalaska (isl.), Alaska, **22/C5**
Ungava (bay), Can., **25/K4**
Ungava (pen.), Que., **25/J3**
Unimak (isl.), Alaska, **22/C4**
Union City, Tenn., **19/L5**
Union of Soviet Socialist Republics, **58-61**
United Arab Emirates, **74/F-G4**
United Arab Republic, see Egypt
United Kingdom, **40-41**
United States, **14-15**
Unterwalden (dist.), Switz., **50/D2**
Upemba Nat'l Pk., Zaire, **84/E5**
Upernavik, Greenl., **96/B8**
Upolu (isl.), W. Samoa, **89/M8**
Upper Klamath (lake), Oreg., **16/C4**
Upper Tunguska (riv.), U.S.S.R., **58/K4**
Upper Volta, **82/D6**
Uppsala, Sweden, **39/K7**
Ural (mts.), U.S.S.R., **58/F5**
Ural (riv.), U.S.S.R., **58/F5**
Uranium City, Sask., **24/F4**
Urbana, Ill., **18/L5**
Urmia, Iran, **74/D2**
Urmia (lake), Iran, **74/E2**
Uruguay, **34/J10**
Uruguay (riv.), S. Amer., **34/J9**
Ürümqi (Urumchi), China, **65/C3**
Ushuaia, Arg., **34/G14**
Ussuri (riv.), Asia, **65/M2**
Ustí nad Labem, Czech., **48/C1**
Utah (state), U.S., **14/D3**
Utica, N.Y., **20/P4**
Utrecht, Neth., **42/G4**
Uvalde, Texas, **19/H7**
Uxmal (ruins), Mex., **26/H4**
Uzbek S.S.R., U.S.S.R., **59/G5**

V

Vaal (riv.), S. Africa, **86/D5**
Vaasa, Fin., **39/M5**
Vadodara, India, **72/C4**
Vaduz (cap.), Liecht., **50/E1**
Valdez, Alaska, **22/E3**
Valdivia, Chile, **34/F11**
Val-d'Or, Que., **25/J6**
Valdosta, Ga., **21/N7**
Valencia, Spain, **53/F3**
Valencia, Ven., **32/G2**
Valladolid, Spain, **53/D2**
Vallejo, Calif., **14/B3**
Valletta (cap.), Malta, **54/E7**
Valley City, N. Dak., **18/J3**
Valparaíso, Chile, **34/F10**
Van Buren, Ark., **19/K6**
Vancouver, Br. Col., **24/D6**
Vancouver (isl.), Br. Col., **24/D6**
Vandalia, Ill., **18/L5**
Vänern (lake), Sweden, **39/H7**
Van Horn, Texas, **19/G7**
Vanua Levu (isl.), Fiji, **88/H7**
Vanuatu, **88/G7**
Van Wert, Ohio, **20/M4**
Varanasi, India, **72/E3**
Vardar (riv.), Europe, **56/E5**
Varna, Bulg., **56/H4**
Västeras, Sweden, **39/K7**
Vatican City, **54/B6**
Västervik, Sweden, **39/J7**
Vegreville, Alta., **24/E5**
Veliko Türnovo, Bulg., **56/G4**
Venda (aut. rep.), S. Africa, **86/E3**

Venezia, Italy, see Venice
Venezuela, **32/F-H2**
Venice, Italy, **54/D2**
Ventura, Calif., **17/D6**
Veracruz, Mex., **26/F4**
Vercelli, Italy, **54/B2**
Verde (riv.), Ariz., **17/F6**
Verde (cape), Sen., **82/A6**
Verdun, France, **44/F3**
Vereeniging, S. Africa, **86/D5**
Vermilion (lake), Minn., **18/K2**
Vermillion, S. Dak., **18/J4**
Vermont (state), U.S., **15/M2**
Vernon, Br. Col., **24/E5**
Vernon, Tex., **19/J6**
Vero Beach, Fla., **21/N8**
Verona, Italy, **54/C2**
Versailles, France, **44/A2**
Vesuvius (vol.), Italy, **54/E4**
Viborg, Den., **39/F8**
Vicenza, Italy, **54/C2**
Vichy, France, **44/E4**
Vicksburg, Miss., **19/L6**
Victoria (Mosi-Oa-Tunya) (falls), Afr., **86/D3**
Victoria (lake), Afr., **85/F4**
Victoria (state), Austr., **92/A-D5**
Victoria (cap.), Br. Col., **24/D6**
Victoria (cap.), Hong Kong, **65/H7**
Victoria (isl.), N.W.T., **24/E1**
Victoria (str.), N.W.T., **24/G2**
Victoria, Tex., **19/J7**
Vidalia, Ga., **21/N6**
Vienna (cap.), Austria, **49/D2**
Vientiane (cap.), Laos, **68/D3**
Vietnam, **68/E-F 2-5**
Vigo, Spain, **52/B1**
Vijayawada, India, **72/D5**
Vila (cap.), Vanuatu, **88/G7**
Vila de Sena, Moz., **86/E4**
Vila Fontes, Moz., **86/E3**
Vila Real, Port., **52/C2**
Villarrica, Par., **34/J9**
Vilna, U.S.S.R., **60/C3**
Viña del Mar, Chile, **34/F10**
Vincennes, France, **44/B2**
Vincennes, Ind., **20/M5**
Vinita, Okla., **19/K5**
Virgin (isls.), N. Indies, see detailed map p. 29
Virginia (state), U.S. **15/L3**
Virginia, Minn., **18/K3**
Virginia Beach, Va., **20/P5**
Virginia City, Nev., **16/D5**
Virunga Nat'l Pk., Afr., **84/F4**
Visakhapatnam, India, **72/E5**
Visalia, Calif., **17/D5**
Viscount Melville (sound), N.W.T., **24/F1**
Vistula (riv.), Pol., **51/D2**
Viti Levu (isl.), Fiji, **88/H7**
Vitoria, Spain, **53/E1**
Vladimir, U.S.S.R., **60/F3**
Vladivostok, U.S.S.R., **59/O5**
Vlissingen (Flushing), Neth., **42/C6**
Vlorë, Alb., **56/D5**
Vltava (riv.), Czech., **48/B2**
Vohimena (cape), Madag., **87/G5**
Volga (riv.), U.S.S.R., **60/G5**
Volgograd, U.S.S.R., **60/F5**
Vologda, U.S.S.R., **60/E3**
Vólos, Greece, **56/F6**
Volta (lake), Ghana, **80/D7**
Volta Redonda, Braz., **34/M8**
Vorkuta, U.S.S.R., **60/K1**
Voronezh, U.S.S.R., **60/E4**
Voroshilovgrad, U.S.S.R., **60/E5**
Vosges (mts.), France, **44/G3**
Voyageurs Nat'l Pk., Minn., **15/H1**
Vyborg, U.S.S.R., **60/C2**

W

Wabash (riv.), U.S., **15/J2**
Wabush Lake, Newf., **25/K5**
Waco, Tex., **19/J7**
Wad Medani, Sudan, **81/F5**
Wager (bay), N.W.T., **24/G3**
Wagga Wagga, Austr., **92/D4**
Wagon Mound, N. Mex., **19/G5**
Wahiawa, Hawaii, **23/B4**
Wahpeton, N. Dak., **18/J3**
Waialua, Hawaii, **23/B3**
Waikiki, Hawaii, **23/C4**
Wailua, Hawaii, **23/B1**
Wailuku, Hawaii, **23/B4**
Waimanalo (bay), Hawaii, **23/D4**
Waimea, Hawaii, **23/B2**
Waipahu, Hawaii, **23/B4**
Wajir, Kenya, **85/H3**
Wake (isl.), Pacific, **88/G4**
Wakeham (Maricourt), Que., **25/J3**
Wales, **41/E4-5**
Walla Walla, Wash., **16/D3**
Wallis & Futuna, **88/J7**
Walterboro, S.C., **21/N6**
Walvis Bay, S. Africa, **86/A4**
Wanganui, N.Z., **94/F3**
Wankie, Zim., **86/C3**

Warangal, India, **72/D5**
Warmbad, Namibia, **86/B5**
Warren, Ohio, **20/N4**
Warren, Pa., **20/O4**
Warrensburg, Mo., **18/K5**
Warrnambool, Austr., **92/B6**
Warroad, Minn., **18/K2**
Warsaw, Ind., **20/M4**
Warsaw (cap.), Pol., **51/E2**
Warwick, Eng., **41/F4**
Wasatch (range), U.S., **16/F4-5**
Wasco, Calif., **17/D6**
Wash, The (bay), Eng., **41/G4**
Washington, Iowa, **18/L4**
Washington, Mo., **18/L5**
Washington, N.C., **21/O6**
Washington, Pa., **20/O5**
Washington (state), U.S., **14/B1**
Washington, D.C. (cap.), U.S.,
    15/L3
Waterford, Ire., **41/C4**
Waterloo, Belg., **43/E7**
Waterloo, Iowa, **18/L4**
Waterton-Glacier Int'l Peace Pk.,
    N. Amer., **16/E2**
Watertown, N.Y., **20/P4**
Watertown, S. Dak., **18/J3**
Waterville, Maine, **20/R3**
Watford City, N. Dak., **18/H3**
Watling (San Salvador) (isl.),
    Bah., **28/C2**
Watrous, Sask., **24/F5**
Watson Lake, Yukon, **24/D3**
Watsonville, Calif., **16/C5**
Wau, Sudan, **81/E6**
Waukegan, Ill., **18/L4**
Waukesha, Wis., **18/L4**
Waupun, Wis., **18/L4**
Wausau, Wis., **18/L3**
Wauwatosa, Wis., **18/L4**
Waverly, Iowa, **18/K4**
Waxahachie, Tex., **19/J6**
Waycross, Ga., **21/N7**
Wayne, Nebr., **18/J4**
Waynesboro, Ga., **21/N6**
Waynesboro, Va., **20/O5**
Weatherford, Okla., **19/J6**
Webster City, Iowa, **18/K4**
Weimar, E. Ger., **47/D3**
Weirton, W. Va., **20/N4**
Wellington, Kans., **19/J5**
Wellington (cap.), N.Z., **94/E4**
Wellsboro, Pa., **20/O4**

Welwyn, Eng., **41/F5**
Wenatchee, Wash., **16/C3**
Wenzhou, China, **65/J6**
Weser (riv.), W. Ger., **47/C2**
Weslaco, Tex., **19/J8**
West Allis, Wis., **18/L4**
West Bank, Near East, **76/C3**
West Bend, Wis., **18/L4**
Westbrook, Maine, **20/R4**
West Des Moines, Iowa, **18/K4**
Wessington Sprs., S. Dak., **18/J3**
Western Australia (state), Austr.,
    91/B-D 4-5
Western Sahara, **82/B3-4**
Western Samoa, **89/M8**
West Frankfort, Ill., **18/L5**
West Indies, **28-29**
West Monroe, La., **19/K6**
Weston, W. Va., **20/N5**
West Palm Beach, Fla., **21/N8**
West Plains, Mo., **19/L5**
West Point, Miss., **19/L6**
West Virginia (state), U.S., **15/K3**
Wetaskiwin, Alta., **24/E5**
Wetterhorn (mt.), Switz., **50/D2**
Wetzlar, W. Ger., **47/C3**
Wexford, Ire., **41/C4**
Weyburn, Sask., **24/F6**
Whangarei, N.Z., **94/E1**
Wheeling, W. Va., **20/N5**
White (sea), U.S.S.R., **60/E1**
Whitefish (bay), N. Amer., **20/M3**
Whitehorse (cap.), Yukon, **24/C3**
White Nile (riv.), Afr., **81/F5**
White Russian S.S.R., U.S.S.R.,
    58/C4
White Sulphur Sprs., Mont.,
    16/F3
Whitney (mt.), Calif., **17/D5**
Wichita, Kans., **18/J5**
Wichita Falls, Tex., **19/J6**
Wickenburg, Ariz., **17/E6**
Wickiup (res.), Oreg., **16/C4**
Wicklow, Ire., **41/C4**
Wien (Vienna), Austria, **48/D2**
Wiener Neustadt, Austria, **49/D3**
Wiesbaden, W. Ger., **47/C3**
Wight (isl.), Eng., **41/F5**
Wigtown (bay), Scot., **40/D3**
Wildwood, N.J., **20/P5**
Wilhelm-Pieck-Stadt, E. Ger.,
    47/F3
Wilhelmshaven, W. Ger., **47/B2**

Wilkes-Barre, Pa., **20/P4**
Wilkinsburg, Pa., **20/O4**
Willemstad (cap.), Neth. Ant.,
    28/E4
Williamsburg, Va., **20/O5**
Williams Lake, Br. Col., **24/D5**
Williamson, W. Va., **20/N5**
Williamsport, Pa., **20/O4**
Williston, N. Dak., **18/H2**
Willmar, Minn., **18/K3**
Wilmington, Del., **20/P5**
Wilmington, N.C., **21/O6**
Wilrijk, Belg., **42/E6**
Wilson, N.C., **21/O6**
Winchester, Eng., **41/F5**
Winchester, Ky., **20/N5**
Winchester, Va., **20/O5**
Wind Cave Nat'l Pk., S. Dak.,
    18/G4
Winder, Ga., **21/N6**
Windhoek (cap.), Namibia, **86/B4**
Wind River (range), Wyo., **16/F4**
Windsor, N.S., **25/K7**
Windsor, Ont., **25/H7**
Windward (isls.), W. Indies,
    29/G4-5
Winfield, Kans., **18/J5**
Winnemucca, Nev., **16/D4**
Winnfield, La., **19/K7**
Winnipeg (cap.), Man., **24/G6**
Winnipeg (lake), Man., **24/G5**
Winnipegosis (lake), Man., **24/F5**
Winnsboro, La., **19/L6**
Winona, Minn., **18/L4**
Winona, Miss., **19/L6**
Winslow, Ariz., **17/F6**
Winston-Salem, N.C., **21/N5**
Winter Haven, Fla., **21/N7**
Winter Park, Fla., **21/N7**
Winterthur, Switz., **50/D1**
Wisconsin (state), U.S., **15/H1**
Wisconsin (riv.), Wis., **15/H2**
Wisconsin Rapids, Wis., **18/L3**
Wismar, E. Ger., **47/D2**
Wittenberg, E. Ger., **47/E3**
Wittenoom Gorge, Austr., **91/B4**
Witwatersrand (reg.), S. Africa,
    86/H7
Wolfsburg, W. Ger., **47/D2**
Wollongong, Austr., **92/F4**
Wolverhampton, Eng., **41/E4**
Wŏnsan, N. Korea, **66/C4**
Wood Buffalo Nat'l Pk., Can., **24/E4**

Woodland, Calif., **16/C5**
Woods, Lake of the, N. Amer.,
    15/G1
Woodstock, N. Br., **25/K6**
Woodward, Okla., **19/J5**
Woomera, Austr., **91/F6**
Worcester, Eng., **41/E4**
Worcester, Mass., **20/R4**
Worland, Wyo., **16/F3**
Worms, W. Ger., **47/C4**
Worthington, Minn., **18/K4**
Wrangell, Alaska, **22/F4**
Wrangell (mts.), Alaska, **22/E3**
Wrocław, Pol., **51/C3**
Wuhan, China, **65/H5**
Wuhu, China, **65/J5**
Wuppertal, W. Ger., **47/B3**
Würzburg, W. Ger., **47/C4**
Wye (riv.), U.K., **41/E4**
Wynne, Ark., **19/L6**
Wynyard, Sask., **24/F5**
Wyoming (state), U.S., **15/E2**
Wyoming (range), Wyo., **16/F4**

X

Xai-Xai, Moz., **86/E5**
Xánthi, Greece, **56/G5**
Xenia, Ohio, **20/N5**
Xiamen, China, **65/J7**
Xi'an, China, **65/G5**
Xi Jiang (riv.), China, **65/H7**
Xingu (riv.), Braz., **32/K4**
Xining, China, **65/E4**
Xinjiang Uygur Zizhiqu (aut. reg.),
    China, **65/B3**
Xinxiang, China, **65/H4**
Xizang (reg.), China, **65/B5**
Xuzhou, China, **65/J5**

Y

Yablonovyy (range), U.S.S.R.,
    59/M4
Yakima, Wash., **16/C3**
Yakutat, Alaska, **22/F4**
Yakutsk, U.S.S.R., **59/N3**

Yalu (riv.), Asia, **63/R5**
Yamaguchi, Japan, **66/E6**
Yan'an, China, **65/G4**
Yangtze Kiang (riv.), China, see
    Chang Jiang
Yankton, S. Dak., **18/J4**
Yantai, China, **65/K4**
Yaoundé (cap.), Cameroon, **84/B3**
Yap (isl.), Fed. States of
    Micronesia, **88/D5**
Yarkand, China, see Shache
Yarmouth, N.S., **25/K7**
Yaroslavl', U.S.S.R., **60/E3**
Yathkyed (lake), N.W.T., **24/F3**
Yavne, Isr., **76/B4**
Yazd, Iran, **74/F3**
Yazoo (riv.), Miss., **15/H4**
Yazoo City, Miss., **19/L6**
Yellow (sea), Asia, **65/K4**
Yellow (riv.), China, see Huang He
Yellowknife (cap.), N.W.T., **24/E3**
Yellowstone (riv.), U.S., **15/E1**
Yellowstone (lake), Wyo., **14/D2**
Yellowstone Nat'l Pk., U.S.,
    16/E2
Yemen Arab Republic, **74/D6-7**
Yemen, People's Democratic
    Republic of, **74/D-F 6-7**
Yenan, China, see Yan'an
Yenisey (riv.), U.S.S.R.,
    58/J4
Yerington, Nev., **16/D5**
Yinchuan, China, **65/G4**
Yirga Alam, Eth., **81/G6**
Yogyakarta, Indon., **70/D7**
Yoho Nat'l Pk., Can., **24/D5**
Yokohama, Japan, **67/J6**
Yonkers, N.Y., **20/P4**
York (cape), Austr., **91/G2**
York, Eng., **41/F4**
York, Nebr., **18/J4**
York, Pa., **20/O5**
York Factory, Man., **24/G4**
Yorkton, Sask., **24/F5**
Yosemite Nat'l Pk., Calif.,
    14/D3
Youngstown, Ohio, **20/N4**
Ypres (Ieper), Belg., **43/B7**
Yreka, Calif., **16/C4**
Yuba City, Calif., **16/C4**
Yugoslavia, **56/B-E 3-4**
Yukon (terr.), Can., **24/C3**
Yukon (riv.), N. Amer., **22/D3**

Yuma, Ariz., **17/E6**
Yunnan (prov.), China, **65/F7**

Z

Zaandam, Neth., **42/F4**
Zabrze, Pol., **51/A4**
Zacatecas, Mex., **26/D3**
Zagazig, Egypt, **81/J3**
Zagreb, Yugo., **56/C3**
Zagros (mts.), Iran, **74/E3**
Zahedan, Iran, **75/H4**
Zaire, **84/D-E4**
Zambezi (riv.), Afr., **86/E3**
Zambia, **84/E-F 6-7**
Zamboanga, Phil., **71/G4**
Zamora, Spain, **53/D2**
Zanesville, Ohio, **20/N5**
Zanzibar, Tanz., **85/G5**
Zaporozh'ye, U.S.S.R., **60/E5**
Zaragoza, Mex., **26/E2**
Zaragoza (Saragossa), Spain,
    53/F2
Zaria, Nigeria, **83/F6**
Zawia, Libya, **80/B1**
Zefat (Safad), Isr., **76/C2**
Zermatt, Switz., **50/C2**
Zhdanov, U.S.S.R., **60/E5**
Zhengzhou, China, **65/H5**
Zhitomir, U.S.S.R., **60/C4**
Zibo, China, **65/J4**
Ziguinchor, Sen., **83/A6**
Zilten, Libya, **80/C1**
Zimbabwe, **86/D-E3**
Zimbabwe Nat'l Pk., Zim., **86/E4**
Zinder, Niger, **82/F6**
Zion Nat'l Pk., Utah, **14/D3**
Zomba, Malawi, **85/G7**
Zoulrât, Maur., **82/B4**
Zug, Switz., **50/D1**
Zugspitze (mt.), Europe, **47/D5**
Zululand (reg.), S. Africa, **86/E5**
Zuni, N. Mex., **17/F6**
Zuni (riv.), U.S., **17/F6**
Zürich, Switz., **50/D1**
Zwickau, E. Ger., **47/E3**
Zweibrücken, W. Ger., **47/B4**
Zwolle, Neth., **42/J3**